Historic Preservation

ART AND ARCHITECTURE INFORMATION GUIDE SERIES

Series Editor: Sydney Starr Keaveney, Associate Professor, Pratt Institute Library, Brooklyn

Also in this series:

AMERICAN ARCHITECTS TO THE FIRST WORLD WAR—*Edited by Lawrence Wodehouse*

AMERICAN ARCHITECTS FROM THE FIRST WORLD WAR TO PRESENT— *Edited by Lawrence Wodehouse*

AMERICAN DECORATIVE ARTS AND OLD WORLD INFLUENCES—*Edited by David M. Sokol*

AMERICAN DRAWING—*Edited by Lamia Doumato*

AMERICAN PAINTING—*Edited by Sydney Starr Keaveney*

AMERICAN SCULPTURE—*Edited by Janis Ekdahl*

ART EDUCATION—*Edited by Clarence Bunch*

BRITISH ARCHITECTS, 1840-1976—*Edited by Lawrence Wodehouse*

COLOR THEORY—*Edited by Mary Buckley*

INDIGENOUS ARCHITECTURE WORLDWIDE—*Edited by Lawrence Wodehouse*

POTTERY AND CERAMICS—*Edited by James E. Campbell*

STAINED GLASS—*Edited by Darlene A. Brady and William Serban**

TWENTIETH-CENTURY EUROPEAN PAINTING—*Edited by Ann-Marie Cutul*

*in preparation

The above series is part of the
GALE INFORMATION GUIDE LIBRARY

The Library consists of a number of separate series of guides covering major areas in the social sciences, humanities, and current affairs.

General Editor: Paul Wasserman, Professor and former Dean, School of Library and Information Services, University of Maryland

Managing Editor: Denise Allard Adzigian, Gale Research Company

Historic Preservation

A GUIDE TO INFORMATION SOURCES

Volume 13 in the Art and Architecture Information Guide Series

Arnold L. Markowitz

Elmer Holmes Bobst Library
New York University

Gale Research Company
Book Tower, Detroit, Michigan 48226

Library of Congress Cataloging in Publication Data

Markowitz, Arnold L
   Historic preservation.

   (Art and architecture information guide series ;
v. 13) (Gale information guide library)
   Includes indexes.
   1. Historic sites—United States—Conservation and
restoration—Bibliography. 2. Historic sites—Conservation and restoration—Bibliography. 3. Historic
buildings—United States—Conservation and restoration—Bibliography. 4. Historic buildings—Conservation—Bibliography. I. Title.
Z1251.A2M37 [E159] 016.3636'9   80-14313
ISBN 0-8103-1460-6

VITA

Arnold L. Markowitz is a reference librarian at the Elmer Holmes Bobst Library, New York University, where he is also the art bibliographer. Before entering a career in librarianship, he was office manager of the New York architectural firm of J. Sanford Shanley and W. Knight Sturges, a firm active in preservation work and the preservation movement.

After attending St. John's College, Annapolis, Markowitz completed his bachelor's degree at the New School for Social Research, New York. He earned a master's degree in librarianship at Columbia University and a master's degree in art history at Hunter College, the City University of New York. He subsequently studied at Columbia University, in the Department of Art and Archaeology and in the Program in Historic Preservation of the Graduate School of Architecture and Planning.

Mr. Markowitz has published a bibliography of the architect and art historian Paul Zucker, which appeared in PAPERS XII of the American Association of Architectural Bibliographers, and an article on doctoral dissertations in the field of historic preservation, which appeared in the JOURNAL OF ARCHITECTURAL EDUCATION. He is general editor of Garland Bibliographies in Architecture and Planning.

As an active member of organizations concerned with architectural history, librarianship, and historic preservation, he has served as chairman of the Museums, Arts, and Humanities Group of the New York Chapter--Special Libraries Association and as vice-president of the New York Chapter--Society of Architectural Historians.

CONTENTS

Contents

Contents

INTRODUCTION

Historic Preservation is a term which covers, to paraphrase the old expression, "a multitude of blessings." It is concerned with the preservation, maintenance, repair, restoration, and sometimes the replication or reconstruction of such elements of the human environment as buildings and other structures, complexes of buildings, sites, and entire towns. It is also concerned with their description and documentation and with their use in promoting an understanding of past cultures. It is concerned with maintaining the vitality of urban centers while keeping their historic and traditional ambience intact. It is concerned with neighborhoods; with gardens, farms, and scenic views; with legal devices and taxation; with tools, building materials, and craftmanship; with modes of transportation; with early industry and early industrial settings; with ruins; and with the continued and adaptive use of all manner of buildings. Historic preservation is a hybrid.

Some of the concerns of historic preservation have reached out beyond structures, sites, and artifacts, to include other manifestations of the cultural patrimony. While these aspects are usually touched upon in the overall interpretation of historic buildings and sites, they sometimes occupy a strong and distinct position in preservation policy. Japan, for example, provides a major instance of a national preservation policy which covers a broad array of cultural manifestations, tangible and intangible. There, the Law for the Protection of Cultural Properties includes provisions for the art and skill employed in drama and music, as well as manners related to food, clothing, housing, and religious faiths (see entry 74).

Traditionally, historic preservation has been the concern of architects, antiquarians, historians, specialists in building materials and building technology, and specialists in the decorative arts. More recently, however, these ranks have grown to include landscape architects, lawyers, urban planners, sociopolitical activists, real estate developers, and all manner of bureaucrats.

Paralleling the growth of interest and activity in historic preservation, there has been in recent years a proliferation of courses and programs in historic preservation on the college and university level. With this increasing academic interest and an increase of occupational employment directly concerned with aspects of historic preservation, claims have been made for an emerging professional group of "historic preservationists." Counterclaims have been made that historic preservation,

hybrid such as it is, is not a profession, but an "activity," an activity in which
roles are played by participants from a wide variety of callings. At the same time,
there are those who claim that preservationists have taken on too many concerns,
and would prefer a return to a concentration on historic houses and "architectural
preservation and restoration." The intention here is not to argue one view or another,
but to organize and record what has been written. Nevertheless, the observation
might be made that the content of this bibliography substantiates two of the generally
accepted criteria for determining whether an activity might be judged a profession:
1) that there is a substantial body of literature related to that activity and 2)
that there is a substantial recorded history related to that activity. Another
criterion, degree programs on the graduate level, is also being met.

In the United States, the two major agencies for historic preservation are the
Heritage Conservation and Recreation Service and the National Trust for
Historic Preservation. The former is a division of the U.S. Department of the
Interior and the latter is a private organization which operates under congres-
sional charter. Known as the National Park Service until 1978, the Heritage
Conservation and Recreation Service was renamed to reflect more fully its con-
cerns and responsibilities. Within the Heritage Conservation and Recreation
Service, and formerly within the National Park Service, the Office of Archeol-
ogy and Historic Preservation has had primary responsibility for the administra-
tion of historic sites and the administration of programs directly concerned with
historic preservation. Among these programs are the Historic American Buildings
Survey (HABS), the Historic American Buildings Survey Inventory (HABSI), the
Historic American Engineering Record (HAER), and the National Register of
Historic Places.

Since its founding in 1949, the National Trust for Historic Preservation has
experienced tremendous growth. Much of this growth has occurred during the
past 12 years, with a membership of 12,000 in 1967 and 160,000 in 1979, including individuals, organizations, corporations, and foundations. Its concerns
over the years have reflected the development of the preservation movement, in
general, starting with an interest in historic houses and historic house museums
and branching out to such interests as industrial archaeology, neighborhood conservation, and maritime conservation.

The Heritage Conservation and Recreation Service and the National Trust for
Historic Preservation are two of the major producers and disseminators of information concerning historic preservation. Their publications, ranging from brochures
and leaflets to books and series, represent a substantial and essential portion of
the literature of the field. On the international level, the United Nations
Educational, Scientific and Cultural Organization (UNESCO) and its affiliate,
the International Council on Monuments and Sites (ICOMOS), are two agencies
that play a major role in historic preservation and in the publication and distri-
bution of relevant literature. Two organizations that play a similar role in more
regionally limited spheres are the Council of Europe and the Organization of
American States.

This survey of the literature of historic preservation aims to cite, fairly comprehensively, the classic works and the indispensable works, and, selectively, examples of the wide variety of publications related to the many aspects of the topic. It is intended to be of use to students of historic preservation, to practitioners of the various professions and occupations concerned with historic preservation, and to members of organizations concerned with historic preservation, from local groups to government agencies.

The items listed in this information guide are primarily books, pamphlets, and other separate publications, including entire periodical issues devoted to historic preservation or closely related themes. With a very few exceptions, individual periodical articles and individual contributions to collected works have not been included. The few that have been listed include two articles in CURATOR by Stephen W. Jacobs, which describe preservation history in Europe (see entry 41) and the government role in preservation in the United States (see entry 84), included because of their particular usefulness as concise, readily available articles covering overviews of two areas of major concern to the student of historic preservation. Among other exceptions are a bibliography by Hans Huth (see entry 8) and the summary of a round table discussion on the preservation of historical architectural monuments (see entry 48), both of which appeared in 1941 in the journal of the fledgling American Society of Architectural Historians and are included here as landmark documents in the history of historic preservation in the United States.

The literature cited is overwhelmingly in the English language, mostly of American origin, and concerned primarily with the United States. Some emphasis has been placed on literature concerned with Great Britain and countries such as Australia, Canada, and South Africa, where preservation philosophy and practice have their basis in the British experience. The items in other languages are mostly proceedings of international conferences and overviews of preservation history, philosophy, and practice in European and Latin American countries.

In chapters 1 through 12 the arrangement is thematic and all entries are annotated, starting with "General Reference Works" and "Historic and Current Overviews," and moving through the various specialized aspects of historic preservation, as well as several closely related disciplines and areas of interest. Chapter 13, a listing of periodicals, is divided into two sections, the first containing general periodicals relevant to historic preservation and the latter containing statewide periodicals. Chapter 14 is a checklist of publications related to the Historic American Buildings Survey, with cross-references, wherever applicable, to annotated entries in the earlier chapters. Each entry in the bibliography has been assigned a number to facilitate cross-referencing and indexing. Although a number of entries might well have been included in more than one of the thematic chapters, there are no duplications. Reliance has been placed, instead, on indexing and cross-referencing to exclude the possibility of their being overlooked.

All annotated entries, that is to say all of the entries in the first twelve chapters, are cited on the basis of personal examination. The items in the final two chapters have been included partly on the basis of personal examination and partly on the basis of information contained in lists issued by the Historic American Buildings

Introduction

Survey, the International Council on Monuments and Sites, and the National Trust for Historic Preservation. Annotations are for the most part not critical, but are intended to elucidate the nature and content of the publications cited, sometimes by direct quotation or paraphrase of the text. Where practicable, annotations to collected works give the names of contributors and the titles of their contributions, but this is not done in all instances. Where it is done, the authors and titles are listed in the author index and the title index.

Citations refer to the specific editions examined and do not preclude the existence of earlier, later, or variant editions. Similarly, the inclusion or exclusion of the note "paper." (indicating a paperback edition) does not preclude the existence of an alternate format.

A number of unpublished doctoral dissertations have been included. Their citations conclude with a note which indicates the volume and page of DISSERTATION ABSTRACTS INTERNATIONAL in which the abstract appears, and also the academic field under which D.A.I. lists the abstract.

An appendix, "Developing the Historic Preservation Library," by Brigid Rapp, Library Services Coordinator, National Trust for Historic Preservation, concludes with a select list for initiating preservation collections. This is followed by an author index, an organization index, a title index, and a subject index. The author index lists the names of editors, translators, illustrators, and contributors of forewords and introductions, as well as the names of contributors to collected works if they have been mentioned in the entry. The organization index functions partly as a "directory of organizations," listing firms, government departments, organizations, and agencies which are either the authors of publications or the sponsors of publications, conferences, programs, surveys, or studies. The title index, a short-title listing, includes titles of contributions to multiauthored works and titles of individual volumes of multivolume works only if they are mentioned in the entry. The titles of publications included in the "Select List" are distinguished in the title index by an asterisk. The subject index, along with the table of contents, is the thematic key to the bibliography. It should be noted that some individuals listed in the author index and organizations listed in the organization index also appear in the subject index.

The span of dates for the publications cited extends from roughly the turn of the century through 1978. Apologies are offered for some publications of 1978 and earlier years which have been excluded, not without regret, because of the author's inability to locate them within the constraints of the publication deadline. It is hoped that, even with these omissions, the materials cited and the organization of this bibliography will serve as a guide to further sources of information about historic preservation. For current publications, the reader is advised to consult the book reviews and the lists of new publications in the various journals and newsletters cited, as well as the MONTHLY CATALOG OF UNITED STATES GOVERNMENT PUBLICATIONS, and catalogs of the Preservation Bookshop of the National Trust for Historic Preservation.

Introduction

I am indebted to Brigid Rapp and the staff of the Library of the National Trust
for Historic Preservation for making available to me not only the publications
in the library's collection, but also the list of subject headings which they have
developed, the lists of periodicals and newsletters which they have compiled,
and the lists of acquisitions with which they have regularly supplied me and
which have so often alerted me to publications for inclusion in this bibliography.
I am especially thankful to Brigid Rapp for her advice and encouragement and
for her willingness to write the appendix, "Developing the Historic Preservation
Library," and to choose from the publications listed in this bibliography the
"Select List" of titles recommended for the basic historic preservation collection.

Most of the publications described were examined at Avery Architectural and
Fine Arts Library, Columbia University. I am grateful to Adolf K. Placzek,
Avery Librarian, and to the staff of Avery Library for making my work there
so pleasurable and rewarding.

My colleagues at the Elmer Holmes Bobst Library were ever thoughtful and
generous in calling new publications to my attention. To them and to Carlton
C. Rochell, dean of libraries at New York University, I offer sincere thanks
for facilitating a sabbatical leave during which a substantial portion of my work
on this book was realized.

To Sydney Starr Keaveney, editor of the Art and Architecture Information Guide
Series, and to the editorial staff of Gale Research Company, my thanks for
their confidence, patience, and generous assistance.

A.L.M.
New York

Chapter 1

GENERAL REFERENCE WORKS

Here are listed those bibliographies, directories, and other reference tools which relate to the broad topic of historic preservation and related areas. Reference works concerned with more specific aspects of historic preservation are included in the pertinent chapters.

1   American Association for State and Local History. DIRECTORY OF HISTORICAL SOCIETIES AND AGENCIES IN THE UNITED STATES AND CANADA. 11th ed. Compiled and edited by Donna McDonald. Nashville: 1978. 474 p. Paper.

> Includes thousands of entries describing organizations that are working to preserve and disseminate knowledge about the past. Gives the name, mailing address, and telephone number of each institution; the name of its director or elected official to whom mail should be addressed; information on membership, paid staff, and volunteer staff; titles of periodical publications; and information on major programs.

2   Christopher, Gary, and Junkin, Dorothy, comps. "Preliminary Bibliographical Inventory of Park Historical and Architectural Studies." Washington, D.C.: U.S. Department of the Interior, National Park Service, Division of History, Office of Archaeology and Historic Preservation, 1971. xiii, 169 p. Mimeographed. Paper.

> Arranged by site, identifies four decades of documentation in the National Park Service. Includes typescript reports along with mimeographed and published materials.

3   Cline, William Erich. "Historic Preservation Literature--1969-1977: Selected References." Exchange Bibliography 1457. Monticello, Ill.: Council of Planning Librarians, 1978. 51 p. Mimeographed.

> Directed particularly to the interests of preservation planners. Emphasis is placed on literature produced in the United States, with a bias toward materials pertaining to Arizona and the Southwest. Most entries are annotated, however those relating to periodicals or periodical articles are not. Concludes with

sections on "Preservation Pieces from the Law Reviews," "Law
Review Historic Preservation Symposiums," and "Federal Register Reports."

4   Committee for the Preservation of Architectural Records. ARCHITEC-
TURAL RESEARCH MATERIALS IN NEW YORK CITY: A GUIDE TO RE-
SOURCES IN ALL FIVE BOROUGHS. New York: 1977. Part I, 114
unnumbered pages. Part II, 118 unnumbered pages. Loose-leaf.

Part I begins with a detailed guide to the New York City
Department of Buildings, and part II with a "User's Guide to
Property Records." Together, these introductions perform an
invaluable service for the uninitiated. The resources of well-
known and little-known libraries, historical societies, museums,
and other institutions are described systematically. Information
includes: scope of collection, major holdings, admission policy,
hours, transportation, duplication processes available, and finding aids.

5   Creigh, Dorothy Weyer. A PRIMER FOR LOCAL HISTORICAL SOCI-
ETIES. Nashville: American Association for State and Local History,
1976. ix, 153 p. Illus., paper.

Includes a chapter on "Preservation of Buildings," another on
"Restoration," and appendixes listing agencies and organizations
of interest to local historical societies in the United States and
Canada. Provides information regarding criteria for inclusion
in the National Register. Lists state historic preservation officers.

6   Eubanks, Sharon Y. A BIBLIOGRAPHY OF BOOKS, PAMPHLETS, AND
FILMS LISTED IN THE LIVING HISTORICAL FARMS BULLETIN FROM
DECEMBER 1970 THROUGH MAY 1976. Washington, D.C.: Association
for Living Historical Farms and Agricultural Museums, n.d. iv, 73 p.
Paper.

Includes 833 items, representing a consolidation of all entries
that appeared in the "Recent Publications" section of the
BULLETIN from the first issue through May 1976. Items listed
under eight topical headings, corresponding to the headings
used in the BULLETIN: (1) "Arts and Crafts," (2) "Crops and
Livestock," (3) "Earth and Water," (4) "Gardens and Orchards,"
(5) "Hearth and Home," (6) "Money and Records," (7) "Odds
and Ends," and (8) "Places and People." Fully indexed.

7   Haynes, Robert E., and Pribanic, Kenneth T., comps. and eds. A
BIBLIOGRAPHY OF HISTORIC PRESERVATION: SELECTED PUBLICATIONS
OF THE OFFICE OF ARCHEOLOGY AND HISTORIC PRESERVATION.
Washington, D.C.: National Park Service, 1977. 10 p. Paper.

Arranged according to specific programs of the Office of
Archeology and Historic Preservation: "Historic American
Buildings Survey," "Historic American Engineering Record,"
"Historic Sites Survey," "National Register of Historic Places,"
"Interagency Archeological Services," and "Technical Preser-
vation Services." Each section begins with a brief note on
the program's activities.

8   Huth, Hans. "Preservationism: A Selected Bibliography." JOURNAL
OF THE AMERICAN SOCIETY OF ARCHITECTURAL HISTORIANS 1,
nos. 3-4 (1941): 33-45.

One of our earliest preservation bibliographies. Divided into
three sections: "General Works," "Special Methods of Preservation," and "Works Dealing with Specific Countries." The
bulk of the entries--from Algeria to Yugoslavia--are in the
last category. Included in a special issue on "Preservation of
Historic Monuments" (see entry 46).

9   Lugo, Lelahvon, comp. LIBRARY RESOURCES IN WASHINGTON, D.C.,
RELATING TO HISTORIC PRESERVATION. Washington, D.C.: Preservation Press, 1977. 55 p. Paper.

Compiled as a project of the Library of the National Trust
for Historic Preservation. A guide to information on archaeology, architecture, the arts, conservation, history, land use,
legislation, museology, real estate, restoration, and urban
and community planning. Covers academic, government, museum, and organization libraries.

10   Menges, Gary L. "Historic Preservation: A Bibliography." Exchange
Bibliography 79. Monticello, Ill.: Council of Planning Librarians,
May 1969. 61 leaves. Mimeographed.

Focuses on the preservation of historic buildings, sites, and
towns. Includes only English-language publications, and emphasizes preservation in the United States. Lists case studies
and architectural surveys by state. Also includes sections on
legal aspects, restoration and maintenance, and environmental
aesthetics. Reflects the resources of the Cornell University
Libraries, especially the Fine Arts Library.

11   National Trust for Historic Preservation. A GUIDE TO FEDERAL PRO-
GRAMS: PROGRAMS AND ACTIVITIES RELATED TO HISTORIC PRES-
ERVATION. A project of the National Trust for Historic Preservation
with the cooperation and assistance of the Advisory Council on Historic
Preservation and the Legislative Reference Service, Library of Congress.
Nancy D. Schultz, principal consultant. Washington, D.C.: 1974.
398 p. Paper.

Covers programs, services, and activities of forty-nine perma-
nent departments, agencies, boards, and commissions of the
federal government as of 30 June 1974. Does not include ad
hoc or other temporary committees and organizations of the
federal government, private organizations, or nonfederal public
agencies.

12   _____. A GUIDE TO FEDERAL PROGRAMS FOR HISTORIC PRESERVA-
TION: 1976 SUPPLEMENT. Compiled by Nancy D. Schultz. Washington, D.C.: Preservation Press, 1976. 110 p. Paper.

An interim updating of the 1974 edition. Incorporates certain
programs and activities initiated since the guide was first published as well as others not originally included that have since
come to the editor's attention.

13   Preservation League of New York State. PRESERVATION DIRECTORY:
A GUIDE TO PROGRAMS, ORGANIZATIONS AND AGENCIES IN
NEW YORK STATE. Albany: 1977. 125 p. Paper.

Lists and describes national and statewide organizations and
federal and state agencies. Provides information on legislative
and educational programs, and concludes with a detailed directory of local organizations.

14   Rath, Frederick L., Jr., and O'Connell, Merrilyn Rogers, comps.
GUIDE TO HISTORIC PRESERVATION, HISTORICAL AGENCIES, AND
MUSEUM PRACTICES: A SELECTIVE BIBLIOGRAPHY. Cooperstown:
New York State Historical Association, 1970. xvi, 369 p.

Includes a descriptive directory of organizations and the related bibliography. Like its predecessor publication, NYSHA
SELECTIVE REFERENCE GUIDE TO HISTORIC PRESERVATION
(see entry 16), which was published in 1966, presents bibliographic entries without annotation, but includes copious explanatory notes at the beginnings of the chapters and their
subdivisions. Succeeded by the same authors' HISTORIC
PRESERVATION (see below).

15   _____. HISTORIC PRESERVATION. A Bibliography on Historical Organization Practices, vol. 1. Nashville: American Association for State
and Local History, 1975. ix, 141 p.

Cites and annotates books and articles through 1973, with some
major references in 1974. Includes chapters on (1) "Historic
Preservation in Perspective," (2) "Preservation Law," (3) "Urban Development and Redevelopment," (4) "Preservation Research and Planning," and (5) "Preservation Action." An outgrowth of the editors' earlier publications, NYSHA SELECTIVE
REFERENCE GUIDE TO HISTORIC PRESERVATION, 1966 (see
below), and GUIDE TO HISTORIC PRESERVATION, HISTORI-

CAL AGENCIES, AND MUSEUM PRACTICES: A SELECTIVE BIBLIOGRAPHY, 1970 (see above). The first in a five-volume work of which the second and third volumes have also appeared: volume 2, CARE AND CONSERVATION OF COLLECTIONS, compiled by Rosemary S. Reese and edited by Rath and O'Connell, published in 1977, and volume 3, INTERPRETATION, compiled by Reese and edited by Rath and O'Connell, published in 1978.

16   Rath, Frederick L., Jr., and Rogers, Merrilyn. NYSHA SELECTIVE REFERENCE GUIDE TO HISTORIC PRESERVATION. Cooperstown: New York State Historical Association, 1966. viii, 133 p. Paper.

A directory of U.S., foreign, and international preservation organizations, followed by a bibliography of books and periodical articles, classified as follows: "General Reference," "History and Background," "Administration," "Study and Care of Collection," "Research," and "Interpretation." Without annotations, but includes introductory statements to each chapter and subsection.

17   Romaine, Lawrence B. A GUIDE TO AMERICAN TRADE CATALOGS 1744-1900. New York: R.R. Bowker Co., 1960. xxiii, 422 p.

Authoritative, descriptive bibliography of American trade catalogs. Gives library locations for the items listed, organized by product, profession, or trade, from "Agricultural Implements & Machinery" through "Windmills." Concludes with a list of bibliographical suggestions and an index listing the firms mentioned in the main body of the work.

18   Smith, John F. A CRITICAL BIBLIOGRAPHY OF BUILDING CONSERVATION: HISTORIC TOWNS, BUILDINGS, THEIR FURNISHINGS AND FITTINGS. London: Mansell, 1978. xxv, 207 p.

Lists and annotates 2,238 books and articles within a rigorously classified organizational scheme. Compiled at the Institute of Advanced Architectural Study, University of York, with a grant from the Radcliffe Trust.

19   Sokol, David M., ed. AMERICAN ARCHITECTURE AND ART: A GUIDE TO INFORMATION SOURCES. American Studies Information Guide Series, vol. 2. Detroit: Gale Research Co., 1976. xii, 341 p.

Broad bibliography including entries of interest indexed under "historic preservation," "architecture, conservation and restoration," "architecture, history of (by place)," and "domestic architecture, history of (by place)."

20   Travers, Jean, and Shearer, Susan. GUIDE TO RESOURCES USED IN
      HISTORIC PRESERVATION RESEARCH. Washington, D.C.: Preservation
      Press, 1978. 26 p. Paper.

      Prepared for the Library of the National Trust for Historic
      Preservation. Introduces a wide range of print and nonprint
      material helpful in the pursuit of historic preservation research.
      Describes each type of resource (from architectural plans and
      specifications to wills) and its usual format; gives locations
      where such materials might be found; and explains the partic-
      ular application and usefulness of each type.

21   Tubesing, Richard. ARCHITECTURAL PRESERVATION IN THE UNITED
      STATES, 1941-1975: A BIBLIOGRAPHY OF FEDERAL, STATE, AND
      LOCAL GOVERNMENT PUBLICATIONS. New York and London:
      Garland Publishing, 1978. xvii, 452 p.

      Developed from a publication of similar title but more limited
      scope published in June 1975 by the Council of Planning Librar-
      ians as "Exchange Bibliography 812-13" (see below). Covers
      the full range of government publications from posters, tourist
      brochures, and maps to state historic preservation plans and
      federal agency annual reports. Listings sometimes based on
      personal examination and sometimes on secondary information,
      in which case date and pagination are occasionally noted as
      "unavailable." Includes an appendix listing names and ad-
      dresses of federal agencies, commissions, and departments
      responsible for historic preservation. Also includes an appen-
      dix listing names and addresses of state and territorial his-
      toric preservation officers and sources of information.

22   _____. "Architectural Preservation in the United States, 1965-1974:
      A Bibliography of Federal, State and Local Government Publications."
      Exchange Bibliography 812-13. Monticello, Ill.: Council of Planning
      Librarians, 1975. 93 p. Mimeographed.

      Lists materials ranging from scholarly studies to tourist brochures
      to miscellaneous ephemera, for a period of heavy publication
      activity in this field. Includes Puerto Rico and the Virgin
      Islands. Chapters include: "Architectural Preservation,"
      "Historic Sites Registers," "Historic Structures," and "Preser-
      vation Legislation." (See also preceding citation.)

Chapter 2

HISTORICAL AND CURRENT OVERVIEWS

Contemporary preservation practice evolved, essentially, from two variant but compatible philosophies, that which developed in Great Britain and that which developed in France. The British model, based on private initiative, has been the prototype which has served in America and in the English-speaking world, in general, while the more governmentally centralized model set by France has served in most continental European countries and in their former colonies and dependencies. This chapter is divided into two sections. The first, General and International, includes materials of a general nature and materials with a broad international focus. The second, National and Regional, includes materials which deal with individual countries or with groups of countries within geographic regions.

GENERAL AND INTERNATIONAL

23   Bailly, G.H.   THE ARCHITECTURAL HERITAGE: LOCAL AUTHORITIES AND THE POLICY OF INTEGRATED CONSERVATION.   Vevey, Switzerland: Editions Delta Vevey, 1975.   102 p.   Paper.

Prepared for the Council of Europe and the European Conference of Local Authorities; product of European Architectural Heritage Year (1975). Sets forth the dangers that exist for the architectural heritage, and proposes policy objectives for combatting these dangers. Proposes the need for a coherent policy of integrated conservation, which demands "conscious, organised, concerted and persevering action on the part of local and regional authorities."

24   Cantacuzino, Sherban, ed.   ARCHITECTURAL CONSERVATION IN EUROPE.   New York: Whitney Library of Design, 1975.   138 p.   Illus.

In celebration of European Architectural Heritage Year (1975), a collection of articles on a variety of preservation themes: the city, the country town, the village and countryside, the coastline, and the care and neglect of churches. Presents examples from Eastern and Western Europe. Also includes two articles dealing with training for conservation and conservation legislation, the latter giving a chronological overview of

7

legislation in thirteen European countries and/or regions. Part of the material first published in a special issue of THE ARCHITECTURAL REVIEW, January 1975.

25   Ceschi, Carlo. TEORIA E STORIA DEL RESTAURO [Theory and history of restoration]. Rome: Mario Bulzoni Editore, 1970. 225 p. Illus., bibliog.

Traces the theory and history of preservation and restoration, primarily in terms of the French and Italian experience, but including also a chapter on John Ruskin. Includes a chronological overview of the development of Italian policy, legislation, and education.

26   Christie, Trevor L. ANTIQUITIES IN PERIL. Philadelphia: Lippincott, 1967. 151 p. Illus.

A popular, but informative, world survey of preservation problems, successes, and failures—past, present, and future.

27   CONGRÈS INTERNATIONAL DES ARCHITECTES ET TECHNICIENS DES MONUMENTS HISTORIQUES, PARIS, 6-11 MAI 1957 [International Congress of the Architects and Technicians of Historic Monuments]. Paris: Vincent, Fréal & Cie., 1960. 491 p. Illus.

Proceedings of a major international congress, including presentations by members of various French governmental agencies related to monument preservation, as well as by delegates from UNESCO. Six sessions, each dealing with a separate specific theme. In French.

28   Council of Europe. PAST IN FUTURE. Liege, Belgium: 1969. 79 p. Illus., paper.

Published on the occasion of the European Conference of Ministers responsible for the preservation of the cultural architectural heritage, organized by the Belgian government under the auspices of the Council of Europe. Describes the nature of Europe's immovable cultural property: monuments and groups of buildings of historical or artistic interest, and sites. Describes the various dangers threatening the cultural heritage, and proposes solutions at the governmental level, at the level of local authority, and by various educational means. Includes appendixes describing actions taken by the council as well as recent European legislation to promote the preservation and rehabilitation of immovable cultural property.

29   _____. THE PRESERVATION AND DEVELOPMENT OF ANCIENT BUILDINGS AND HISTORICAL OR ARTISTIC SITES. Strasbourg, France: 1963. 82 p. Illus., paper.

A report of the Cultural and Scientific Committee on the Pres-

ervation and Development of Ancient Buildings, submitted by
Ludwig Weiss. An overview of the council's philosophy, activity, and recommendations on behalf of historic preservation
in Europe. Also includes reports on policy and activity in
some member nations, the texts of some council recommendations and resolutions, and various reports, resolutions, and
orders of UNESCO and other organizations and conferences.

30 _____. PRESERVATION AND REHABILITATION OF THE CULTURAL
HERITAGE OF MONUMENTS AND SITES: EUROPEAN PROSPECTIVES.
Reprinted from Information Bulletin No. 1/1970 of the Documentation
Center for Education in Europe, pp. 18-85.

A selection of texts from five symposia, presenting the work
and outcome of the Conference of European Ministers responsible for the preservation and rehabilitation of the cultural heritage of monuments and sites, which was held at Brussels 25-27
November 1969. Helps to place this conference in its historical context and to grasp the evolution of the ideas which have
led to a global conception of the problems involved and to a
new policy, which has been summed up in the publication
PAST IN FUTURE (see entry 28).

31 Council of Europe. Committee on Monuments and Sites. "European
Program of Pilot Projects." Strasbourg, France: 1975. iii, 110 p.
Illus. Mimeographed.

Describes conservation projects, with information on the national legislative context, in each of seventeen countries--from the
United Kingdom in the West to Turkey in the East.

32 Fawcett, Jane, ed. THE FUTURE OF THE PAST: ATTITUDES TO CON-
SERVATION 1174-1974. London: Thames and Hudson, 1976. 160 p.
Illus.

A potpourri of essays by John Betjeman, Nikolaus Boulting,
Hugh Casson, Jane Fawcett, Mark Girouard, Osbert Lancaster,
Nikolaus Pevsner, and Robin Winks. Boulting reviews British
legislation and activity in conservation, 1174 to 1974; Pevsner,
in "Scrape and Anti-Scrape," describes the opposing Victorian
views to restoration; Wink, in "Conservation in America: National Character as Revealed by Preservation," offers a philosophical look at American preservation practice seen in the
international context.

33 "The Future of the Past." PROGRESSIVE ARCHITECTURE 53, no. 11
1972: entire issue.

A guest editorial by Arthur Cotton Moore is followed by ex-
cerpts of a preservation symposium cosponsored at the Metropolitan Museum of Art on May 30, 1972, by PROGRESSIVE
ARCHITECTURE and the Italian Art and Landscape Foundation.

Additional materials include a survey of preservation approaches in Louisville, Seattle, Lockport, and Lowell; an article by Peter Melvin, "Conservation and the Built Environment," describing United Kingdom conservation laws, economic viability, and design criteria for fitting new buildings into old sites; a portfolio of projects that "reuse, rescue, refurbish, restore, redecorate, preserve, polish, and protect"; and an article by Walter Kidney on the reuse of Pittsburgh's redundant North Side Post Office as the home of the Pittsburgh History and Landmarks Museum.

34   Giovannoni, Gustavo. IL RESTAURO DEI MONUMENTI [The restoration of monuments]. Rome: Cremonese, 1946(?). 94 p. Illus., paper.

A brief overview of preservation and restoration theory and practice by one of Italy's landmark figures in the field.

35   Glenn, Marsha. HISTORIC PRESERVATION: A HANDBOOK FOR ARCHITECTURE STUDENTS. Washington, D.C.: American Institute of Architects, 1974. iv, 60 p. Bibliog., paper.

A students' introduction to the field of historic preservation. Describes the purpose and process of preservation practice, national and international organizations, and educational opportunities. The result of the author's participation in a summer project for the A.I.A. Institute Scholar Program, 1974.

36   Harvey, John Hooper. CONSERVATION OF BUILDINGS. London: John Baker; Toronto: University of Toronto Press, 1972. 240 p. Illus., bibliographical note.

By a veteran professional in the field of preservation. Discusses: "What to Save and How to Save It--The Town, The Village, The Church and Churchyard"; "Craftsmanship and Materials--Craftsmanship, Masonry and Brickwork, Timberwork, Roofs, Decorations, Fittings and Furniture"; and "Continuing Conservation--The Past, The Present, Looking Forward." A classic history and contemporary review of preservation in Great Britain and Europe.

37   Huxtable, Ada Louise. KICKED A BUILDING LATELY? New York: Quadrangle/New York Times Book Co., 1976. xvi, 304 p. Illus.

An anthology of writings by America's foremost architectural critic, containing a number of selections dealing with various aspects of preservation.

38 International Council on Monuments and Sites. SYMPOSIUM ON
MONUMENTS AND SOCIETY, LENINGRAD, 2-8.IX.1969. Paris:
1971. 153 p. Paper.

A topic of vast proportions addressed by a panel of international
participants. Some reports in English, others in French.

39 International Federation for Housing and Planning. Standing Committee
for Historic Urban Areas. ACTES DE LA RÉUNION DE VENISE. VENICE
MEETING ACTS. SITZUNGSURKUNDEN--VENEDIG. Publication, no.
1. Turin: Urbanistica, 1964(?). 115 p. Illus.

Contributions by an international panel on historic centers
from Bergamo to Bratislava, from Stepney to Split. Articles
in English, French, or German, with summaries in the other
two languages.

40 International Museum Office. LA CONSERVATION DES MONUMENTS
D'ART & D'HISTOIRE/THE CONSERVATION OF ARTISTIC & HISTORI-
CAL MONUMENTS. Paris: 1933. 487 p. Illus.

Comprises the communications presented to the Conférence
Internationale d'Experts pour la Protection et la Conservation
des Monuments d'Art et d'Histoire, held in Athens, 21-30
October 1931. Gives the agenda and the conclusions of the
conference in French, English, German, Spanish, and Italian.
Includes an appendix (pp. 417-54) giving an analytic table
of contents to the papers, agenda, and conclusions of this
most significant landmark conference.

41 Jacobs, Stephen W. "Architectural Preservation in Europe: French and
English Contributions." CURATOR 9, no. 3 (1966): 196-215.

An essay presented at the Conference on Architecture and
Legislation for its Preservation and Excellence, held by the
New York State Council on the Arts at Arden House, Harri-
man, New York, 16 January 1966. Recalls that as early as
1793, the Revolutionary Convention of France expressed concern for the protection of "the monuments of the arts, of
history and of instruction"; the current Commission des Monuments Historiques is descended directly from the Committees
of the Convention. Explains that France, with its long tradition of centralized governmental control of the national heritage, has served as a model for most European countries;
while in England, dedicated amateurs, independent scholars,
and nongovernmental professionals have led the preservation
movement. Explains that England has been the model for the
United States, where sectional and local initiatives have been
the source of the preservation movement, with the federal and
state governments playing a modest role.

42   Kennet, Wayland [Young, Wayland Hilton, Baron Kennet]. PRESERVA-
      TION. London: Temple Smith, 1972. 224 p. Illus.

      Moves from Pope Benedict XIV's edict forbidding further de-
      struction of Rome's Colosseum, through the history of preserva-
      tion in England, to the author's personal involvement during
      1966-70 in the development of legislation, policy, and finance
      on the preservation of buildings of historic and architectural
      interest, during service in the Ministry of Housing and Local
      Government. Describes current French and Italian practice,
      and compares that with English practice. Includes chapter of
      advice to amenities societies and a chapter presenting case
      histories of some recent preservation battles. Lists relevant
      bodies and organizations in an appendix.

43   Museum (Paris). MONUMENTS ET SITES D'ART ET D'HISTOIRE ET
      FOUILLES ARCHÉOLOGIQUES: PROBLEMES ACTUELS/MONUMENTS
      AND SITES OF HISTORY AND ART AND ARCHAEOLOGICAL EXCA-
      VATIONS: PROBLEMS OF TODAY. UNESCO Publications No. 729.
      Paris: 1950. 99 p. Illus.

      Articles which first appeared in MUSEUM 3, no. 1 (1950),
      reporting on a meeting of international experts held at UNESCO,
      Paris, on 17-19 October 1949. A major postwar move to
      establish international cooperation in the preservation and
      restoration of monuments, buildings, glass, and architectural
      sculpture. Entire text in both English and French.

44   North American International Regional Conference, Williamsburg, Vir-
      ginia, and Philadelphia, 1972. PRESERVATION AND CONSERVATION:
      PRINCIPLES AND PRACTICES. Edited by Sharon Timmins. Washington,
      D.C.: Preservation Press, 1976. xxi, 547 p. Illus.

      Proceedings of a meeting conducted under the auspices of the
      International Centre for Conservation, Rome, and the Inter-
      national Centre Committee of the Advisory Council on Historic
      Preservation; 140 leading architectural preservationists and
      museum conservators convened to learn more about one another's
      practices and problems and to explore areas where one group
      might be able to assist the other. Includes sessions on occu-
      pations and organizations, materials and techniques, standards,
      and education.

45   "Preservation and Conservation: Perspectives, Programs, Projects."
      JOURNAL OF ARCHITECTURAL EDUCATION 30, no. 2 (1976): 32 p.

      An issue devoted to preservation and conservation. Includes
      descriptions of preservation education at Columbia University,
      George Washington University, the International Centre for
      Conservation Studies (Rome), the University of Florida, and

the University of Vermont. Also includes other articles dealing with the architect as developer, aspects of neighborhood
preservation, individual preservation cases, adaptive reuse,
and urban design.

46   "Preservation of Historic Monuments." JOURNAL OF THE AMERICAN
      SOCIETY OF ARCHITECTURAL HISTORIANS 1, nos. 3-4 (1941).

      The Society of Architectural Historians (known briefly in its
      early days as "The American Society of Architectural Histori-
      ans") has since its inception been concerned with architectural
      preservation. This early special issue of its journal is an
      anthology of preservation-related articles by a distinguished
      roster of contributors: "Introduction to the Preservation Issue"
      by Turpin C. Bannister, "The Evolution of Preservationism in
      Europe" by Hans Huth, "The Care of Historic Monuments in
      France" by Kenneth J. Conant, "The Preservation Movement
      in America" by Fiske Kimball, "The National Park Service
      and the Preservation of Historic Sites and Buildings" by Newton
      B. Drury, "The Society for the Preservation of New England
      Antiquities and Its Work" by William Sumner Appleton, "An
      Architectural Inventory for Charleston" by Helen G. McCormack,
      "The Museum of American Architecture: A Progress Report" by
      Charles E. Peterson, "The Heritage of Our Planned Communi-
      ties" by Carl Feiss, "Some Hard Facts on Practical Preserva-
      tion" (a letter to the New York City Board of Estimate) by
      Robert Moses, New York City Parks Commissioner, and "Pres-
      ervationism: A Selected Bibliography" (see entry 8) by Hans
      Huth.

47   "Restoration and Preservation of Historic Buildings." BUILDING RE-
      SEARCH 1, no. 5 (1964): 4-57.

      An issue of the journal of the Building Research Institute pre-
      senting a series of brief articles by leaders in the field of
      historic preservation. Based on presentations at the BRI Forum
      on Restoration and Preservation of Historic Buildings, held at
      Washington, D.C., on 11-12 June 1964. From the most
      philosophical and general to the most practical and specific.

48   "Summary of the Round Table Discussion on the Preservation of Historical
      Architectural Monuments: Held Tuesday, May 18, 1941, in the Library
      of Congress, Washington, D.C. " JOURNAL OF THE AMERICAN
      SOCIETY OF ARCHITECTURAL HISTORIANS 1, no. 2 (1941): 21-24.

      A landmark event in the history of historic preservation in the
      United States. Chaired by Henry-Russell Hitchcock, the meet-
      ing was a continuation of that held during the annual meeting
      of the College Art Association at Chicago, 29 January - 1
      February 1941. Those present at this historic roundtable were,

in addition to the chairman: Turpin C. Bannister, Rose T.
Briggs, Marian Comings, Albert H. Good, F. A. Gutheim,
John Davis Hatch, Jr., Leceister B. Holland, Walter Read
Hovey, Hans A. Huth, Donald C. Kline, Richard Krautheimer,
John McAndrew, C. L. V. Meeks, Ulrich Middeldorf, Richard
K. Newman, Jr., Frederick D. Nichols, Charles W. Porter,
Esther Isabel Seaver, Myron B. Smith, Robert T. Smith,
Elizabeth Read Sunderland, Thomas C. Vint, and Paul Zucker.

49   United Nations Educational, Scientific and Cultural Organization.   PRE-
SERVING AND RESTORING MONUMENTS AND HISTORIC BUILDINGS.
Museums and Monuments, No. 14.   Paris: 1972. 267 p.   Illus.

Presents a survey of the field in thirteen chapters by six inter-
nationally prominent preservationists: Ernest A. Connally,
Hiroshi Daifuku, Hans Foramitti, Piero Gazzola, Piero
Sanpaolesi, and Masaru Sekino.   Includes such topics as historical background, national legislation, international agreements, present programs, documentation, survey methods,
problems of deterioration, and restoration principles and
techniques.   Suggests that this volume be used in conjunction
with THE CONSERVATION OF CULTURAL PROPERTY, volume
9 in the same series, which deals in detail with problems and
solutions in the preservation of building materials such as
stone, wood, brick, and glass.

50   _____. PROTECTION OF MANKIND'S CULTURAL HERITAGE: SITES
AND MONUMENTS. Unesco and Its Programme. Paris: 1970. 73 p.
Illus., paper.

Part of a series describing UNESCO's various programs, presents a digest of that organization's action in the protection of
monuments and sites.   Covers the following subjects: "Legal
Protection"; "Scientific Cooperation"; "UNESCO Missions for
Monuments"; "The International Campaign to Save the Monuments of Nubia"; "The International Campaign for Florence
and Venice"; "Cultural Tourism"; "Six Projects for Cultural
Tourism"; and "The International Campaign for Monuments."

NATIONAL AND REGIONAL

The Americas

51   "Old Cities of the New World." Proceedings of the Pan American
Symposium on the Preservation and Restoration of Historic Monuments,
St. Augustine, Florida, 20-25 June 1965. Sponsored by the Organiza-
tion of American States, National Trust for Historic Preservation, St.
Augustine Historical Restoration & Preservation Commission. San Agustín
Antiguo: 1967. Mimeographed. 150 leaves (various paginations). Illus.

A major conference on the preservation of Ibero-American architecture and sites. Presents a distinguished group of experts from North and South America surveying the architecture worth preserving in the United States and Latin America, considering related problems of techniques in preservation and restoration, and discussing protective legislation in effect in such countries as the United States, Mexico, Brazil, and Guatemala. Concludes with the text of the "Charter of Venice," the resolution of the Second International Congress of Historic Monument Architects and Technicians, held in Venice, 25-31 May 1964. Some of the papers of this symposium later published in PATRIMONIO CULTURAL/CULTURAL PROPERTY, PRESERVACIÓN DE MONUMENTOS/PRESERVATION OF MONUMENTS, no. 1 (see below).

52   Organization of American States. Department of Cultural Affairs. Division of Cultural Relations. PATRIMONIO CULTURAL/CULTURAL PROPERTY, PRESERVACIÓN DE MONUMENTOS/PRESERVATION OF MONUMENTS. No. 1. Washington, D.C.: 1966. 78 p. Illus., Paper. No. 2. Washington, D.C.: 1968. 49 p. Illus., Paper.

Number 1: a selection of the papers presented to the Pan American Symposium on the Preservation and Restoration of Historical Monuments (see preceding citation). Number 2: a report of the Meeting on the Preservation and Utilization of Monuments and Sites of Historical Value, held in Quito, Ecuador, 29 November to 2 December 1967. Includes the text of the important result of that meeting, "Las Normas de Quito," or "The Quito Standards," the specifically American equivalent of the "Charter of Venice," which sets forth the goals and standards for the protection and use of the cultural and historic patrimony in the Americas, with special emphasis on the Hispanic heritage.

Australia

53   Australia. The National Estate Committee of Inquiry. REPORT OF THE NATIONAL ESTATE: REPORT OF THE COMMITTEE OF INQUIRY INTO THE NATIONAL ESTATE. Canberra: Australian Government Publishing Service, 1974. 415 p. Illus., paper.

The work of a committee charged by the Prime Minister to present a report on Australia's national patrimony. Includes five parts: part I concerns itself with defining the "National Estate"; part II reports on the condition of the natural environment, the built environment, aboriginal sites and other special areas, and cultural property; part III speaks of the role of government, constitutional constraints, taxation, and the present role and new tasks for the Australian government;

part IV, entitled, "People," has a chapter on "Education for
Conservation" and one on "Voluntary Organizations"; and
part V, the conclusion, presents "Findings and Recommendations."

Austria

54   Austria. Bundesdenkmalamt. DENKMALPFLEGE IN ÖSTERREICH,
      1945-1970   [Monument protection in Austria, 1945-1970]. Informations-
      schau des Bundesdenkmalamtes, Secession Wien, 16 Oktober--15 Nov-
      ember 1970. Vienna: 1970. 279 p. Illus., bibliog., paper.

      Published in connection with an exhibition in Vienna review-
      ing and documenting preservation activity in Austria in the
      twenty-five-year period following the end of World War II.
      Includes articles on all aspects of this activity, contributed
      by a number of experts involved in monuments preservation
      in Austria. Includes an appendix listing Austrian preservation
      legislation and a directory of organizations and personnel in
      the Bundesdenkmalamt (the organization of monuments bureaus).

Caribbean

55   Carlozzi, Carl Anthony. "Conservation of Natural, Scenic, and His-
      toric Areas in the Lesser Antilles." Ph.D. dissertation, University of
      Michigan, 1965. 274 p. (DISSERTATION ABSTRACTS INTERNATIONAL,
      Vol. 26, Part 11, p. 6276--Agriculture, Forestry and Wildlife.)

      Based on field investigation on twenty-two islands in the Lesser
      Antilles from September 1962 to July 1964, to compile a quali-
      fied inventory of sites suitable for national parks, nature re-
      serves, historic sites, and outdoor recreation, and to suggest
      possible means for the protection of the sites in the inventory
      in the context of present social, economic, and political
      conditions on the islands. Includes three parts: part I reviews
      the natural and human history of the islands; part II presents
      an island by island inventory of sites in each class; part III
      discusses the factors that have impeded the conservation of
      natural and historic areas in the islands. Concludes that the
      natural and historic resources of the islands would best be
      conserved through a system of international cooperation that
      would pool existing interest and talent and would provide a
      means for acquiring funds from outside the islands. Proposes
      a model international organization, and discusses the role of
      tourism.

56 National Trust for Historic Preservation. A CARIBBEAN CRUISE IN
CONSERVATION AND PRESERVATION. Washington, D.C.: n.d.
48 p. Bibliog., paper.

Report of the January 1974 Preservation Clinics in the Carrib-
bean, sponsored by the National Trust along with the Island
Resources Foundation and the Caribbean Conservation Association, both of St. Thomas, Virgin Islands. Reports that representatives of the National Park Service and the sponsoring
organizations visited the islands of Antigua, Barbados, Grenada,
Jamaica, St. Croix, St. Eustatius, St. Kitts, St. Lucia, and
St. Vincent, where they met in workshops with participants
representing local organizations and agencies.

Central and Eastern Europe

57 Society of Architectural Historians, and the National Trust for Historic
Preservation. SEMINAR ON ARCHITECTURE AND HISTORIC PRESER-
VATION IN CENTRAL AND EASTERN EUROPE, NEW YORK, 1975.
n.d. 25 p.

Synopses of papers read at a seminar held in New York, at
the Carnegie International Center, 28-30 November 1975,
cosponsored by the Society of Architectural Historians and the
National Trust for Historic Preservation. Concerns architectural heritage and preservation activity in Czechoslovakia, Hungary, Poland, Romania, Russia, and Yugoslavia.

Germany (Federal Republic of Germany)

58 Mielke, Friedrich. DIE ZUKUNFT DER VERGANGENHEIT: GRUND-
SÄTZE, PROBLEME UND MÖGLICHKEITEN DER DENKMALPFLEGE
[The future of the past: principles, problems and possibilities of monu-
ments protection]. Stuttgart: Deutsche Verlags-Anstalt, 1975. 328 p.
Illus., bibliog., paper.

By the director of the Institute for Monument Protection in
West Berlin's Technical University, where Denkmalpflege has
been a subject of study since 1908. Published in European
Architectural Heritage Year, 1975. Reviews the foundations,
problems, and possibilities of historic preservation. Considers
every philosophical and practical aspect. Gives an outline
for a teaching program. Includes a directory of West German
bureaus for monument protection and of West German schools
and universities where this is taught.

Germany (German Democratic Republic)

59   Institut für Denkmalpflege. Arbeitsstelle Erfurt. DENKMALE IN
      THÜRINGEN: IHRE ERHALTUNG UND PFLEGE IN DEN BEZIRKEN
      ERFURT, GERA UND SUHL [Monuments in Thüringen: their preserva-
      tion and protection in the districts of Erfurt, Gera and Suhl]. Weimar:
      Hermann Böhlaus Nachfolger, 1973. 398 p. Illus.

      Concerns landmarks preservation in the German Democratic
      Republic. A publication of the Erfurt branch of the Institute
      for Monuments Protection. Presents sixteen reports of activity
      in Thüringen, particularly in the districts named. Discusses
      the role and history of monument protection in Socialist phi-
      losophy; the conservation of specific materials, such as paint
      colors and stone; archaeological investigation; and specific
      building types, including ruins, churches, palaces, and town
      houses. Includes a review of preservation activity from the
      founding of the Institut für Denkmalpflege in 1963 to the year
      1971. Concludes with a directory of work undertaken, by
      locality.

Great Britain

60   Bailey, K[enneth]. V. EDUCATION AND HERITAGE: A REPORT ON
      THE SIGNIFICANCE AND OUTCOME OF EUROPEAN ARCHITECTURAL
      HERITAGE YEAR IN ENGLISH EDUCATION. London: Heritage Edu-
      cation Group, Civic Trust, 1976. 96 p. Paper.

      A broad account of educational activity in England relating
      to European Architectural Heritage Year, in the schools, in
      adult education, and on the part of the museums, broadcasting
      authorities, and others.

61   Briggs, Martin Shaw. GOTHS AND VANDALS: A STUDY OF THE
      DESTRUCTION, NEGLECT AND PRESERVATION OF HISTORICAL
      BUILDINGS IN ENGLAND. London: Constable, 1952. 251 p. Illus.,
      bibliog.

      From the most ancient times to the twentieth century, records
      destruction in the name of religious suppression, destruction
      in the name of improvement, destruction in the name of resto-
      ration, and so forth. Presents a record of preservation and
      recording activity in Britain until after World War II. Re-
      views acts of Parliament for monument protection, beginning
      in 1873. Includes a select bibliography listing publications
      chronologically from 1850 to 1950.

62   Dixon-Scott, J. ENGLAND UNDER TRUST: THE PRINCIPAL PROPER-
      TIES HELD BY THE NATIONAL TRUST IN ENGLAND AND WALES.
      Foreword by G.M. Trevelyan. London: Alexander Maclehose & Co.,
      1937. xx, 339 p. Illus.

From the vantage point of four decades, presents a document
in the history of the National Trust, founded in Great Britain
in 1895. Describes a number of the trust's natural and built
properties.

63   Fedden, Robin. THE CONTINUING PURPOSE: A HISTORY OF THE
NATIONAL TRUST, ITS AIMS AND WORK. London: Longmans, Green
and Co., 1968. xi, 226 p. Illus.

A detailed account of the history, purpose, methods, and
achievements of England's National Trust from its founding to
the time of publication. Revised in 1974 as THE NATIONAL
TRUST: PAST AND PRESENT (see below).

64   _____. THE NATIONAL TRUST: PAST AND PRESENT. London:
Jonathon Cape, 1974. 191 p. Illus., paper.

A revision of the author's 1968 detailed history of the National Trust titled THE CONTINUING PURPOSE (see above), which
was a fairly full record of the first seventy years, containing,
according to the author, "detailed information unlikely to
interest the general reader." Presents a revision of the earlier
book, which "tells the same story in briefer compass and
broader outline, and brings it up to date." Contains a history of the National Trust and a description of its purpose
and operation.

65   Freeman, Edward Augustus. THE PRESERVATION AND RESTORATION
OF ANCIENT MONUMENTS. A paper read before the Archaeological
Institute at Bristol on July 29, 1851, with notes. Oxford and London:
John Henry Parker; Bristol: T. Kerslake and O. Lasbury, 1852. iv,
66 p.

By an author noted as "Late fellow of Trinity College, Oxford;
Local Secretary of the Institute for Gloucestershire." Presents
a plea against the "restorations" of the time, "...this daemon
of destruction veiled in the garb of the angel of preservation
...". Reviews some contemporary restorations, and recommends
different treatment for antiquities whose value lies only in
their antiquity and beauty and for those antiquities whose use
continues to the present. "The former class I conceive to be
objects for simple preservation, while the latter, whenever
they require it, should be faithfully and reverentially restored."

66   Great Britain. Preservation Policy Group. REPORT TO THE MINISTER
OF HOUSING AND LOCAL GOVERNMENT, MAY, 1970. London:
Her Majesty's Stationery Office, 1970. iv, 54 p. Paper.

By the Preservation Policy Group, which was set up in 1966
to coordinate the special studies of historic areas in five towns;
to review experience of action to preserve the character of
other historic towns; to consider measures adopted in other

Historical and Current Overviews

countries (France, Belgium, Denmark, and The Netherlands)
for preserving the character of historic towns and villages; to
consider legal, financial, and administrative arrangements for
preservation, including the planning and development aspects;
and to make recommendations. Presents a result of the group's
study, with the original five towns reduced to four: Bath,
Chester, Chichester, and York. Includes a review of the
Civic Amenities Act of 1967, the Town and County Planning
Act of 1968, the Transport Act of 1968, and the Housing
Act of 1969.

67   Hill, William Thompson. OCTAVIA HILL, PIONEER OF THE NATIONAL
      TRUST AND HOUSING REFORMER. Foreword by Lionel Curtis. London:
      Hutchinson, 1956. 208 p. Illus., bibliog.

      Biography of Octavia Hill, 1838-1912, a young friend of
      John Ruskin, who became a major force in the fight for
      housing and preservation in Great Britain, and who was a
      founder of Britain's National Trust.

68   Kelsall, Moultrie R., and Harris, Stuart. A FUTURE FOR THE PAST.
      Edinburgh and London: Oliver and Boyd, 1961. vii, 151 p. Illus.

      States that this is a book written in wrath and hope, "wrath
      at the monumental wastage of old buildings that goes on in
      Scotland today: hope that it may yet be possible to stop it
      by marshalling the overwhelming arguments for reconstruction
      and showing how a satisfactory reconstruction may be achieved."
      In the first part, reviews the advantages of reconstruction as
      a local and national policy; in the second part, discusses the
      technique of reconstruction, with typical examples. Gives
      case histories of specific restored and rehabilitated structures.

69   Lees-Milne, James, ed. THE NATIONAL TRUST: A RECORD OF FIFTY
      YEARS' ACHIEVEMENT. Introduction by G.M. Trevelyan. London:
      B. T. Batsford, 1945. xii, 132 p. Illus.

      A half-century progress report in the form of essays by a num-
      ber of contributors. The subjects are all manner of buildings,
      sites, landscapes, and shrines which are the concern of the
      National Trust. An appendix describes the work of the Trust.

Hungary

70   Dercsenyi, Dezso. HISTORICAL MONUMENTS IN HUNGARY: RES-
      TORATION AND PRESERVATION. Budapest: Corvina, 1969. 96 p.
      Illus.

      A historical survey of preservation legislation and practice in
      Hungary, divided into three parts: the period from 1863 to
      1934, the period from 1934 to 1949, and the period from 1949

20

onward. Describes the differences in philosophy, policy, and methodology in these three major periods. Presents a survey of current restoration projects covering ruins, castles, country places and manor houses, public buildings, ecclesiastical buildings, dwelling houses, rural and industrial buildings, and statues and mural paintings.

Italy

71 Cantone, Alfredo. DIFESA DEI MONUMENTI E DELLE BELLEZZE NATURALI [Protection of monuments and of natural beauty]. 2d ed. Naples: Fausto Fiorentino Editore, 197?. vi, 670 p. Paper.

A manual and guide to Italian agencies, practice, and legislation relating to all aspects of the protection and management of the artistic, cultural, and natural scenic patrimony.

72 Gurrieri, Francesco, comp. TEORIA E CULTURA DEL RESTAURO DEI MONUMENTI E DEI CENTRI ANTICHI [Theory and culture of the restoration of monuments and antique centers]. Florence: CLUSF (Cooperativa Libraria Universitatis Studii Florentini), 1974. 329 p. Illus., paper.

An anthology of articles, all of which appeared earlier in various periodicals, by leading Italian preservationists and architectural historians.

73 Santoro, Lucio. RESTAURO DEI MONUMENTI E TUTELA AMBIENTALE DEI CENTRI ANTICHI [The restoration of monuments and protection of the ambience of historic centers]. Cava dei Tirreni: Di Mauro Editore, 1970. 222 p. Bibliog., paper.

Theory and practice of the preservation of historic centers, with primary emphasis on Italy. From Viollet-le-Duc, Ruskin, and Morris to the more recent past: the post World War II period, the Charter of Venice, and current international cooperation through such bodies as the International Council on Monuments and Sites and the Council of Europe. Includes a chronological bibliography, mostly Italian, from 1781 to 1970.

Japan

74 Japan. Bunkazai Hogo Iinkai [National Commission for Protection of Cultural Properties]. ADMINISTRATION FOR PROTECTION OF CULTURAL PROPERTIES IN JAPAN. Tokyo: National Commission for Protection of Cultural Properties, 1962. 101 p. Illus., paper.

Reports that in 1950, Japan established the National Commission for Protection of Cultural Properties. In part I, describes in detail the definition of cultural property and its application

to all aspects of Japanese cultural heritage, including traditional foods, theatre, music, and costume, which are categor-
ized as (1) tangible cultural properties, (2) intangible cultural
properties, (3) folk culture, and (4) monuments with historic,
scientific, or scenic significance. Under the first heading,
includes buildings, pictures, sculpture, calligraphy, books,
ancient documents, etc.; under the second, includes the art
and skill employed in drama, music, and the applied arts;
under the third, includes manners and customs related to food,
clothing, housing, occupations, religious faiths, festivals,
clothes, implements, and houses; and under the fourth, includes shell mounds, tombs, sites, places of scenic value,
bridges, gardens, seashores, and mountains. In part II, presents the "Law for the Protection of Cultural Properties," law
number 214 of 30 May 1950.

Poland

75   Zachwatowicz, Jan. PROTECTION OF HISTORICAL MONUMENTS IN
      POLAND. Warsaw: Polonia Publishing House, 1965. 147 p. Illus.,
      paper.

      Best described by its contents: (1) "The Heritage of Polish
      Culture," (2) "Protection of Historical Monuments and Objects
      of Art before the Second World War," (3) "The Second World
      War--The Nazi Occupation," (4) "Protection of Historical
      Monuments after the Second World War: Principles, Legislation,
      Education, Financing of a Conservation Program," (5) "Recon-
      struction of Historical Urban Centers: Warsaw, Gdańsk,
      Szczecin, Wrocław, Poznań, Lublin, Opole, etc.," (6) "Aims
      and Objectives with Regard to Immovable Objects," (7) "Aims
      and Objectives with Regard to Movable Objects," (8) "Poland's
      Part in International Cooperation on the Protection and Conser-
      vation of Historic Monuments."

South Africa

76   Immelman, R.F.M., and Quinn, G.D., eds. THE PRESERVATION AND
      RESTORATION OF HISTORIC BUILDINGS IN SOUTH AFRICA. Cape-
      town: A.A. Balkema, 1968. xii, 98 p. Illus.

      Based on a symposium held in Capetown, 16-27 November 1959,
      instituted by the Cape Provincial Institute of Architects in col-
      laboration with the South African National Society. Includes
      papers on: "Preservation Policy of the Cape Provincial Admin-
      istration," "Aims and Procedures in Restoration and Preservation
      of Historic Buildings," "British Influence in South African
      Architecture," "Design Sources for Historic Buildings at the
      Cape," "The Practical Relation of Restoration and Preservation

of Historic Buildings to Town Planning," "The Aesthetic Relation of Restoration and Preservation of Historic Buildings to
Town Planning," and others.

Switzerland

77   Knoepfli, Albert. SCHWEIZERISCHE DENKMALPFLEGE: GESCHICHTE
      UND DOKTRINEN [Swiss monuments protection: history and doctrines].
      BEITRÄGE ZUR GESCHICHTE DER KUNSTWISSENSCHAFT IN DER
      SCHWEIZ. 1 [Contributions to the History of Art Scholarship in Switzer-
      land, 1]. Zurich: Schweizerisches Institut für Kunstwissenschaft, 1972.
      240 p. Illus., bibliog.

      A historical and current overview of Swiss theory and practice
      in the protection of monuments and sites, published in collab-
      oration with the Eidgenössische Technische Hochschule, Zurich,
      the Institut für Denkmalpflege, and the Gesellschaft für
      Schweizerische Kunstgeschichte. In German, with summaries
      in English, French, and German.

Union of Soviet Socialist Republics

78   U.S. Historic Preservation Team. A REPORT BY THE U.S. HISTORIC
      PRESERVATION TEAM OF THE U.S.-U.S.S.R. JOINT WORKING
      GROUP ON THE ENHANCEMENT OF THE URBAN ENVIRONMENT.
      Washington, D.C.: U.S. Department of the Interior, 1975. x, 93 p.
      Illus., paper.

      Concerns the visit of the U.S. Historic Preservation Team to
      the Soviet Union, 25 May - 14 June 1974, as part of a
      project titled "Improvement of environment with regard to
      historic places and monuments." Reports that the purpose of
      the visit was to study the current principles, policies, and
      practices of Soviet historic preservation, with emphasis upon
      the procedural and legal aspects involved in the registration,
      protection, and adaptive use of historic monuments; and on
      the role of the private and academic sectors in Soviet preser-
      vation. Includes a series of papers by members of the team
      on various aspects of their findings. Includes appendixes
      describing the program and the tour, listing the Soviet partici-
      pants, and listing the documents taken to the U.S.S.R. by the
      team.

United States

79   Advisory Council on Historic Preservation. THE NATIONAL HISTORIC
      PRESERVATION PROGRAM TODAY. Washington, D.C.: 1976. vii,
      111 p. Pamphlet.

Prepared by the council at the request of Senator Henry M. Jackson, chairman of the Senate Committee on Interior and Insular Affairs, for presentation to the committee in the bi-centennial year, during the second session of the 94th Congress. Surveys and critically examines the national historic preservation program and identifies current and future needs for the preservation of the national heritage. Describes official preservation policy in Great Britain, U.S.S.R., Japan, the Netherlands, and Canada.

80   Finley, David E. HISTORY OF THE NATIONAL TRUST FOR HISTORIC PRESERVATION. Washington, D.C.: National Trust for Historic Preservation, 1965. v, 115 p. Illus.

A short, informal history of the National Trust, from its founding in 1947 to 1963. By one of the founders, who was a director of the National Gallery of Art at the time of the National Trust's inception. Includes bylaws and other documents in appendixes. (For update see entry 89.)

81   Hosmer, Charles Bridgham, Jr. "Old Houses in America: The Preservation Movement to 1926." Ph.D. dissertation, Columbia University, 1961. 465 p. (DISSERTATION ABSTRACTS INTERNATIONAL, vol. 22, part 5, p. 1593--History.)

Proposes that the preservation of a large number of houses in the United States before 1926 was not merely the result of scattered efforts, but the work of a broad and interrelated movement which was distinctly American. Reports that the huge majority of people who supported preservation work were amateurs with little or no idea what other countries were doing in the field, pointing out the indigenous character of the movement. Proposes that the people who preserved old buildings were motivated by a romantic notion that historical landmarks could be important in patriotic education and by various subordinate motives as well, particularly local pride and the utilitarian purpose of locating a suitable headquarters for a local historical or patriotic society. Examines and documents the history of the preservation movement in the United States from the rescue and preservation of Mount Vernon to the reconstruction of Colonial Williamsburg. Served as the basis for the author's book, PRESENCE OF THE PAST: A HISTORY OF THE PRESERVATION MOVEMENT IN THE UNITED STATES BEFORE WILLIAMSBURG (see below).

82   _____. PRESENCE OF THE PAST: A HISTORY OF THE PRESERVATION MOVEMENT IN THE UNITED STATES BEFORE WILLIAMSBURG. New York: G.P. Putnam's Sons, 1965. 386 p. Illus., bibliog.

The classic chronicle of the preservation movement in the
United States until 1926. Based on the author's doctoral dissertation done at Columbia University in 1961 (see preceding
citation). A sequel by the author, bringing the chronicle
up to date, is awaiting publication.

83   Jacobs, Stephen William. "Architectural Preservation: American Development and Antecedents Abroad." Ph.D. dissertation, Princeton
University, 1966. 555 p. (DISSERTATION ABSTRACTS INTERNATIONAL,
vol. 27-A, part 9, p. 2962--Fine Arts.)

A dissertation written at a time when massive losses occurring
as a result of large scale renewal and highway programs brought
the rapid decimation of the stock of architectural landmarks to
the attention of a broad citizenry. In light of the need for
greater effort and new methods for architectural preservation,
proposes to account for what the author sees as the unsatis-
factory results of a century of work in architectural preservation. Sees much of the difficulty as deriving from the use
of inappropriate methods developed in Europe and the failure
to recognize the special conditions and opportunities which
exist in the United States. Presents a historical review of
Old World concern for the preservation of buildings, concluding with a description of preservation methods developed
in France and in the British Isles since the late eighteenth
century. Reviews the experience of architectural preservation
in the United States, and discusses state and local efforts at
preservation and the role of recently evolving planning techniques. Concludes that European approaches to architectural
preservation must be radically modified for use in the United
States.

84   _____. "Architectural Preservation in the United States: the Government's Role." CURATOR 9, no. 4 (1966): 307-30.

An essay prepared for the Seminar on Preservation and Restoration held by the National Trust for Historic Preservation and
Colonial Williamsburg at Williamsburg, Virginia, 8-11 September 1963, and also published in HISTORIC PRESERVATION
TODAY (see entry 93). Compares U.S. preservation history
to that of Great Britain, and contrasts it with that of France
and most European countries. Presents a review of the history
of preservation in the United States, from its beginnings to
the date of the essay.

85   Lee, Ronald F. THE ANTIQUITIES ACT OF 1906. Washington, D.C.:
U.S. National Park Service, Office of History and Historic Architecture,
Eastern Service Center, 1970. iv, 120 p. Paper.

Starting with the establishment by Congress of the Bureau of
Ethnology in the year 1879, traces the public interest in
American Indian antiquities and related legislation and activity to the year 1969. Gives the text of the 1906 act. Includes tables which show historic areas, scientific areas, and
national monuments established from 1906 to 1969.

86   _____. UNITED STATES: HISTORICAL AND ARCHAEOLOGICAL
MONUMENTS. Instituto Panamericano de Geografía e Historia,
Comision de Historia, Publicación no. 30; Monumentos históricos y
arqueológicos, 2.; Instituto Panamericano de Geografía e Historia,
Publicación no. 117. Mexico City: I.P.G.H., 1951. 121 p.
Illus.

By the then assistant director of the U.S. National Park Service, a major figure in the founding of the National Trust
for Historic Preservation. Describes preservation in the United
States from 1850, "when the State of New York acquired the
Hasbrouck House, General Washington's headquarters at New-
burgh, New York, and placed it in the hands of the village
trustees for preservation and exhibition--the first publicly-
owned historic house museum in the country." From the background of the preservation movement, moves to legislative
procedures, survey and classification, preservation and restoration policies, educational policies and program, administration,
and recent trends. One of a number of volumes about preservation of monuments in various American nations published by
the Panamerican Institute of Geography and History in its
series MONUMENTOS HISTÓRICOS Y ARQUEOLÓGICOS.

87   Lord, Clifford L., ed. KEEPERS OF THE PAST. Chapel Hill: University of North Carolina Press, 1965. 241 p.

Biographical essays, by a number of contributors, of notable
American figures connected with historical societies, public
archives, historical museums, special collections, and historic site preservation.

88   Miner, Ralph W. CONSERVATION OF HISTORIC AND CULTURAL
RESOURCES. American Society of Planning Officials, Planning Advisory
Service Report No. 244. Chicago: A.S.P.O., 1969. 56 p. Illus.,
bibliog., paper.

Sets forth the purpose of the report as "to define historic and
cultural conservation, trace the changing emphasis of the preservation movement as it has evolved in the United States,
outline an approach to historic and cultural conservation within
the perspective of key issues and problems, and describe the
basic components of a comprehensive local conservation program." Covers broad aspects of historic and cultural conser-

vation within an urban planning framework. Discusses historic
district zoning in terms of a traditional approach and a more
flexible approach. Also discusses easements, urban renewal,
federal assistance programs, tax incentives, and architectural
review guidelines.

89   Mulloy, Elizabeth D. THE HISTORY OF THE NATIONAL TRUST FOR
      HISTORIC PRESERVATION, 1963-1973. Washington, D.C.: Preservation
      Press, 1976. xvi, 301 p. Illus.

      Updates David E. Finley's HISTORY OF THE NATIONAL TRUST
      FOR HISTORIC PRESERVATION (1947-1963) (see entry 80). De-
      scribes activity and involvement of the National Trust for a decade
      of the organization's explosive growth.

90   National Trust for Historic Preservation. AMERICA'S FORGOTTEN
      ARCHITECTURE. Edited by Tony P. Wrenn and Elizabeth D. Mulloy.
      New York: Pantheon Books, 1976. 311 p. Illus., bibliog.

      A bicentennial book which looks, through photographs, at
      many aspects of the built environment, extant and destroyed,
      and describes the philosophy and methods of preservation.

91   _____. HISTORIC PRESERVATION TOMORROW: REVISED PRINCIPLES
      & GUIDELINES FOR HISTORIC PRESERVATION IN THE UNITED STATES.
      Washington, D.C.: 1967. xi, 57 p. Illus., bibliog., paper.

      A revision of the guidelines originally prepared at the Seminar
      on Preservation and Restoration held in Williamsburg, Virginia,
      in 1963, and included in its publication HISTORIC PRESERVA-
      TION TODAY (see entry 93). Prepared at a workshop held in
      Williamsburg on 3-5 March 1967, sponsored by the National
      Trust and Colonial Williamsburg. Reports that, because the
      history of the preservation movement in the United States,
      with its European background, was presented at the first work-
      shop and published in HISTORIC PRESERVATION TODAY, with
      another full account in WITH HERITAGE SO RICH (see entry
      96), the intent of the second workshop was to revise only the
      "Principles and Guidelines" section of the report in the light of
      1966 federal legislation directly affecting the preservation move-
      ment.

92   _____. A REPORT ON PRINCIPLES AND GUIDELINES FOR HISTORIC
      PRESERVATION IN THE UNITED STATES: OBSERVATIONS ON THE
      PRESENT STATE OF AFFAIRS, TOGETHER WITH A STATEMENT OF
      PRINCIPLES INVOLVED AND SOME RECOMMENDATIONS FOR IM-
      PROVEMENTS BY A COMMITTEE APPOINTED FOR THAT PURPOSE.
      Preservation Leaflet Series. Washington, D.C.: 1964. 23 p. Paper.

Published as a contribution to International Monuments Year, reports conclusions based on the joint Seminar on Preservation and Restoration held at Williamsburg, 8-11 September 1963.

93   National Trust for Historic Preservation, and the Colonial Williamsburg Foundation. HISTORIC PRESERVATION TODAY: ESSAYS PRESENTED TO THE SEMINAR ON PRESERVATION AND RESTORATION, WILLIAMS-BURG, VIRGINIA, SEPTEMBER 8-11, 1963. Charlottesville: University Press of Virginia, 1966. x, 265 p. Paper.

Presents the proceedings of a three-day conference of a group of 160 persons active in the American preservation movement. Reports that their purpose was "to review the history of Ameri-can preservation (including its European background), to ana-lyze its philosophical basis, examine its present effectiveness, and to discuss ideal ways to shape its future." Indicates that distinguished foreign participants included Jacques Dupont, Inspecteur Général des Monuments Historiques, Paris; Sir John Summerson, Curator of Sir John Soane's Museum, London; Stanisław Lorentz, Director of The National Museum, Warsaw; and Peter Michelsen, Director of the Frilandsmuseet, Copen-hagen. Concludes with "A Report on Principles and Guidelines for Historic Preservation in the United States." For an update and revision of these guidelines, see HISTORIC PRESERVATION TOMORROW (see entry 91).

94   President's Council on Recreation and Natural Beauty. FROM SEA TO SHINING SEA: A REPORT ON THE AMERICAN ENVIRONMENT--OUR NATURAL HERITAGE. Washington, D.C.: U.S. Government Printing Office, 1968. 304 p. Illus., bibliog., paper.

A massive report concerned with every aspect of the built and natural environment of rural and urban areas, parks, and shorelines. Outlines progress in environmental programs since the 1965 White House Conference on Natural Beauty, described in its publication titled BEAUTY FOR AMERICA (see entry 98). Presents proposals and recommendations to stimulate federal, state, local, and private action to further enhance the qual-ity of the environment and the beauty of the nation. Presents a guide for action by local officials, citizens groups, and individuals. Contains a section on neighborhood conservation. Lists agencies and organizations, public and private, which can be of assistance.

95   Schneider, J. Thomas. REPORT TO THE SECRETARY OF THE INTERIOR ON THE PRESERVATION OF HISTORIC SITES AND BUILDINGS. Wash-ington, D.C.: U.S. Department of the Interior, 1935. iii, 185 p. Charts, paper.

Extremely significant report of a survey which led to the
drafting of the U.S. Historic Sites Act of 1935. In part I,
"Present Interest and Activities," describes the then current
growing interest in the historic background of the United
States on the part of its citizenry, the activity at Williamsburg and Greenfield Village, efforts on the state and local
government level, and federal activities. In part II, "European Survey," describes the development of legislation abroad;
current legislation abroad; current legislation in six European
countries and Japan; current problems abroad; technical methods
employed abroad; unofficial organizations in Belgium, England,
France, and Sweden; and international cooperation. In part
III, "Legislation and Recommendations," describes the drafting
of the 1935 act, and develops recommendations to support and
fulfill the purpose of the act.

96   U.S. Conference of Mayors. Special Committee on Historic Preservation.
       WITH HERITAGE SO RICH: A REPORT. New York: Random House,
       1966. xvi, 230 p. Illus., bibliog.

       Includes essays by Helen Duprey Bullock, Carl Feiss, Robert
       R. Garvey, Jr., Richard H. Howland, Sidney Hyman, Chris-
       topher Tunnard, Walter Muir Whitehill, and George Zabriskie.
       Also includes the findings and recommendations of the Special
       Committee on Historic Preservation, generally credited with
       being the major impetus to the enactment of the U.S. Historic
       Preservation Act of 1966.

97   WASHINGTON PRESERVATION CONFERENCE, SMITHSONIAN INSTI-
       TUTION MUSEUM OF NATURAL HISTORY, FRIDAY AND SATURDAY
       14-15 APRIL 1972. Sponsored by The Society of Architectural Historians-
       Latrobe Chapter and The National Trust for Historic Preservation. Wash-
       ington, D.C.: 1972. iv, 210 p. Cartoon illus., bibliog., paper.

       Although focusing on the federal city, explores the broad
       spectrum of preservation and urban rehabilitation activity.
       Includes appendixes giving a register of landmark structures
       and places in the national capital and a directory of preser-
       vation organizations, both national and district.

98   White House Conference on Natural Beauty, Washington, D.C., 24-25
       May 1965. BEAUTY FOR AMERICA. Washington, D.C.: 1965.
       782 p. Paper.

       Proceedings of a broad conference which included historic
       preservation among the topics discussed. For progress from
       this conference to the year 1968, see the publication, FROM
       SEA TO SHINING SEA (see entry 94).

Yugoslavia

99   Moor, Jay Haden. "Historic Preservation in Slovenia: A Case Study
      of the Need for Continuity." Ph.D. dissertation, University of Wash-
      ington, 1974. 257 p. (DISSERTATION ABSTRACTS INTERNATIONAL,
      Vol. 35-A, Part 7, p. 4747--Urban and Regional Planning.)

> Concerns cultural identity in a world of rapid change. Focuses
> on historic preservation in Slovenia, a region of ancient ethno-
> cultural identity which became, in the recent past, incorporated
> into the newly formed multinational state of Yugoslavia. Reports
> that, since World War II, historic preservation in Yugoslavia
> has been part of a broader cultural conservation function, felt
> to be necessary in order to avoid an internal split along the
> diverse lines of nationality. Indicates that, in great measure,
> the conservation of the cultures that make up Yugoslavia con-
> tributes to its political and social stability; this has been par-
> ticularly important in the Slovenian Republic, where industrial-
> ization, urbanization, and changes in ownership patterns have
> been the cause of stress. Includes in appendixes, translations
> of Yugoslav and Slovene conservation legislation and an inven-
> tory of cultural monuments in the Ljubljana urban region.

Chapter 3

FINANCIAL, LEGAL, AND PLANNING ASPECTS

Here are included writings about legislation concerned specifically with historic preservation as well as writings which demonstrate how preservation can be supported through the use of the existing legal and planning framework. Economic incentives and advantages are covered, as are preservation plans on the state and local levels.

GENERAL BACKGROUND—GREAT BRITAIN AND THE UNITED STATES

100   Advisory Council on Historic Preservation. GUIDELINES FOR STATE HISTORIC PRESERVATION LEGISLATION. Historic Preservation Workshop, National Symposium on State Environmental Legislation, March 15-18, 1972. Washington, D.C.: 1972. 61 p. Paper.

Guidelines for state historic preservation legislation drafted by the Advisory Council, based on the needs brought about by the enactment of the National Historic Preservation Act of 1966, which were submitted as a working draft to the Historic Preservation Workshop of the National Symposium on State Environmental Legislation. Represents the combined efforts of participants from the states, the federal establishment, and the private preservation movement.

101   Cambridgeshire and Isle of Ely County Council. County Planning Department. A GUIDE TO HISTORIC BUILDINGS LAW. 2d ed., rev. Cambridge: 1970. 54 p.

A booklet which sets out in simple note form the essence of British laws and regulations regarding historic buildings and sites, excluding special provisions (such as those specifically for the City of London, Wales, or Scotland) which do not pertain to Cambridgeshire and the Isle of Ely. Refers, in nonlegal language, to acts of Parliament dealing not only with planning law, but with ancient monuments, housing, and the National Trust. Discusses redundant churches and procedures under the "Pastoral Measure."

102   Greater London Council. Historic Buildings Board. THE WORK OF THE HISTORIC BUILDINGS BOARD OF THE GREATER LONDON COUNCIL. London: 1970. 61 p. Illus., paper.

Includes cartoons by Osbert Lancaster and verses by Sir John Betjeman, adding charm to this book which explains the role of the Historic Buildings Board in preserving the beauty and character of London.

103   National Trust for Historic Preservation. ECONOMIC BENEFITS OF PRESERVING OLD BUILDINGS. Washington, D.C.: Preservation Press, 1976. 164 p. Illus.

Papers from the Economics of Preserving Old Buildings Conference, sponsored by the National Trust, Seattle, Washington, 31 July - 2 August 1975. Presents the Seattle experience along with activity in Salt Lake City, New Orleans, and Savannah. Discusses municipal action and the role of the governmental and private sectors.

104   _____ . A GUIDE TO STATE HISTORIC PRESERVATION PROGRAMS. Researched and compiled by Betts Abel. Edited by Jennie B. Bull. Washington, D.C.: Preservation Press, 1976. 533 p. Paper.

A bicentennial edition, presenting information for each of the fifty states, the District of Columbia, Puerto Rico, Guam, the Virgin Islands, American Samoa, and the Trust Territory of the Pacific Islands. Divides the information for each into three major sections; preservation framework, state historic preservation office, and preservation programs. Concerns legislation, fiscal periods, agencies, review boards, annual preservation program status, National Register nomination process, budget, publications, technical assistance, training and education, historic sites, and other topics. Sections for individual states available separately.

105   _____ . HISTORIC PRESERVATION PLANS: AN ANNOTATED BIBLIOGRAPHY. Washington, D.C.: Preservation Press, 1976. 42 p. Paper.

Lists ninety-one historic preservation plans and reports published in the United States, including plans that address the general issue of historic preservation as well as those that provide recommendations and methods for implementation. Includes district plans, municipal plans, regional plans, state plans, ethnic area plans, open space plans, historic waterfront plans, and others. Provides source for obtaining each plan. In an appendix, gives the policy statement of the American Institute of Planners on "Conservation/Historic Preservation."

106   Pyke, John S., Jr. LANDMARK PRESERVATION. 2d ed. New York: Citizens Union Research Foundation, Inc., of the City of New York, 1972. 32 p. Illus., bibliog.

Produced by an organization established in 1948 to study and report to the public on issues concerning urban areas. A primer on the subject of landmark preservation, which aims to "persuade concerned citizens that landmark structures from the past can and must be saved for the future." Describes the economic benefits and the intangible benefits of landmarks, and discusses the landmarks preservation movement, with emphasis on the New York City Landmarks Preservation Commission and the law under which it operates.

107   "Symposium: Perspectives on Historic Preservation." CONNECTICUT LAW REVIEW 8, no. 2 (Winter 1975-76): 199-411.

An issue of a periodical published by the University of Connecticut School of Law, devoted to historic preservation. Eight articles on various economic, legal, and tax aspects of historic and neighborhood preservation, conservation, and rehabilitation.

108   U.S. Department of Housing and Urban Development. Division of Technical Standards. PRESERVING HISTORIC AMERICA. Washington, D.C.: U.S. Government Printing Office, 1966. 80 p. Illus., bibliog.

Demonstrates examples of preservation through the U.S. urban renewal program and the open-space land projects. Gives guidelines for a successful local historic preservation program.

109   U.S. National Park Service. Office of Archaeology and Historic Preservation. Division of Grants. HISTORIC PRESERVATION GRANTS-IN-AID CATALOG: THE NATIONAL HISTORIC PRESERVATION ACT OF 1966. Washington, D.C.: 1976. 237 p. Paper.

Lists and describes preservation of privately and publicly owned buildings on the National Register, with details regarding each project and grant.

BUILDING CODES

110   Massachusetts Institute of Technology. AN INVESTIGATION OF THE REGULATORY BARRIERS TO THE RE-USE OF EXISTING BUILDINGS. Cambridge: 1978. 117 p. Bibliog., paper.

A team investigation sponsored by the National Bureau of Standards Center for Building Technology. Concludes that existing buildings pose a significant problem for code interpretation and enforcement, and suggests that further investigations in a variety of areas will be necessary before a code can be developed which responds clearly to existing buildings.

111   National Trust for Historic Preservation. PRESERVATION AND BUILD-
ING CODES. Washington, D.C.: Preservation Press, 1975. 96 p.
Paper.

Presents a variety of current issues and solutions in papers
from the Preservation and Building Codes Conference sponsored
by the National Trust in Washington, D.C., in May 1974.
Lists examples of state and national code provisions relating
to historic buildings.

EASEMENTS, FINANCE, AND TAX INCENTIVES

112   Ipswich Historical Commission. SOMETHING TO PRESERVE: A REPORT
ON HISTORIC PRESERVATION BY THE ACQUISITION OF PROTECTIVE
AGREEMENTS ON BUILDINGS IN IPSWICH, MASSACHUSETTS. Ipswich:
1975. 111 p. Illus., glossary, paper.

Presents Ipswich's specific experience, set in the context of
Massachusetts and New England.

113   Nannen, Howard. A GUIDE TO THE FINANCING AND DEVELOPMENT
OF SMALL RESTORATION PROJECTS. Hartford, Conn.: Hartford Architecture Conservancy, 1976. 43 p. Paper.

A manual specifically designed for people interested in buying
and rehabilitating a deteriorated older building in the city of
Hartford for private residence and/or rental. In part I, explains terms and procedures relating to buying and financing
this type of real estate. In part II, provides forms for all
relevant information that may be used for particular projects
and needs.

114   Property Tax Forum, Washington, D.C., 1975. PROPERTY TAX INCEN-
TIVES FOR PRESERVATION: USE-VALUE ASSESSMENT AND THE PRES-
ERVATION OF FARMLAND, OPEN SPACE, AND HISTORIC SITES.
Studies in Property Taxation. International Association of Assessing
Officers, 1975. vii, 135 p. Paper.

Includes presentations on: "Differential Assessment and the
Preservation of Farmland, Open Space, and Historic Sites";
"Property Tax Incentives to Preserve Farming in Areas of
Urban Pressure"; "The Impact of Ad Valorem Assessment on the
Preservation of Open Space and the Pattern of Urban Growth";
"The Impact of Differential Assessment Programs on the Tax
Base"; "A Planner's Perception of the Effects of Farmland and
Vacant Fringe Land Assessment Practice on Urban Development";

"Use of Soil Information in Market-Value and Use-Value
Assessment Programs"; "When Urban Landmarks Commissions
Come to the Assessor"; "Transferable Development Rights:
Impact on Real Property Tax Assessments"; and "Emerging
Trends in Agricultural Retention and Open Space Preservation."

115   Ziegler, Arthur P., Jr.; Adler, Leopold II; and Kidney, Walter C.
        REVOLVING FUNDS FOR HISTORIC PRESERVATION: A MANUAL OF
        PRACTICE. Pittsburgh: Ober Park Associates, 1975. 111 p. Illus.,
        glossary, paper.

        Derived from the deliberations of the Advisory Committee to
        the Revolving Fund of the National Trust for Historic Pres-
        ervation.   Intended as a guide to the preservationist in his
        "inevitable role as businessman." Explains the revolving fund
        as a preservation device, and presents some basic related in-
        formation concerning real estate, finance, fund raising, and
        surveys. Includes case studies on Charleston, Savannah,
        Pittsburgh, and Annapolis; also a development fund, Action
        Housing, Inc., and a loan fund, Neighborhood Housing
        Services, Inc., both located in Pittsburgh.

LEGAL FRAMEWORK

116   Gammage, Grady, Jr.; Jones, Philip N.; and Jones, Stephen L.
        HISTORIC PRESERVATION IN CALIFORNIA: A LEGAL HANDBOOK.
        Stanford, Calif.: Stanford Environmental Law Society [and the National
        Trust for Historic Preservation], 1975. 146 p. Biblio., paper.

        A companion volume to THE CALIFORNIA LAND USE PRIMER,
        published by the society in 1972. Intended to provide guid-
        ance and assistance to preservationists, attorneys, and public
        officials in legal approaches to historic preservation.   Goes
        beyond the limits of the state of California in its discussions
        of the rationale and implementation of preservation law.   Re-
        views legislation on the federal, state, and local levels.

117   "Historic Preservation." LAW AND CONTEMPORARY PROBLEMS 36,
        no. 3 (1971). Bibliography.

        An issue of a quarterly of the Duke University School of Law
        is devoted to the publication of a selection of papers from a
        conference on historic preservation law sponsored by the
        National Trust for Historic Preservation in May 1971. Papers
        discuss federal and state legislation in the United States as
        well as contemporary developments in British law and practice;
        and, on the local level, the preservation framework in New
        York City and Philadelphia. Additional papers discuss archi-
        tectural controls, standing to sue in preservation cases, con-

trolling the surroundings of historic sites, blacks and historic
preservation, and historic preservation in the context of environmental law. The concluding bibliography covers periodical
literature relating to the law of historic preservation.

118   Kettler, Ellen L., and Reams, Bernard D., Jr. HISTORIC PRESER-
       VATION LAW: AN ANNOTATED BIBLIOGRAPHY. Washington, D.C.:
       Preservation Press, 1976. v, 115 p. Paper.

       A highly classified and fully annotated and indexed bibliog-
       raphy. Primarily journal literature, but including all other
       formats, in a thorough coverage of this relatively new field.

119   Morrison, Jacob H. HISTORIC PRESERVATION LAW. Rev. ed. Wash-
       ington, D.C.: National Trust for Historic Preservation, 1965. xii,
       198 p. Illus.

       An enlarged and revised version of a work first published in
       1957. Surveys the history of preservation law from the
       Emperor Majorian (453 A.D.) to its comparatively recent be-
       ginnings in the United States. Discusses the preservation of
       public and private property at the national, state, and local
       levels as well as the concept and enactment of historic dis-
       tricts. Digests or analyzes laws, statutes, and ordinances of
       various states and localities. Contains a "Table of Cases,
       Authorities and Laws."

120   New Hampshire. Office of State Planning. PLANNING ENABLING
       LEGISLATION IN NEW HAMPSHIRE. Concord: 1972. 101 p. Paper.

       A compilation of laws of the state of New Hampshire which
       permit communities to enact planning ordinances. Describes
       the "Authority to Establish Historic Districts."

121   "The Police Power, Eminent Domain, and the Preservation of Historic
       Property." COLUMBIA LAW REVIEW 63, no. 4 (April 1963): 708-32.

       Reports that of the state's four great powers--war, taxation,
       police, and eminent domain--the powers of police and eminent
       domain are the primary means of compelling preservation. As
       a "Note" in Columbia University's law review, draws upon
       specific American examples to elucidate how these two powers
       are so employed.

PRESERVATION PLANNING

122   Allsopp, Bruce, ed. HISTORIC ARCHITECTURE OF NEWCASTLE-UPON-
       TYNE. 2d ed. Sponsored by the Northumberland and Newcastle Soci-
       ety and the City Council. Newcastle-upon-Tyne, Engl.: Oriel Press,

1968. 96 p. Illus.

Describes the monuments, streetscape, buildings, and industrial structures of Newcastle-upon-Tyne, from Roman times to the twentieth century, in photographs and text, in the hope that it will help the people of Newcastle to appreciate what is theirs, "to decide how much of the history of their famous city is to be preserved," and "to make wise decisions, setting real values against financial expedience."

123   Bell, Dennis R., et al. BARRIO HISTORICO, TUCSON. Tucson: College of Architecture, University of Arizona, 1972. ii, 171 p. Illus., glossary, paper.

A study of the history, architecture, and population of the Barrio, with proposals for its preservation and rehabilitation. Prepared by students in the College of Architecture, University of Arizona, in response to the Barrio's being threatened by a highway proposal.

124   Delaware Valley Regional Planning Commission. A REPORT ON HISTORIC PRESERVATION. Philadelphia: 1969. 61 p. Illus., bibliog.

Provides information on the setting for historic preservation and the historical background for historic preservation in the United States. Moves to a discussion of preservation in the Delaware Valley, describing achievements and recommendations, and setting forth guidelines for implementing plans. Discusses legal action, federal and state funding programs, private involvement, and governmental involvement on all levels. Includes survey forms for the Pennsylvania Historical and Museum Commission Register of Historic Sites and Landmarks.

125   Dobby, Alan. CONSERVATION AND PLANNING. The Built Environment Series. London: Hutchinson of London, 1978. 173 p. Illus., bibliog. refs., paper.

An up-to-date report of the state-of-the-art of preservation of buildings and districts in Britain. Includes chapters on conservation practice in the United States and a number of Eastern and Western European countries, and on European Architectural Heritage Year, 1975.

126   Falkner, Ann. WITHOUT OUR PAST?: A HANDBOOK FOR THE PRESERVATION OF CANADA'S ARCHITECTURAL HERITAGE. Toronto and Buffalo: University of Toronto Press, 1977. x, 242 p. Illus., bibliog.

Surveys "Heritage Preservation" in Canada in its many aspects. Covers federal, provincial, and municipal preservation policy

and legislation as well as the many private organizations involved in the cause of preservation in Canada. Describes
various means of preservation action. Published in association
with the Ministry of State for Urban Affairs and Publishing
Centre, Supply and Services, Ottawa.

127 Montague, Robert L. III, and Wrenn, Tony P. PLANNING FOR
PRESERVATION. Chicago: American Society of Planning Officials
[and National Trust for Historic Preservation], 1964. 42 p. Bibliog.,
paper.

Presents an overview of U.S. preservation planning at the
time.

128 New York City. Mayor's Office of Lower Manhattan Development.
TO PRESERVE A HERITAGE: THE RESTORATION AND UTILIZATION
OF HISTORIC SITES IN LOWER MANHATTAN. New York: 1975.
78 p. Illus., paper.

Mostly discusses officially designated New York City landmarks.
Projects for their preservation, restoration, and utilization have
been developed by the city in cooperation with such groups as
the New York Landmarks Conservancy, the Friends of Cast-
Iron Architecture, Sons of the Revolution, South Street Seaport Museum, the Custom House Institute, and the Downtown-
Lower Manhattan Association.

129 Ramirez, Constance Werner. "Urban History for Preservation Planning:
The Annapolis Experience." Ph.D. dissertation, Cornell University,
1975. 484 p. (DISSERTATION ABSTRACTS INTERNATIONAL, Vol.
36-A, Part 6, p. 4079-- . Urban and Regional Planning.)

Reports that Annapolis, Maryland, is a city which, by reason
of remote location and continuity of function from colonial
days to the present, has maintained a distinct conformity.
Indicates that in recent times this historical identity has been
threatened by pressures resulting from easier accessibility, the
pressures of expanding space needs of governmental and other
institutions, and the encroachments of contemporary life.
Studies the growth and change of the historic district of
Annapolis, which demonstrates the background and insight
that are necessary for preservation planning versus other forms
of physical planning. Aims to document the history of the
physical city in order to understand its contemporary form and
to provide a framework for decisions concerning future changes.
Presents a study undertaken at a time when changes in
Annapolis, more extensive in scale and costs than ever before, were not sympathetic to the city's visual image. While
not a "plan," introduces a strategy for both the private and
the public sector to help safeguard the visual reminders of
the city's history.

130   Southeastern Connecticut Regional Planning Agency. OPPORTUNITIES
       FOR HISTORIC PRESERVATION: SOUTHEASTERN CONNECTICUT
       REGION. Norwich: 1968. 99 p. Illus., paper.

       Stresses the importance of historic preservation considerations
       in the regional and local planning process. Presents a regional
       view of the very large number of architecturally significant
       buildings and sites in southeastern Connecticut, and discusses
       the needs, opportunities, and methods for their preservation.
       Covering a 560-square-mile region, presents a basic town-by-
       town inventory, and describes the climate for preservation,
       town-by-town. Describes and illustrates the major historical
       styles of the region.

131   Taylor, Ray; Cox, Margaret; and Dickins, Ian, eds. BRITAIN'S PLAN-
       NING HERITAGE. London: Croom Helm, for Royal Town Planning
       Institute, 1975. ix, 230 p. Illus., glossary, bibliog.

       Presents a guide to planning in England, Scotland, Northern
       Ireland, and Wales, frequently with historic connotations.

132   Tishler, William H., and Garber, Randy, eds. and comps. "Historic
       Preservation and the Cultural Landscape: An Emerging Land Use Planning
       Process." Occasional Paper 1976-77. Madison: University of Wisconsin,
       College of Agriculture and Life Sciences, School of Natural Resources,
       Department of Landscape Architecture and the Environmental Awareness
       Center. 141 leaves. Illus. Mimeographed.

       Papers on a variety of topics which all deal with the broader
       aspects of conserving historic values in rural and urban environ-
       ments. Includes an assessment of preservation issues in rural
       areas, an analysis of the evolution of historic district desig-
       nations, a comparative study of historic resource evaluation
       procedures, a suggested methodology for determining the
       economic feasability of historic sites, the utilization of re-
       mote sensing imagery for surveys, an examination of the
       cultural landscape of two important ethnic groups (Finnish
       and Polish), and the historic site significance of an urban
       park.

133   U.S. National Park Service. Office of Archaeology and Historic
       Preservation. GRANTS FOR HISTORIC PRESERVATION: A GUIDE FOR
       STATE PARTICIPATION. Washington, D.C.: 1969. 75 p. Paper.

       Provides the guidance and standards necessary to translate the
       National Historic Preservation Act of 1966 into a cooperative
       historic preservation effort between state and local governments,
       private groups and individuals, and the federal government.
       Includes application forms and report forms.

134   Worskett, Roy. THE CHARACTER OF TOWNS: AN APPROACH TO
       CONSERVATION. London: Architectural Press, 1969. 271 p. Illus.,
       bibliog.

       Based on the author's experience working in the United King-
       dom's Ministry of Housing and Local Government, and in
       response to the greater attention given to the conservation of
       the character and identity of towns, following the passage of
       the Civic Amenities Act of 1967. Seeks to "...suggest a
       method of approach to conserving the character and identity
       of towns; to provide a check list of some of the things to
       look for in your town and of the policies that will help to
       maintain its character."

135   Wright, Russell. TECHNIQUES FOR INCORPORATING HISTORIC
       PRESERVATION OBJECTIVES INTO THE HIGHWAY PLANNING
       PROCESS. Washington, D.C.: U.S. Department of Transportation,
       1972. 258 p. Illus., bibliog., paper.

       Prepared for the National Trust for Historic Preservation and
       the Department of Transportation. States that "The contents
       of this report reflect the views of the National Trust for
       Historic Preservation, which is responsible for the facts and
       the accuracy of the data presented herein. The contents do
       not necessarily reflect the official views or policy of the
       Department of Transportation. This report does not constitute
       a standard, specification or regulation." Calls for "Historic
       and Cultural Resources Inventory" that goes beyond the
       National Register of Historic Places. Part I outlines the
       inventory, part II describes the potential uses of the inventory,
       and part III presents guidelines for minimizing the environ-
       mental impact of proposed highway construction activities.

TDR—TRANSFER OF DEVELOPMENT RIGHTS

136   Chavooshian, B. Budd, and Norman, Thomas. TRANSFER OF DEVELOP-
       MENT RIGHTS: A NEW CONCEPT IN LAND USE MANAGEMENT.
       New Brunswick, N.J.: Rutgers University, 1973. 20 p. Paper.

       Asks how New Jersey, the most densely populated state in the
       nation, can preserve open space and ensure the quality of
       life which its residents desire. Intends to describe the new
       concept of land use controls--transfer of development rights--
       an uncomplicated idea, yet very different from traditional
       philosophies of land ownership and development.

137   Costonis, John J. SPACE ADRIFT: SAVING URBAN LANDMARKS
       THROUGH THE CHICAGO PLAN. Urbana: University of Illinois

Press for the National Trust for Historic Preservation, 1974. xx, 207 p. Illus., bibliog., paper.

Relates preservation to urban land use planning and urban design. Documents many specific cases in Chicago and elsewhere. Describes the establishment of a "development rights bank" for the depositing of condemned development rights as well as rights deposited by private owners of landmarks and transferred from publicly owned landmarks. The city would meet its preservation costs by selling these pooled rights from time to time, subject to the same planning controls that apply to private owners. Compares development rights transfers to zoning bonuses. Based on four actual Chicago School landmarks, serving as "models for determining the type and amount of costs that would result from the acquisition of preservation restrictions in landmark properties." Proposes that private donations of rights would be inspired by tax deduction incentives, as an alternative to the private sale of rights. Also published as SPACE ADRIFT: LANDMARK PRESERVATION AND THE MARKETPLACE, same publisher and same date as above.

138   Costonis, John J., and DeVoy, Robert S. THE PUERTO RICO PLAN: ENVIRONMENTAL PROTECTION THROUGH DEVELOPMENT RIGHTS TRANSFER. Washington, D.C.: Urban Land Institute, 1975. x, 52 p. Illus., paper.

A study sponsored by the Conservation Trust of Puerto Rico. Applies TDR (Transfer of Development Rights) to environmental protection in the Puerto Rican context through the transfer of rights from "Protected Environmental Zones" in natural areas to "Transfer Districts" in urban areas. See Costonis's SPACE ADRIFT (above).

139   Costonis, John [J.], and Schlaes, Jared. DEVELOPMENT RIGHTS TRANSFERS: A SOLUTION TO CHICAGO'S LANDMARKS DILEMMA. Chicago: Chicago Chapter Foundation of the American Institute of Architects, 1971. 52 p.

Study commissioned by the Chicago Chapter Foundation of the American Institute of Architects and the National Trust for Historic Preservation. An examination of the legal and economic aspects of development rights transfer as a tool for historic preservation.

140   Rose, Jerome G., ed. THE TRANSFER OF DEVELOPMENT RIGHTS: A NEW TECHNIQUE OF LAND USE REGULATION. New Brunswick, N.J.: Rutgers University, Center for Urban Policy Research, 1975. 341 p.

An anthology of writings on development rights transfer, from historical precedent to current practice and future possibilities.

STATE PRESERVATION PLANS

Florida

141   Florida. Department of State. Division of Archives, History, and
Records Management. Bureau of Historic Sites and Properties. OUR
PAST . . . OUR FUTURE: FLORIDA'S COMPREHENSIVE HISTORIC
PRESERVATION PLAN. Tallahassee: 1973. 96 p. Paper.

     In format, scope, and content, follows guidelines established
by the Office of Archaeology and Historic Preservation,
National Park Service: part I, historical background and
philosophy of preservation in the state, with a projection of
preservation needs in the future; part II, an inventory by
theme and by county; part III, a report of the status of state
preservation programs, with long-range and short-range proposals.

Maryland

142   Maryland Historical Trust. THE STATE OF MARYLAND HISTORIC
PRESERVATION PLAN: 1970 PLAN. 3 vols. Prepared with the
assistance of Maryland Department of State Planning and Raymond,
Parish, Pine & Plavnick. Annapolis: 1970. Illus., paper.

     Submitted under the terms of the National Historic Preservation
Act of 1966, presents the program of one of the states richest
in historic buildings, sites, and towns.

Texas

143   Texas Historical Commission. HISTORIC PRESERVATION IN TEXAS;
THE COMPREHENSIVE STATEWIDE HISTORIC PRESERVATION PLAN
FOR TEXAS. Vol. I. The Commission and the Office of Archaeology
and Historic Preservation, U.S. Dep't. of the Interior, 1973. xi, 126
p. Illus., paper.

     Includes: "Historical Summary"; "Review of Preservation Efforts
in Texas (a) Public Sector, (b) Private Sector, (c) Current
Status of Preservation Law in Texas"; "Growth of Preservation
Philosophy in Texas"; "Relation of Preservation Planning to
Other State Planning"; "Preservation Problems"; and "Historic
Survey--Methods and Results." In an appendix, includes the
texts of the Act Creating Texas Historical Commission and
the Antiquities Code of Texas.

Wisconsin

144   Wisconsin State Historical Society. "Wisconsin's Historic Preservation

Plan." 2d ed. 2 vols. Madison: 1973. Vol. I: "The Historical Background," 95 leaves; Vol. II: "The Inventory," 150 leaves. Mimeographed.

"Submitted to the U.S. Department of the Interior, National Park Service, Office of Archaeology and Historic Preservation, the National Register of Historic Places, in compliance with requirements of the National Historic Preservation Act of 1966 (P.L. 89-665)." In the first volume, contains sections on historical summary, preservation history, preservation philosophy, preservation planning, preservation problems, and historical surveys; in the second, a county inventory and a thematic inventory.

LOCAL PRESERVATION PROGRAMS

145 Berkeley-Charleston-Dorchester Regional Planning Council. HISTORIC PRESERVATION PLAN. Charleston, S.C.: 1972. vi, 95 p. Illus., paper.

Excluding the city of Charleston, but including the county, presents a regional preservation plan prepared by the council in conjunction with the South Carolina Department of Archives and History, financed in part through the National Historic Preservation Act of 1966. In section A, "Historical Background," gives (1) historical summary, (2) preservation history, (3) preservation philosophy, (4) historical survey, (5) historic preservation planning's relation to other state planning, and (6) major historical preservation problems. In section B, gives an inventory for each of the three counties, illustrated by photographs.

146 Carper, Robert L. A PLAN FOR HISTORIC PRESERVATION IN DENVER. Prepared by the Denver Planning Office, City and County of Denver; assisted by the Denver Landmark Preservation Commission, Historic Denver, Inc., and the State Historical Society of Colorado. Denver: Denver Planning Office, 1974. 82 p. Bibliog., paper.

Aside from its particular application to Denver and to Colorado, also presents an overview of historic preservation in all of its aspects--historical, philosophical, methodological, legal, and financial.

147 Delgado Mercado, Osiris. "Proyecto para la Conservación del San Juan Antiguo" [Project for the conservation of Old San Juan]. San Juan, Puerto Rico: Instituto de Cultura Puertorriqueña, 1956. 77 leaves. Illus. Mimeographed.

An early document in one of the most successful preservation programs in the Americas; the walled city of San Juan is a model for historic district legislation and management. Outlines the total district and its various component parts, such as the historic-commercial zone.

148   Garrett, Billy G., and Garrison, James W. PLAN FOR THE CREATION OF A HISTORIC ENVIRONMENT IN TOMBSTONE, ARIZONA. Tombstone: Tombstone Restoration Commission, 1972. xi, 181 p. (77 p. plus a "Workbook" of various paginations.) Illus.

A report prepared under provisions of the National Historic Preservation Act of 1966. Study and proposals for the "Schieffelin Historic District," with an 1885 restoration reference date. Gives an action plan, showing completion by 1985. Includes a five-part workbook covering: "Community Policies," "Building Appearance," "Legal Requirements," "Support Systems," and "Financial Assistance."

149   Historic Landmarks Foundation of Indiana. THE LOWER CENTRAL CANAL: A PRESERVATION PROGRAM. Prepared for the Waterways Task Force of the Greater Indianapolis Progress Committee, 1975. 130 p. Illus., bibliog., paper.

Presents a recommended program, including adaptive reuse proposals, urban linear park development concepts, and historic districting.

150   Housing Authority of Savannah. HISTORIC PRESERVATION PLAN FOR THE CENTRAL AREA--GENERAL NEIGHBORHOOD RENEWAL AREA, SAVANNAH, GEORGIA. Washington, D.C.: U.S. Department of Housing and Urban Development, 1973. 32 p. Illus., paper.

A plan which deals specifically with the General Neighborhood Renewal Area, but whose results have application to the entire Old Savannah area. Emphasis on preservation of the flavor of the Savannah squares through controlled urban renewal, design standards, preservation, and restoration.

151   Lowell, Massachusetts. Historic Districts Study Committee. FINAL REPORT. Lowell: City Development Authority, 1973. 23 p. Appendix, 11 p. Bibliog.

Once the major textile manufacturing city of the world, Lowell has canal systems, mill buildings, houses, and sites which are a living document to the early days of the American industrial revolution. Includes recommendations for the establishment of two historic districts, the "City Hall Historic District" and the "Locks and Canals Historic District," and urges support of the Urban National Cultural Park proposal.

152   Lowell, Massachussetts. Human Services Corporation. LOWELL URBAN
       PARK DEVELOPMENT PROGRAM. Lowell: 1974. 48 p. Illus.,
       paper.

       Proposes one of the earliest successfully planned industrial
       communities in the world as a new model for an Urban Nation-
       al Cultural Park Program, with the partners in the program
       being: state investment program for the park; private founda-
       tion investment; National Park Service investment program;
       private downtown adaptive restoration; NERC-Economic Devel-
       opment Stimulation Programs; Corps of Engineers, Merrimack
       and Concord River Programs; state transportation study and
       improvements; and city park and capital programs.

153   Miller, Hugh C. THE CHICAGO SCHOOL OF ARCHITECTURE: A
       PLAN FOR PRESERVING A SIGNIFICANT REMNANT OF AMERICA'S
       ARCHITECTURAL HERITAGE. Washington, D.C.: U.S. National Park
       Service, 1973. v, 36 p. Illus., bibliog., paper.

       Describes the development of the Chicago School of Architec-
       ture, the evolution of the skyscraper as a new form, and town
       planning--architecture in the landscape. Presents a plan for
       a new park concept, the proposed establishment of an Urban
       Park in Chicago by the National Park Service in cooperation
       with the city of Chicago and with the private sector. Pro-
       poses that the National Park Service would provide inter-
       pretive services, the city would provide landmark designations
       and administer a "development rights bank," and the private
       sector would administer a private preservation revolving fund.

154   Providence, Rhode Island. City Plan Commission. COLLEGE HILL:
       A DEMONSTRATION STUDY OF HISTORIC AREA RENEWAL. 2d ed.
       Conducted by the Providence City Plan Commission in cooperation with
       the Providence Preservation Society and the Department of Housing and
       Urban Development. Providence: 1967. x, 230 p. Illus., paper.

       Following a chapter which reviews and describes preservation
       in America, describes survey techniques and sets forth detailed
       proposals for the renewal of this historic area of Providence
       through preservation and restoration. Recommends various
       governmental and private programs to facilitate the realization
       of these programs. Originally published in 1959, now presents
       an additional chapter, part IV, "Progress Since 1959," which
       describes the major recommendations, urban renewal activities,
       private restoration efforts, institutional activities, and impact
       elsewhere.

155   Sag Harbor Historic Preservation Commission. SAG HARBOR: PAST,
       PRESENT AND FUTURE. Prepared by Robert H. Pine. Sag Harbor,
       N.Y.: 1973. 76 p. Illus., paper.

A proposed historic preservation program for the village of
Sag Harbor, with drawings by Joan Baren, photographs by
Otto Fenn, and architectural analysis by Ellen Rosebrock.
Presents a history of the village from 1730 to 1914, followed
by a description of the period from 1918 to date. Concludes
with a discussion of preservation techniques, federal and state
preservation programs, and recommendations for planning and
preservation.

156 THE URBAN DESIGN PLAN, HISTORIC HILL, NEWPORT, RHODE
ISLAND. Prepared by the Providence Partnership, Providence, Rhode
Island, and Russell Wright, A.I.P., Reston, Virginia. Project No.
R.I. R-23. Newport: Redevelopment Agency of the City of Newport,
1971. 44 p. Illus., paper.

Examines and describes Historic Hill, a registered national
historic landmark, in terms of its history, its architecture,
and its current status. Presents a design plan consisting of
design objectives, a proposed land use map, an illustrative
site plan, detailed design proposals, and a program for public
improvements. The first and foremost design goal of the plan
is to preserve and protect Historic Hill as an active, living
historic district.

Chapter 4

DESCRIPTION AND DOCUMENTATION

Description and documentation are the first steps, and vital steps, in the preservation process. Frequently, highlighting the historical and/or architectural significance of a structure or site is the means by which constructive action is promoted. This is invariably a requirement, at any level of government, in the process of nomination to landmark status. In the case of buildings later damaged or destroyed, this provides the necessary basis for repair, restoration, or reconstruction; or, as a last resort, it provides a detailed historical record of that which was.

ARCHITECTURAL BIBLIOGRAPHIES, GLOSSARIES, AND STYLE GUIDES

157   Blumenson, John J.-G. IDENTIFYING AMERICAN ARCHITECTURE: A PIC-
TORIAL GUIDE TO STYLES AND TERMS, 1600-1945. Foreword by Sir Nikolaus Pevsner. Nashville: American Association for State and Local History,
1977. viii, 118 p. Illus., bibliog.

A handbook intended "primarily for the tourist or traveler," but
certainly of value to the preservationist in compiling historic
buildings inventories or surveys. Identifies, illustrates, and
describes thirty-nine American architectural styles. Includes a
pictorial glossary of building details and photographic illustrations
drawn primarily from the Historic American Buildings Survey.

158   Hall, Robert de Zouche, ed. A BIBLIOGRAPHY ON VERNACULAR
ARCHITECTURE. Newton Abbot, Engl.: David & Charles, 1972. 191 p.

Covers rural and urban regional buildings of England, Ireland,
Scotland, Wales, and Channel Islands. Sponsored by the
Vernacular Architecture Group.

159   Harris, Cyril M. HISTORIC ARCHITECTURE SOURCEBOOK. New York:
McGraw-Hill, 1977. vii, 581 p. Illus.

Includes five thousand definitions and twenty-one hundred line
drawings elucidating terms relating to the major geographic and
temporal divisions of the history of architecture, covering a

span of five thousand years. Defines and describes building complexes, complete buildings, and minute details.

160 _____, ed. DICTIONARY OF ARCHITECTURE AND CONSTRUCTION. New York: McGraw-Hill, 1975. xv, 553 p. Illus.

Includes fifty-three contributing editors, representing fields as diverse as "Greek, Hellenistic, and Roman Architecture," "Law," "Carpeting," "Fire Protection," "Theatre Technology," and "Sanitary Engineering, Plumbing." A unique reference book including definitions of terms and abbreviations, accompanied by over seventeen hundred illustrations.

161 Hitchcock, Henry-Russell. AMERICAN ARCHITECTURAL BOOKS: A LIST OF BOOKS, PORTFOLIOS, AND PAMPHLETS ON ARCHITECTURE AND RELATED SUBJECTS PUBLISHED IN AMERICA BEFORE 1895. 3d rev. ed. Minneapolis: University of Minnesota Press, 1962. Reprint. Foreword by Adolf K. Placzek. Appendix by William H. Jordy. New York: Da Capo Press, 1976. xvi, 150 p.

Based on the 1946 third revised edition of a work first published in mimeographed form in 1938/39, to which has been added a chronological short-title list and a list of American architectural periodicals whose starting date precedes 1895. Covers the period between the Revolution and the end of the nineteenth century. The 1,500 entries include builders' guides, house pattern books, theoretical writings, textbooks, dictionaries of terms, and individual architects' sketches and projects.

162 McKee, Harley J. "Amateur's Guide to Terms Commonly Used in Describing Historic Buildings: Following the Order Used by the Historic American Buildings Survey." Rochester, N.Y.: Landmark Society, 1970. 14 p. Illus. Mimeographed.

An enlarged and revised edition of an earlier edition of 1967. The first edition prepared for the Landmark Society of Western New York; and the revised edition for the twenty-third Annual Seminar on American Culture, New York State Historical Association, Cooperstown, New York. Very directly and concisely gives verbal equivalents to the architectural features illustrated in quick pencil sketches. An invaluable aid in the training of amateurs in inventory and survey methods.

163 Neil, J. Meredith. "Architectural Comment in American Magazines 1783-1815." In PAPERS, vol. 5, pp. 15-45. The American Association of Architectural Bibliographers. Charlottesville: The University Press of Virginia, 1968.

Approximately 130 articles devoted primarily to architecture, with an additional 250 travel accounts, book reviews, and other articles with some extensive comment on architecture.

Part I, "General" (by broad geographic division), part II,
"Individual Structures," part III, "Building Types" (including
churches and bridges and other pieces of engineering), and
part IV, "Book Reviews."

164   Park, Helen. A LIST OF ARCHITECTURAL BOOKS AVAILABLE IN
AMERICA BEFORE THE REVOLUTION. Foreword by Adolf K. Placzek.
Los Angeles: Hennessey & Ingalls, 1973. xv, 79 p. Illus.

A revised and enlarged version of a work first published in the
JOURNAL OF THE SOCIETY OF ARCHITECTURAL HISTORIANS
20, no. 3 (1961). The list of 106 books, all but eight of which
carry a British imprint, contains the stylistic, pictorial, and structural sources of much of colonial American architecture. Provides
modern and eighteenth-century locations of the books listed.

165   Roos, Frank J., Jr.   BIBLIOGRAPHY OF EARLY AMERICAN ARCHI-
TECTURE: WRITINGS ON ARCHITECTURE CONSTRUCTED BEFORE 1860
IN EASTERN AND CENTRAL UNITED STATES. Urbana, Chicago,
London: University of Illinois Press, 1968. 389 p.

A revised and enlarged edition of a work first published in
1943. Lists over four thousand books and articles, organized
mostly according to historical period or geographic location.
Includes additional sections on architects, bibliographies, and
general reference, with a subdivision of the last on preservation
and restoration.

166   Whiffen, Marcus. AMERICAN ARCHITECTURE SINCE 1780: A GUIDE
TO THE STYLES. Cambridge: M.I.T. Press, 1969. x, 313 p. Illus.,
glossary, bibliog.

Intended for the "building watcher." Describes and illustrates
the full array of American architectural styles and substyles.
Includes cross references to the bibliography for each stage.

167   Williams, Henry Lionel, and Williams, Ottalie K. A GUIDE TO OLD
AMERICAN HOUSES, 1700-1900. New York: A.S. Barnes and Co.;
London: Thomas Yoseloff, 1962. 168 p. Illus., glossary.

A study of the basic styles of American domestic architecture
to the turn of the century. Considers the migration of these
styles within and from the thirteen original states and the
further development of the styles with French and Spanish influences via Louisiana, Florida, and California.

168   Wodehouse, Lawrence. AMERICAN ARCHITECTS FROM THE CIVIL
WAR TO THE FIRST WORLD WAR: A GUIDE TO INFORMATION
SOURCES. Art and Architecture Information Guide Series, vol. 3.
Detroit: Gale Research Co., 1976. xii, 343 p.

_____. AMERICAN ARCHITECTS FROM THE FIRST WORLD WAR TO THE PRESENT: A GUIDE TO INFORMATION SOURCES. Art and Architecture Information Guide Series, vol. 4. Detroit: Gale Research Co., 1977. xiii, 305 p.

Picks up where Frank J. Roos, Jr., in his BIBLIOGRAPHY OF EARLY AMERICAN ARCHITECTURE (see entry 165) lets off. Contains, in each of the two above volumes, a section of general reference works followed by a selected annotated biographical bibliography of American architects of the period. Also contains, in the volume covering the earlier period, a listing of significant architects about whom little has been written; and in the volume covering the later period, an appendix on "Ada Louise Huxtable and the Location of Her Articles."

GUIDELINES, HISTORIES, TECHNOLOGY OF SURVEYS AND INVENTORIES, FEASIBILITY STUDIES, AND STRUCTURE REPORTS

169   Bailey, Worth. SAFEGUARDING A HERITAGE: AN ACCOUNT OF THE HISTORIC AMERICAN BUILDINGS SURVEY. Washington, D.C.: U.S. National Park Service, 1963. 8 p. Pamphlet.

A resume of the history of HABS, from its birth during the Depression of the 1930s to the date of publication, and a description of "hopeful prospects" for the future. "The program originated with architects of the National Park Service who foresaw the need of such an undertaking. By harnessing federal unemployment relief funds, they proceded to help alleviate the unfortunate plight of their profession." Reports that the 1934 agreement which founded the program was among three parties: the National Park Service, to administer the program; the American Institute of Architects, to provide technical advice; and the Library of Congress, to receive and service the records. Indicates that the program lost ground during World War II but was revitalized in 1957, with MISSION 66.

170   Britz, Billie Sherrill. THE GREENHOUSES AT LYNDHURST: CONSTRUCTION AND DEVELOPMENT OF THE GOULD GREENHOUSE, 1881. Series of the National Trust for Historic Preservation, Research on Historic Properties. Occasional Papers, no. I. Washington, D.C.: Preservation Press, 1977. 48 p. Illus., paper.

First in a series of research reports which will present studies pertaining to various aspects of preservation and research on the structures, sites, and collections maintained by the National Trust for Historic Preservation. A result of the author's research on the greenhouse on Jay Gould's estate at Tarrytown, New York, preparatory to devising a plan for its restoration.

171 Fisher, Perry G. MATERIALS FOR THE STUDY OF WASHINGTON:
     A SELECTED ANNOTATED BIBLIOGRAPHY. G.W. Washington Studies,
     No. 1. Washington, D.C.: George Washington University, 1974.
     63 p. Paper.

     Part of a series focused on the District of Columbia as a
     major urban center rather than as the federal capital. Lists
     general and specialized histories of the city; guidebooks;
     architectural, city, and regional planning works; pictorial
     essays and histories; works on government and political status;
     sociology and social history; and novels with a Washington
     setting. In a concluding directory, describes major collections
     of Washingtoniana and related materials.

172 FORT STANWIX: HISTORY, HISTORIC FURNISHING, AND HISTORIC
     STRUCTURE REPORTS. Washington, D.C.: National Park Service,
     1976. vii, 200 p. Illus., bibliographies., paper.

     The reconstruction of Fort Stanwix, near Rome, New York,
     was a major bicentennial effort of the National Park Service.
     This publication illuminates the process of restoration directed
     research within the Park Service necessary to such an effort.
     The section on construction and military history was contributed
     by John F. Luzader, that on historic furnishings by Louis Torres,
     and the historic structure report by Orville W. Carroll. Archeo-
     logical investigations at the site are reported in CASEMATES
     AND CANNONBALLS (see entry 559).

173 Georgia Department of Natural Resources. Historic Preservation Section.
     HISTORIC PRESERVATION HANDBOOK: A GUIDE FOR VOLUNTEERS.
     Rev. ed. Atlanta: 1974. v. 101 p. Glossary, biblio., paper.

     Updates a 1971 edition. Reviews past and present preservation
     activity in Georgia as well as federal preservation activity
     and procedures. Reproduces forms. Lists Georgia properties
     on the National Register, describes and illustrates Georgia's
     historic architectural styles, and outlines restoration philosophy.
     Lists state, federal, and private organizations with their
     addresses.

174 Historic American Buildings Survey. DOCUMENTING A LEGACY: 40
     YEARS OF THE HISTORIC AMERICAN BUILDINGS SURVEY. Washington,
     D.C.: U.S. Government Printing Office, 1973. Illus., paper.

     Reprinted from the QUARTERLY JOURNAL OF THE LIBRARY
     OF CONGRESS (Oct. 1973): 269-94. Issued in conjunction
     with an exhibition held 1 November 1973 to 31 January 1974
     in the Library of Congress. Describes the activity of HABS,
     and demonstrates that it is directly related to that spurred in
     France by the Revolutionary Convention of 1793. Illustrates
     the wide range of HABS subject matter and the variety of
     HABS technology.

175 _____ . PRESERVATION THROUGH DOCUMENTATION. Washington, D.C.: U.S. Library of Congress, 1968. 16 p. Illus., paper.

Catalog of an exhibition held at the Library of Congress, 25 September 1968 to 1 January 1969, honoring the thirty-fifth anniversary of HABS. Includes a retrospective display of photographs and measured drawings, with explanatory captions, following an introduction by the chairman of the Advisory Council on Historic Preservation.

176 _____ . SPECIFICATIONS FOR THE MEASUREMENT AND RECORDING OF HISTORIC AMERICAN BUILDINGS AND STRUCTURAL REMAINS. Washington, D.C.: 1958. 88 p. Illus., paper.

A manual concerned with measurements and field methods, preparation of drawings and photographs, recording historical and architectural data, and preparation of inventory worksheets and final inventory forms.

177 International Council on Monuments and Sites. APPLICATION OF PHOTOGRAMMETRY TO HISTORIC MONUMENTS, SAINT-MANDE, FRANCE 4-6. VII. 1968. Paris: 1969. 181 p. Bibliog., paper.

Most of these conference reports in French, with some in English. Contains an international "Bibliographie des Applications de la Photogrammetrie a l'Architecture," pages 47-70.

178 _____ . COLLOQUE SUR LE CENTRE DE DOCUMENTATION DE L'ICOMOS. CONFERENCE ON THE ICOMOS DOCUMENTATION CENTRE, BRUXELLES-BRUSSELS, 13-15. XII. 1966. Paris: 1969. 97 p. Paper.

Discusses the need, the objectives, and the means to set up an international center of documentation on monuments and sites. Mostly in French, but some presentations in English. Gives the conference resolutions in both languages.

179 International Symposium on Photogrammetric Surveys of Monuments and Sites. PHOTOGRAMMETRIC SURVEYS OF MONUMENTS AND SITES. Edited by John Badekas. Proceedings of the First International Symposium on Photogrammetric Surveys of Monuments and Sites, Athens, 1974. Amsterdam and Oxford: North-Holland Publishing Co.; New York: American Elsevier Publishing Co., 1975. viii, 176 p. Illus., paper.

Papers on various aspects of photogrammetric surveying: requirements in surveys; instruments, methods, and education; and application and results. Papers mostly in English, and all (including those in English) summarized in English.

180   McKee, Harley J., comp.   RECORDING HISTORIC BUILDINGS.
       Washington, D.C.:   U.S. National Park Service, 1970.   xi, 165 p.
       Illus., bibliog.

       Culmination of a series of guidelines promulgated since 1934.
       States the principles and standards for recording historic archi-
       tecture by the Historic American Buildings Survey.   "The
       present edition incorporates important new material reflecting
       not only the development of HABS practices but the need for
       compiling State and regional catalogs."   Includes sections
       which discuss the HABS inventory, landscape architecture,
       area studies, historic districts, history of planning, civil
       engineering, and industrial archaeology.   Includes: "Organ-
       izing a Survey," "Measured Drawings," "Photographs and
       Graphic Material," "Documentation," "Specialized Record-
       ing Techniques," and "Catalogs."

181   Massey, James C.   THE ARCHITECTURAL SURVEY.   Preservation Leaf-
       let Series.   Washington, D.C.:   National Trust for Historic Preservation,
       [1974].   20 p.   Bibliog., leaflet.

       Describes the process of surveying, from preliminary steps to
       the full range of survey technology: basic broad-scale in-
       ventories; intensive recording of specific buildings; recording
       techniques; documentation; and relation to specialized areas
       such as landscape architecture, engineering history, industrial
       archaeology, and urban planning history.

182   Mendel, Mesick, Cohen, Architects.   THE NOTT MEMORIAL: A
       HISTORIC STRUCTURE REPORT.   Prepared for the Trustees and Alumni
       Council of Union College.   Albany, N.Y.:   1973.   152 p.   Illus.

       Union College, in Schenectady, New York, is one of the
       oldest educational establishments in the United States.   The
       original design for its campus was prepared in 1813 by the
       French architect Joseph Jacques Ramée (1764-1842).   The
       focus of this design, a central rotunda, was not built until
       almost fifty years later, designed by the American architect
       Edward T. Potter.   The structure report on this building, the
       Nott Memorial, is a model for such report writing, incorpora-
       ting thorough historical research with impeccable docu-
       mentation, a current analysis, and a recommended plan of
       action.

183   National Trust for Historic Preservation, and the National Clearing-
       house for Criminal Justice Planning and Architecture.   A COURTHOUSE
       CONSERVATION HANDBOOK.   Washington, D.C.:   Preservation Press,
       1976.   75 p.   Bibliog., paper.

       Produced by the cosponsors as a resource for the National
       Conference on Historic Courthouses, St. Louis, Missouri,
       31 March-2 April 1976.   Reports that the courthouse is a

major element of historic architecture in the United States,
where, in county after county the continued survival of this
most important and symbolic area landmark is endangered.
Presents papers considering urban design; architectural history;
conservation, code, and maintenance; improving obsolete
interior environmental aspects; creating new space; financing
and action to implement programs; and the case study of the
Marshall County Courthouse, Marshalltown, Iowa. Lists
pertinent organizations.

184   New York State. Office of Parks and Recreation. Division for His-
        toric Preservation. HISTORIC RESOURCES SURVEY MANUAL. Rev. ed.
        Albany: 1974. x, 78 p. Illus., bibliog., paper.

        In the first part, discusses new ideas about historic preservation
        and the need to change attitudes in preservation philosophy to
        include the total cultural environment. Discusses adaptive use
        and the preservation of archaeological remains. The second
        part concerned with inventory methods, and the third part with
        action--stressing educational aims of the survey, the protection
        of historic resources before they become threatened, the
        National Register of Historic Places, and the State Preservation
        Plan.

185   New York State Historic Trust (Albany). HISTORIC STRUCTURE REPORTS.
        By John G. Waite and Paul R. Huey. 3 vols. to date. NORTHWEST
        STONEHOUSE, JOHNSON HALL (1971) 29 p. plus illus.; SENATE
        HOUSE (1971) 75 p. plus illus.; HERKIMER HOUSE (1972) 39 p. plus
        illus., paper.

        Volumes in the continuing series, "Historic Structure Reports,"
        relating to historic sites owned by the state of New York.
        Present basic information concerning the physical history of
        the land and the buildings as well as an objective analysis
        of each building in its present condition, as the first step
        toward future detailed research reports on specific subjects
        needed for restoration of the buildings. Johnson Hall in
        Johnstown, Fulton County; Senate House in Kingston, Ulster
        County; and Herkimer House in Danube, Herkimer County.

186   Sykes, Meredith, and Falkner, Ann. CANADIAN INVENTORY OF
        HISTORIC BUILDING: TRAINING MANUAL. 2d ed. Ottawa:
        National Historic Sites Service, National and Historic Parks Branch,
        Department of Indian Affairs and Northern Development, 1971. 57 p.
        Illus., glossary, paper.

        Published to serve as a manual for recording information for
        the Canadian Inventory of Historic Building (CIHB), envisioned
        as a five-year program (1970-75), to record information on
        structures dating from the seventeenth century in Eastern

Canada to the early twentieth century in Western Canada. Reports that the CIHB entails a computerized technique for recording and retrieving information in the first computerized building survey to be implemented on such a large scale anywhere in the world.

187   U.S. Department of the Interior. National Register of Historic Places. GUIDELINES FOR LOCAL SURVEYS: A BASIS FOR PRESERVATION PLANNING. By Anne Derry, H. Ward Jandl, Carol D. Shull, and Jan Thorman. Washington, D.C.: 1977. 82 p. Illus., bibliog., paper.

Provides general guidelines to communities, organizations, federal and state agencies, and individuals interested in undertaking surveys of historic or cultural resources: districts, sites, buildings, structures, or objects. Lists state historic preservation officers with their addresses and telephone numbers. Includes a bibliography divided into six parts: (1) "Survey and Planning Methodology," (2) "Surveys and Inventories," (3) "Preservation Plans," (4) "City/County Architectural Histories and Guidelines," (5) "General Reference," and (6) "Legal Reference Material."

ARCHITECTURAL HISTORIES, INVENTORIES, AND SURVEYS— UNITED STATES

188   Poppeliers, John, ed., with the assistance of Stephens, Deborah. SHAKER BUILT: A CATALOGUE OF SHAKER ARCHITECTURAL RECORDS FROM THE HISTORIC AMERICAN BUILDINGS SURVEY. Washington, D.C.: U.S. Department of the Interior, National Park Service, 1974. 87 p. Illus., bibliographical essay, paper.

Documents eleven Shaker communities in Kentucky, Maine, Massachusetts, New Hampshire, New York, and Ohio.

189   U.S. National Park Service. ADVISORY LIST TO THE NATIONAL REGISTER OF HISTORIC PLACES. Washington, D.C.: 1969. vii, 311 p. Paper.

Lists historic places not part of the NATIONAL REGISTER OF HISTORIC PLACES as of 30 June 1969 which are proposed by the chief of the Office of Archeology and Historic Preservation and the keeper of the National Register as potential entries for the Register. All of the buildings, structures, and sites listed previously recognized in two other historical-archaeological and architectural programs administered by the National Park Service, the National Survey of Historic Sites and Buildings, and the Historic American Buildings Survey. Acknowl-

edges that the places identified may include some which have
been demolished, moved, or so greatly altered as to destroy
their integrity. Arranged by state and, within state, by
county. (See below).

190   . THE NATIONAL REGISTER OF HISTORIC PLACES. Washington,
D.C.: 1969-- . Biennial.

Compiled and issued by Division of the National Register, a
division of the National Park Service's Office of Archaeology
and Historic Preservation, authorized by the National Historic
Preservation Act of 1966. Expands the scope of listings
authorized by the Historic Sites Act of 1935, which provided
for a survey of buildings and sites of national significance, by
including properties of state and local significance. Growing
from a list of 1,500 properties in 1969 edition, consisting
primarily of National Historic Landmarks, 1976 edition lists
12,000 properties, including over 1,000 districts. Nominations
received principally from the state historic preservation officers,
appointed by their governors. Criteria for inclusion, outlined
in the leaflet THE NATIONAL REGISTER OF HISTORIC PLACES,
emphasize the "quality of significance in American history,
architecture, archeology, and culture . . . present in districts, sites, buildings, structures, and objects that possess
integrity of location, design, setting, materials, workmanship,
feeling, and association, and: A. that are associated with
events that have made a significant contribution to the broad
patterns of our history; or B. that are associated with the
lives of persons significant in our past; or C. that embody
the distinctive characteristics of a type, period, or method
of construction, or that represent the work of a master, or
that possess high artistic values, or that represent a significant and distinguishable entity whose components may lack
individual distinction; or D. that have yielded, or may be
likely to yield, information important in prehistory or history."
The official statement informing public and private agencies
and individuals which properties merit preservation. Lists by
county and city within state. THE NATIONAL REGISTER OF
HISTORIC PLACES 1976 edited by Ronald M. Greenberg,
Editor in Chief, Sarah A. Marusin, Editor, and Maricca J.
Lutz, Photo Editor, under the direction of William J. Murtagh,
Keeper of the National Register, contains xvii, 961 pages and
includes maps and illustrations. Additions to the list published
in the FEDERAL REGISTER on the first Tuesday of each month,
with annual cumulation each February. (See also above).

191 THE WHITE PINE SERIES OF ARCHITECTURAL MONOGRAPHS. Edited
by Russell F. Whitehead. Vols. 1-26. New York: 1915-40.

A series sponsored by the American lumber industry which provided a record, in photographs, measured drawings, and text,

of American architecture from the colonial period to the nineteenth century. Examples drawn mostly from New England. The
Early American Society and Arno Press have announced a series,
THE ARCHITECTURAL TREASURES OF EARLY AMERICA, "Pro-
duced from material originally appearing in the famous WHITE
PINE SERIES OF ARCHITECTURAL MONOGRAPHS, revised and
assembled by the editors of EARLY AMERICAN LIFE magazine."
The proposed eight volumes in the new series are described as con-
sisting of 1,792 pages, 8-1/2" x 11"; 2,025 photographic illus-
trations; and 275 measured line drawings. The volumes are: I,
EARLY HOMES OF MASSACHUSETTS; II, COLONIAL HOMES
OF EASTERN MASSACHUSETTS; III, COLONIAL ARCHITEC-
TURE IN NORTHERN NEW ENGLAND; IV, EARLY AMERICAN
HOMES OF RHODE ISLAND; V, GREAT EARLY HOMES OF
NEW ENGLAND; VI, EARLY AMERICAN HOMES OF THE
MID-ATLANTIC STATES; VII, COLONIAL HOMES IN THE
SOUTHERN STATES; and VIII, EARLY AMERICAN DESIGN
SURVEY and index to all volumes.

Alabama

192   Mobile, Alabama. City Planning Commission. NINETEENTH CENTURY
MOBILE ARCHITECTURE: AN INVENTORY OF EXISTING BUILDINGS.
Mobile City Planning Commission and the Historic Mobile Preservation
Society. Prepared under the direction of Arch R. Winter, planning
consultant. Mobile: 1974. ii, 76 p. Illus., glossary, paper.

An illustrated catalog of existing buildings which demonstrates
the evolution of nineteenth-century architecture in Mobile.
Intended to "under-pin a comprehensive program of architectural preservation and to encourage architectural continuity in
the construction and reconstruction of the city."

California

193   Andree, Herb, and Young, Noel. SANTA BARBARA ARCHITECTURE:
FROM SPANISH COLONIAL TO MODERN. Santa Barbara, Calif.:
Capra Press, 1975. 298 p. Illus., glossary, folio.

Illustrates and describes a few hundred examples of Santa
Barbara architecture selected from thousands during a block-
by-block survey. Chronological organization, with style
categories from settlement days to the present. Covers
architects ranging from the most prolific and well known to
the anonymous.

194   Olmsted, Roger R., and Watkins, T.H. HERE TODAY: SAN FRAN-
CISCO'S ARCHITECTURAL HERITAGE. Photographs by Morley Baer
and others. San Francisco: Chronicle Books, 1968. xi, 334 p.
Illus., glossary.

Covers three major divisions, San Francisco, San Mateo County, and Marin County, with each of these then further subdivided geographically. Presents major landmarks within the context of a narrative text, with an additional approximately two thousand buildings given brief description in an appendix. Section of short biographies of architects. Sponsored by the Junior League of San Francisco.

195   Olwell, Carol, and Waldhorn, Judith Lynch. A GIFT TO THE STREET. San Francisco: Antelope Island Press, 1976. xv, 195 p. Illus., paper.

Primarily an album of extremely clear black-and-white photographs by Carol Olwell, of San Francisco's wooden Victorian domestic architecture and its decorative details (including those of iron and of glass). Accompanying commentary by Judith Lynch Waldhorn. Includes illustrations reproduced from historical builders' and suppliers' catalogs, including plans, elevations, interiors, and fittings. In an appendix of drawings, illustrates balloon frame construction and the various San Francisco wooden styles.

196   Smilie, Robert S. THE SONOMA MISSION, SAN FRANCISCO SOLANO DE SONOMA: THE FOUNDING, RUIN AND RESTORATION OF CALIFORNIA'S 21ST MISSION. Fresno, Calif.: Valley Publishers, 1975. 149 p. Illus., bibliog.

A recent addition to the growing body of literature concerning the California missions. Records the last built of the mission chain from its beginnings, through secularization, military occupation, dismantling, revolution, neglect, and final restoration, to the present. Records the role of the Sonoma Valley Woman's Club, the California Historic Landmarks League, the Native Sons and Daughters of the Golden West, and the California Department of Parks and Recreation.

197   Waldhorn, Judith Lynch. HISTORIC PRESERVATION IN SAN FRANCISCO'S INNER MISSION: AND TAKE A WALK THROUGH MISSION HISTORY. Washington, D.C.: U.S. Department of Housing and Urban Development, 1973. 52 p. Illus., bibliog., paper.

In first forty-three pages, presents an inventory and action guide for preservation of the architectural legacy of the Inner Mission neighborhood. In final ten pages, "Take a Walk Through Mission History," contains a series of three walking tours of the Inner Mission. Produced under the auspices of the Stanford Community Development Study.

198   Weinberg, Nathan Gerald. "Historic Preservation and Tradition in California: The Restoration of the Missions and the Spanish-Colonial Revival." Ph.D. dissertation, University of California, Davis, 1974.

236 p. (DISSERTATION ABSTRACTS INTERNATIONAL, Vol. 35-A, Part 4, p. 2411--Sociology, General.)

A study, combining the methods of sociology and architectural history, which addresses itself to the problem of tradition formation in a modern society: California after 1870. Proposes that the processes of tradition formation in California can be seen in the movement to restore the oldest historic buildings in the state, the Spanish missions, and in the related revival of Spanish style architecture. Suggest that the historic preservation movement, which undertakes the preservation of old buildings and monuments, thus influencing our understanding of the past, is a principal mode by which traditions are constructed. Examines the preservationist attitude toward historic buildings, against the development of the movement in the nineteenth century in England, France, Scandinavia, and the United States. Examines the movement to restore the missions from 1870s to the 1940s.

Colorado

199   Brettell, Richard R. HISTORIC DENVER: THE ARCHITECTS AND THE ARCHITECTURE 1858-1893. Denver: Historic Denver, 1973. xii, 240 p. Illus., bibliog.

Describes in greatest detail the major architectural period of nineteenth-century Denver, 1879-93 (the decade and a half preceding the great silver crash). Describes the earlier period to provide background.

Connecticut

200   Larson, Kenneth A., and Yellen, Ira W. A WALK AROUND WALNUT HILL, NEW BRITAIN, CONNECTICUT. Brooklyn, N.Y., and New Britain, Conn.: Kalarson, 1975. 99 p. Illus., bibliog., paper.

An architectural and historical survey, in photographs, drawings, maps, and text, of the buildings and sites in the areas surrounding Walnut Hill Park, 1830-1930. Entries keyed to the historic preservation plan prepared by the New Britain City Plan Commission; also keyed, where applicable, to indicate inclusion in the Walnut Hill Historic District.

201   Nutting, Wallace. CONNECTICUT BEAUTIFUL. Garden City, N.Y.: Garden City Publishing Co., 1935. 256 p. Illus.

A survey of Connecticut's natural and built historic patrimony, by a major figure in the early days of America's consciousness of an historic past. Amply illustrated by the author's own photographs. A later edition of a book first published over a decade earlier.

Description and Documentation

Florida

202   Hoffstot, Barbara D. LANDMARK ARCHITECTURE OF PALM BEACH.
       Introduction by Arthur P. Ziegler, Jr. Pittsburgh: Ober Park Associ-
       ates, 1974. 227 p. Illus.

       Based on the Palm Beach Historical Society's survey for the
       NATIONAL REGISTER; a building-by-building inspection of ev-
       ery street on the island of Palm Beach, Florida--thirteen miles
       long and three quarters of a mile wide at its widest part.
       Divided into three parts, reflecting the north, central, and
       south portions of the island. Stops at approximately 1945.

203   Manucy, Albert. THE HOUSES OF ST. AUGUSTINE (NOTES ON THE
       ARCHITECTURE FROM 1565 TO 1821). St. Augustine, Fla.: St.
       Augustine Historical Society, 1962. 179 p. Illus., glossary, bibliog.

       A detailed study of the locations, design, materials, and
       construction of housing in what is generally acknowledged to
       be the oldest city in the United States.

204   St. Augustine Historical Restoration and Preservation Commission.
       HANDBOOK OF COLONIAL ST. AUGUSTINE ARCHITECTURE. St.
       Augustine, Fla.: 1962. 51 p. Illus., paper.

       In the format of a spiral-bound sketch pad, reproduces pencil
       sketches of a variety of details of St. Augustine architecture.
       Covers such aspects as traditional site planning and floor plans,
       building types, specific buildings, balconies, fences, flooring,
       roof structure and roof covering, and window shutters.

Georgia

205   Gilmore, Janice Haynes. "The Georgia Historical Commission: Its
       History and Its Role in Historic Preservation." Ph.D. dissertation,
       University of Georgia, 1975. 396 p. (DISSERTATION ABSTRACTS
       INTERNATIONAL, Vol. 36-A, Part 12, p. 7694--Architecture.)

       A history of the commission, a state agency from 1951 to
       1973, which served as a pivotal force for historic preservation
       in the state of Georgia. Describes the creation of the com-
       mission by a special act, the commission's financing, its
       policy-making procedures, and its staffing. Describes and
       critically analyzes the historical marker program, under which
       approximately eighteen hundred markers were erected in the
       state. Discusses the commission's site program and its various
       other programs. Discusses the dissolution of the commission
       as a result of the 1972 Executive Reorganization Plan, the
       transfer of its duties and staff to the Georgia Department of
       Natural Resources, as well as the formation of the Georgia

Heritage Trust and the Georgia Trust for Historic Preservation, which came as a result of this transfer. Concludes with a critical evaluation of the commission's role in historic preservation in Georgia.

206 Lane, Mills. SAVANNAH REVISITED: HISTORY, ARCHITECTURE, RESTORATION. 3d ed. Research by Mary Morrison; new photographs by Van Jones Martin. Savannah: Beehive Press, 1977. 214 p. Illus.

The text describing various periods of Savannah's rich history is accompanied by historic and modern photographs and reproductions of graphics and paintings. First published in 1969.

Kansas

207 Topeka-Shawnee County Metropolitan Planning Commission. REMEMBRANCES IN WOOD, BRICK AND STONE: EXAMPLES FROM THE ARCHITECTURAL HERITAGE OF SHAWNEE COUNTY, KANSAS. Topeka: 1974. 207 p. Illus., paper.

A listing of over one hundred buildings and groups of buildings selected from an inventory of existing architecture in Shawnee County, conducted by a special staff from the Topeka-Shawnee County Metropolitan Planning Commission. For each selection, includes a photograph and a caption describing the building's architectural, cultural, or historical significance in the Shawnee County heritage. Introduces a public education program on the possibilities of historic preservation and preservation planning in Shawnee County.

Louisiana

208 Christovich, Mary Louise, et al., eds. NEW ORLEANS ARCHITECTURE. 5 vols. Gretna, La.: Pelican Publishing Co., 1971-77. Illus., bibliog. Vol. I: THE LOWER GARDEN DISTRICT (1971) xvi, 159 p.; Vol. II: THE AMERICAN SECTOR (1972) xii, 243 p.; Vol. III: THE CEMETARIES (1974) x, 198 p.; Vol. IV: THE CREOLE FAUBOURGS (1974) xvi, 184 p.; Vol. V: THE ESPLANADE RIDGE (1977) xx, 172 p.

A series sponsored by the Friends of the Cabildo, recognized for its excellence by awards granted by the American Association for State and Local History and by the Society of Architectural Historians. Contains histories, photographic albums, and inventories to document the rich legacy of the former seat of power of French government in the New World.

209 Swanson, Betsy. HISTORIC JEFFERSON PARISH: FROM SHORE TO SHORE. Foreword by Henry C. Bezou. Introduction by Bethlyn McCloskey. Gretna, La.: Pelican Publishing Co., 1975. xiii, 176 p. Illus., bibliog.

Surveys the natural history, prehistory, and historic monuments and sites of Jefferson Parish, Louisiana, which stretches sixty miles from the shores of Lake Pontchartrain to the sand beaches of the Gulf of Mexico.

Maryland

210   Swann, Don. COLONIAL AND HISTORIC HOMES OF MARYLAND: ONE HUNDRED ETCHINGS. Text by Don Swann, Jr. Foreword by F. Scott Fitzgerald. Baltimore: Johns Hopkins University Press, 1975. 211 p. Illus.

First published in 1939, a survey of historic Maryland houses from the simplest vernacular to the highest of the high style.

Massachusetts

211   Bunting, Bainbridge. HOUSES OF BOSTON'S BACK BAY: AN ARCHI-TECTURAL HISTORY, 1840-1917. Cambridge: Belknap Press of Harvard University Press, 1967. xvii, 494 p. Illus. Paper. ed., 1975.

The architectural history of Back Bay Boston, seen in its cultural background, in the context of the topographical development of Boston, 1790-1965, and as an example of city planning. Significant for nineteenth-century brownstone rowhouse neighborhoods.

212   Lancaster, Clay. THE ARCHITECTURE OF HISTORIC NANTUCKET. Introduction by James C. Massey. New York: McGraw-Hill, 1972. xxxiii, 286 p. Illus., glossary, bibliog.

An in-depth study of the architecture and streetscape of Nantucket town on Nantucket island, Massachusetts; street by street, period by period, and building type by building type. Includes bibliography of source materials on Nantucket architecture and related subjects, including books, articles, albums, photograph and picture collections, and others.

213   Whitehill, Walter Muir. BOSTON: A TOPOGRAPHICAL HISTORY. 2d ed. Cambridge: Belknap Press of Harvard University Press, 1968. xl, 299 p. Illus.

Based on a series of lectures given by the author at the Lowell Institute in 1958. Describes the course of Boston's development from colonial times. In this revised edition, adds a final chapter covering the period of renewal between 1958 and 1968.

Michigan

214   Ferry, W. Hawkins. THE BUILDINGS OF DETROIT: A HISTORY.
Detroit: Wayne State University Press, 1968. xxii, 479 pp. Illus.

An illustrated history of Detroit buildings, from frontier community to skyscraper metropolis.

Missouri

215   Van Ravenswaay, Charles. THE ARTS AND ARCHITECTURE OF GERMAN
SETTLEMENTS IN MISSOURI: A SURVEY OF A VANISHING CULTURE.
Columbia: University of Missouri Press, 1977. xiv, 533 p. Illus.,
bibliog.

Deals with an area about fifty miles wide that extends some
hundred and fifty miles along the lower Missouri River valley,
where the immigrants from the German states began settling
among Anglo-American families about 1831. By the director
emeritus of the Henry Francis du Pont Winterthur Museum, who
spent forty years in preparation for this book, interviewing
craftsmen, studying and photographing their work, and examining documentary materials.

Nebraska

216   Kolberg, Persijs, and Jones, Carl H. A SURVEY OF HISTORIC,
ARCHITECTURAL AND ARCHAEOLOGICAL SITES OF THE ELEVEN
COUNTY EASTERN NEBRASKA URBAN REGION. Lincoln: Nebraska
State Historical Society, 1971. vi, 119 p. Illus., paper.

Prepared for the State Office of Planning and Programming.
Gives summary histories for each of the regions, followed by
surveys of each region's historic, archaeological, and architectural sites. In a final section, describes preservation
accomplishments in the state of Nebraska, discusses the need
for further action, and makes specific recommendations for
certain emergency sites which are at present in disuse or will
shortly be in disuse (with possible future destruction) or are
at present in danger of being destroyed.

New Jersey

217   Thomas, George E., and Doebley, Carl. CAPE MAY, QUEEN OF
THE SEASIDE RESORTS: ITS HISTORY AND ARCHITECTURE. Philadelphia: Art Alliance Press; London: Associated University Press,
1976. 202 p. Illus.

Concerns Cape May, New Jersey (or "Cape Island," as it
was called), which was extolled as a resort from around 1800.

Describes its successive stages, including its Victorian heyday.
In the first part, includes three sections: "Cape May--an
American Resort," "Architecture in Cape May," and "New
Cape May." In the second and third parts presents an
illustrated catalog of thirty buildings and an illustrated check-
list of seventy buildings.

New Mexico

218   Stewart, Ronald L. MONUMENTS OF NEW MEXICO. Photographs
by Alan Pitcairn. Boulder, Colo.: Pruett Publishing Co., 1974. x,
134 p. Illus.

A survey in text and photographs of the national, state, and
local monuments of New Mexico. Covers natural sites,
ancient Indian sites, Hispanic sites, and early Anglo con-
structions. Lists suggested reading at chapter ends.

New York

219   Aurora Historical Society. AURORA'S ARCHITECTURAL HERITAGE.
East Aurora, N.Y.: 1973. 96 p. Illus., glossary.

Concerns Aurora, a town in Erie County, New York, with
significant connections to William Morris and the arts and
crafts movement and a rich architectural heritage dating from
the early nineteenth century. Shows representative examples
in overall and detail photographs.

220   Burham, Alan, ed. NEW YORK LANDMARKS: A STUDY & INDEX
OF ARCHITECTURALLY NOTABLE STRUCTURES IN GREATER NEW YORK.
Foreword by Brendan Gill. Middletown, Conn.: Wesleyan University
Press, 1976. xiv, 430 p. Illus., bibliog., paper.

First published in 1963, under the auspices of the Municipal
Art Society of New York. The outgrowth of an index completed and published in 1957, in a mimeographed edition of
forty pages, under the title "New York Landmarks." A major
publication of its type, representing the significant role of
the Municipal Art Society in landmarks preservation. Indicates
that the society, particularly through the work of its Committee on Historic Architecture, was a primary force in the
founding of the New York City Landmarks Preservation Board
and, ultimately, in the passage of legislation which permitted
the transformation of the board into the New York City Landmarks Preservation Commission. Describes the styles of New
York's historic architecture, illustrates and describes a number
of the city's major landmarks, and provides an "Index of
Architecturally Notable Structures in Greater New York."

221   Dutchess County Planning Board. LANDMARKS OF DUTCHESS COUNTY,
       1683-1867: ARCHITECTURE WORTH SAVING IN NEW YORK STATE.
       New York State Council on the Arts, 1969. 242 p. Illus., glossary,
       paper.

       Provides photographs and descriptions of significant structures,
       as a first step in preserving the county's heritage. Concludes
       with recommendations for additional research and preservation
       action that can be undertaken at the local level. In appen-
       dixes, outlines New York state laws relating to historic pres-
       ervation, and federal, state, and private assistance programs.

222   Everest, Allan. OUR NORTH COUNTRY HERITAGE: ARCHITECTURE
       WORTH SAVING IN CLINTON AND ESSEX COUNTIES. Plattsburgh,
       N.Y.: Tundra Books, 1972. 143 p. Illus., paper.

       Sponsored by the Clinton County Historical Association, with
       the support of the New York State Council on the Arts.
       Presents a survey of the full range of styles and building
       types, from the simple log cabins and other shelters of the
       early settlers to the buildings of the post-Victorian era. In
       a concluding section, describes structures of special historical
       significance; describes rescue efforts, successful, failed, and
       current; and offers advice to the towns of the two counties.

223   Foerster, Bernd. ARCHITECTURE WORTH SAVING IN RENSSELAER
       COUNTY, NEW YORK. Troy, N.Y.: Rensselaer Polytechnic Institute,
       1965. 207 p. Illus., paper.

       Result of a survey by the School of Architecture at Rensselaer
       Polytechnic Institute, supported by the New York State Coun-
       cil on the Arts, to appraise "the architectural character and
       an assessment of buildings prior to 1920 that should be pre-
       served in Rensselaer County." Illustrates and describes spe-
       cific buildings of architectural worth, and makes a plea for
       the survival of total environments in which these buildings
       may remain comfortable and meaningful.

224   Gayle, Margot, and Gillon, Edmund V., Jr. CAST-IRON ARCHI-
       TECTURE IN NEW YORK. New York: Dover Publications, 1974.
       xviii, 190 p. Illus., paper.

       Presents Gillon's photographic survey, accompanied by Gayle's
       text. Includes an index to cast-iron buildings and another
       index to persons mentioned in the text and to firms that
       commissioned and occupied cast-iron buildings.

225   "Historic Fort Greene: A Proposal for the Designation of Fort Greene
       as an Historic District." New York: Presented to the New York City
       Landmarks Preservation Commission by the Fort Green Landmarks Pres-

Description and Documentation

ervation Committee, 30 November 1973.   196 leaves (various paginations).   Maps, bibliog.   Mimeographed.

A full scale survey in support of a petition for historic district
designation. Includes a "Block-by-Block Description" by
Theodore H.M. Prudon and seventy.five research assistants,
preceded by three essays: "The Rationale for Landmark Designation" by James Marston Fitch; "Historic Perspective" by
Albert Fein, Lois Gilman, and Donald Simon; and "Landscape
to Cityscape" by Charles Lockwood. (See entry 230.)

226   Kelly, Virginia B., et al. WOOD AND STONE: LANDMARKS OF
THE UPPER MOHAWK REGION. Utica: Central New York Community
Arts Council, 1974.   120 p. Illus., paper.

The result of field documentation, photography, and historical
research conducted from 1966 to 1971 in Herkimer and Oneida
Counties. Concludes with a master list of all of the historical
and architectural landmarks in the two counties nominated in
the 1965–66 survey and documented from 1966 to 1971. Organized by town, city, or village, within each of the two counties.

227   Lockwood, Charles. BRICKS AND BROWNSTONE: THE NEW YORK
ROW HOUSE, 1783–1929, AN ARCHITECTURAL AND SOCIAL HISTORY.
Introduction by James Biddle. New York: McGraw-Hill, 1972. xxv,
262 p. Illus., bibliog.

Arranged primarily chronologically, treating of the Federal
Style; the Greek Revival Style; the Gothic Revival Style; the
Italianate, Anglo-Italianate, and Second Empire Styles; and
the Neo-Grec, Queen Anne, Romanesque, Renaissance, and
Colonial Revival Styles. Explores their sources and their
application to New York houses. Discusses the development
of various residential neighborhoods.

228   _____. MANHATTAN MOVES UPTOWN: AN ILLUSTRATED HISTORY.
Boston: Houghton Mifflin Co., 1976.   xxi, 343 p. Illus.

Primarily a social history, describing the march of growth up
Manhattan Island, from the end of the Revolutionary War in
1783 to the years at the beginning of the twentieth century.
Describes the evolution of neighborhoods and the development
of architectural types.

229   Malo, Paul. LANDMARKS OF ROCHESTER AND MONROE COUNTY:
A GUIDE TO NEIGHBORHOODS AND VILLAGES. Syracuse: Syracuse
University Press, 1974.   ix, 276 p. Illus., glossary, bibliog., paper.

Presents, in a series of tours, a city and county with an extremely rich architectural tradition. Explores a variety of

styles, periods (including contemporary), building types, and
neighborhood environments. Sponsored by the Landmark Society
of Western New York.

230   New York City. Landmarks Preservation Commission. "Fort Greene
Historic District Designation Report." New York: 1978. 146 leaves.
Illus., bibliography. Mimeographed.

The Fort Greene Historic District, in Brooklyn, was designated
an historic district on 26 September 1978, the thirty-third
historic district to be officially designated by the New York
City Landmarks Preservation Commission. This report of the
commission, and those that follow, have been chosen because
they are representative of the more complex and substantive
of the reports, but other designation reports prepared by the
commission, appropriate to the smaller size of most of the
districts, consist of little more than a few mimeographed leaves.
Fort Greene Park, a site of immense significance in American
history, is the location of Stanford White's Prison Ship Martyrs'
Monument, commemorating the American prisoners of war who
died on prison ships in nearby Wallabout Bay during the Revolutionary War and whose bones were ultimately interred in
what is now the park. It is Fort Greene Park that provides
the central focus for the designated district, a district whose
boundaries are somewhat more limited than those originally
proposed in HISTORIC FORT GREENE: A PROPOSAL FOR THE
DESIGNATION OF FORT GREENE AS AN HISTORIC DISTRICT
(see entry 225).

231   _____. GREENWICH VILLAGE HISTORIC DISTRICT DESIGNATION
REPORT. 2 vols. New York: 1969. 201 p., 219 p. Paper.

Greenwich Village is more than just a collection of Manhattan
neighborhoods--it is a world mecca, with a rich and varied
history. The "Village" is one of the oldest sections of New
York City, laid out for development in the years following
the Revolution and containing still the greatest concentration
of early New York residential architecture to be found anywhere within the five burroughs. The report's historical
description extends from 1790 to "recent developments" and
its architectural description extends from Federal style to
Greek Revival, Gothic Revival, Italianate, French Second
Empire, Queen Anne, Romanesque Revival, etc. The artistic
and cultural history recorded in the report starts with Tom
Paine (1737-1809) and continues unbroken to the present.
This massive document divides the block-by-block descriptions
into nine distinct areas within the district.

232 _____. "Park Slope Historic District Designation Report." New York: 1973. xvii, 147 p. Mimeographed.

Documentation for this report, prepared by a team of neighbor-hood volunteers and contained in ten volumes of photographs and a file of research notes, is abstracted here in 142 pages of block-by-block architectural and historical description. Also included in the report are a description of the district's boundaries, a description of testimony heard at public hear-ings, an overview of Park Slope's historical background, and a description of this Brooklyn neighborhood's building develop-ment and architectural styles.

233 _____. "SoHo-Cast Iron Historic District Designation Report." New York: 1973. x, 231 p. Glossary, bibliog. Mimeographed.

SoHo, an area South of Houston Street in downtown Manhattan, contains a unique collection of cast-iron structures. It is a formerly commercial neighborhood that has become in recent years a center of artistic life in New York City. The hy-phenated name, SoHo-Cast Iron, was chosen for this historic district to reflect both its cultural and its architectural unique-ness. The report is divided into three parts: part I discusses the social and economic history of the area, with background information on cast-iron as a building material; part II contains block-by-block descriptions; and part III contains appendixes, sources and credits, and bibliography--as well as the commis-sion's findings. Among the appendixes is a listing of promi-nent architects whose work is represented in the district, with listings of their buildings in the district and general information on their careers.

234 New York State. Hudson River Valley Commission. HISTORIC RE-SOURCES OF THE HUDSON: A PRELIMINARY INVENTORY. Pre-pared by Lewis C. Rubenstein, Staff Historian. Tarrytown: 1969. 96 p. Illus.

Reports that the historic Hudson Valley is a region coveted by developers and converters of energy. Indicates that the com-mission has attempted, in a three-hundred mile jurisdiction, to identify worthwhile historic resources in an attempt to protect them from death by bulldozer or neglect. Gives background for the region and its stylistic particularities and for the New York State Historic Sites Program and other related historic site inventories.

235 New York State. Office of Planning Coordination. Metropolitan New York District Office. LONG ISLAND LANDMARKS. Edward J. Smits, consultant. Albany: 1969. 122 p. Illus., paper.

Identifies architectural landmarks in Nassau and Suffolk
Counties. Presents guidelines and possibilities for preservation
programs, and identifies sources of information and of technical and financial assistance.

236   Pins, Anita. AN HISTORIC DISTRICT IN MURRAY HILL. New York:
       Murray Hill Committee, 1977. 86 p. Illus., bibliog., paper.

       Prepared in response to the Murray Hill Committee's inquiry
       about historic district legislation and its application to a
       brownstone row within its neighborhood, this report was sub-
       mitted as a studio project in the Program in Historic Preser-
       vation at Columbia University's Graduate School of Archi-
       tecture and Planning. It provides a history of Murray Hill,
       a history of row house development in the district, descriptions
       of the individual buildings under consideration, and proposed
       guidelines for their maintenance and preservation.

237   Sanchis, Frank E. AMERICAN ARCHITECTURE, WESTCHESTER COUNTY,
       NEW YORK: COLONIAL TO CONTEMPORARY. Croton-on-Hudson,
       N.Y.: North River Press, 1977. xii, 564 p. Illus.

       Presents an examination of a county adjoining New York City,
       by a team of investigators sponsored by the Historic Preservation
       Committee of the Bicentennial Committee of Westchester.
       Organized by building use, and within use, by style. Covers
       residential buildings, ecclesiastical buildings, industrial build-
       ings, corporate buildings, commerical buildings, public and
       civic buildings, transportation, engineering, and recreation.

238   Wright, Russell J. THE VISUAL AND THE HISTORIC RESOURCES OF
       THE FINGER LAKES-SOUTHERN TIER REGION, N.Y. Ithaca:
       Office of Regional Resources and Development, Cornell University,
       1968? ix, 169 p. Illus., bibliog., paper.

       Discusses the historic architecture and the unique natural
       features, seen in the many distinctive land forms created by
       the two glaciers that completely covered the region during
       the Ice Age. Considers the extensive system of canals and
       railroads along with historic, archaeological, and Indian sites,
       in a survey of the natural and built environmental patrimony.

Oregon

239   Vaughan, Thomas, and McMath, George A. A CENTURY OF PORTLAND
       ARCHITECTURE. Portland: Oregon Historical Society, 1967. 226 p.
       Illus., glossary, paper.

       Includes photographs and substantial descriptions of Portland's
       notable structures.

Description and Documentation

Pennsylvania

240   Siskind, Aaron. BUCKS COUNTY: PHOTOGRAPHS OF EARLY ARCHI-
       TECTURE. Text by William Morgan. New York: Horizon Press for
       the Bucks County Historical Society, 1974. 112 p. Illus.

       Surveys a Pennsylvania county rich in history and architectural
       heritage, as a step in its preservation planning.

241   Stotz, Charles Morse. THE ARCHITECTURAL HERITAGE OF EARLY
       WESTERN PENNSYLVANIA: A RECORD OF BUILDING BEFORE 1860.
       Pittsburgh: University of Pittsburgh Press, 1966. xix, 293 p. Illus.,
       bibliog.

       Originally published in 1936 as THE EARLY ARCHITECTURE OF
       WESTERN PENNSYLVANIA. In the later version, includes a
       new introduction by Stotz and retains the original introduction
       by Fiske Kimball as the foreword. Records the work of the
       Western Pennsylvania Architectural Survey of 1932-35, which
       grew out of the Committee for the Preservation of Historic
       Monuments of the Pittsburgh Chapter, American Institute of
       Architects, of which Stotz was chairman. Remains a model for
       historic architecture surveys.

242   Van Trump, James D., and Ziegler, Arthur P., Jr. LANDMARK ARCHITEC-
       TURE OF ALLEGHENY COUNTY, PENNSYLVANIA. The Stones of Pitts-
       burgh, no. 5. Pittsburgh: Pittsburgh History and Landmarks Foundation, 1967.
       viii, 294 p. Illus., bibliog.

       A register of preservation areas and individual buildings, both
       within the city of Pittsburgh and in the surrounding county,
       which are proposed for preservation and, when necessary, re-
       habilitation. Covers areas ranging from the old village of
       Sewickley to inner city neighborhoods; individual buildings
       ranging from H.H. Richardson's Allegheny County Court House
       and Jail to simple log houses. States, "Our endeavor is to
       compile an initial list that provides an overview of the County's
       notable buildings. In this way we will have the future work
       of preservation planning and historical research delineated."

Rhode Island

243   Downing, Antoinette F., and Scully, Vincent J., Jr. THE ARCHI-
       TECTURAL HERITAGE OF NEWPORT, RHODE ISLAND, 1640-1915.
       2d ed., rev. New York: Clarkson N. Potter, 1967. xvi, 526 p.
       Illus.

       First published in 1952 by the Harvard University Press for
       the Preservation Society of Newport County. Describes in
       detail Newport's rich and varied architectural history. In-
       cludes many illustrations, strong documentation, and "spot
       restoration proposals."

Tennessee

244   Graham, Eleanor, ed. NASHVILLE: A SHORT HISTORY AND SELECT-
ED BUILDINGS. Maps and design by Gary Gore. Nashville: Historical
Commission of Metropolitan Nashville-Davidson County, 1974. 288 p.
Illus., bibliog.

> A history of the founding and development of Nashville,
> followed by a guide to the city in eight parts--each part
> covering a distinct section of town or environs, with a map,
> a narrative introduction, and an illustrated survey of signifi-
> cant structures. Includes a list of Davidson County buildings
> listed in the National Register of Historic Places, a list of
> buildings which have been presented awards by the Historical
> Commission, a list of Nashville and Tennessee organizations
> for historic preservation, and an index of place names.

Texas

245   Williamson, Roxanne Kuter. AUSTIN, TEXAS: AN AMERICAN ARCHI-
TECTURAL HISTORY. San Antonio: Trinity University Press, 1973.
xxii, 161 p. Illus.

> Presents the architectural history of Austin (or the history of
> Austin told through its architecture) over a period of 133
> years. Includes seven chapters, ranging from "The Creation
> of Austin" to "A Postscript on the Present: Austin, 1940-
> 1970." Concentrates on style changes, especially as they
> are demonstrated on the exteriors and facades of buildings.
> Makes only occasional note of interiors, and even less of
> the occupants or owners of the structures discussed.

Virginia

246   Cox, Ethelyn. HISTORIC ALEXANDRIA, VIRGINIA, STREET BY STREET:
A SURVEY OF EXISTING EARLY BUILDINGS. Alexandria: Historic
Alexandria Foundation, 1976. xxi, 216 p. Illus., paper.

> Reports that Alexandria a city rich in eighteenth- and nine-
> teenth-century architecture, has since 1946 had a local zon-
> ing ordinance defining the Old and Historic Alexandria Dis-
> trict, one of the first such local actions in the United States
> to restrict the changes permitted by private property owners.
> A pocket format guidebook, one of several projects sponsored
> by the Historic Alexandria Foundation to encourage interest
> in the renovation and restoration of early buildings in that
> city. Describes buildings of special architectural or histori-
> cal significance and also buildings which, alone, would be
> of minor importance but, which, standing together, retain
> the ambience of an earlier period of history.

Description and Documentation

247   Dulaney, Paul S. THE ARCHITECTURE OF HISTORIC RICHMOND.
        Charlottesville: University Press of Virginia, 1968. 208 p. Illus.

        A pocket guide to the historic areas of Richmond, based on
        a survey and inventory conducted in 1965 under the direction
        of members of the School of Architecture, University of
        Virginia. Presents photographic and textual descriptions of
        the various historic areas, followed by an essay on historic
        preservation, with particular application to Richmond. In
        concluding appendixes, describes and indexes the surveys:
        survey 1, "Inventory of Historic Buildings," and survey 2,
        "Aesthetic Resources."

Wisconsin

248   Sheboygan, Wisconsin. Redevelopment Authority. PROSPECTS FOR
        THE PAST: A STUDY OF NOTABLE ARCHITECTURE, SHEBOYGAN
        RENEWAL AREA--1972. Washington, D.C.: U.S. Department of
        Housing and Urban Development, 1973. 35 p. Illus., bibliog., paper.

        While presenting only the most notable architecture in a
        limited area of Sheboygan, highlights the need to intensify
        and broaden such activity in that city. Contains a survey
        and inventory, recommendations for urban renewal, and rec-
        ommendations for local activities to help assure effective
        preservation.

Washington, D.C.

249   Maddex, Diane. HISTORIC BUILDINGS OF WASHINGTON, D.C.
        Historic Buildings of America: A Selection from the Records of the
        Historic American Buildings Survey, National Park Service, U. S.
        Department of the Interior. Foreword by Arthur Cotton Moore. Pitts-
        burgh: Ober Park Associates, 1973. 191 p. Illus., bibliog.

        Reviews past and present preservation activity and future
        prospects for preservation in Washington, and describes the
        role of the Historic American Buildings Survey in that effort.
        Includes HABS drawings and photographs to illustrate the
        histories of standing and demolished structures in the federal
        city. In appendixes lists District of Columbia sites recorded
        by HABS, District of Columbia landmarks designated by the
        Joint Committee on Landmarks, and District of Columbia Sites
        in the National Register of Historic Places.

250   U.S. Commission of Fine Arts. MASSACHUSETTS AVENUE ARCHI-
        TECTURE. 2 vols. Washington, D.C.: U.S. Government Printing
        Office. Vol. 1, 1973, 427 p.; vol. 2, 1975, 272 p. Illus.

        Indicates that the purpose behind this study was essentially to
        preserve and record a unique collection of architecture threat-
        ened by development and change in an area lacking formal sta-

tus as a historic district. Surveys and catalogs some of America's most imposing domestic and ambassadorial architecture (standing and demolished), with architectural description, drawings, and interior and exterior photographs.

251 _____. SIXTEENTH STREET ARCHITECTURE. Vol. I. Prepared by Sue A. Kohler and Jeffrey R. Carson. Washington, D.C.: U.S. Government Printing Office, 1978. xix, 571 p. Illus., gloss., paper.

Celebrates Beaux Arts design, along the so-called "Presidents Avenue."

Puerto Rico

252 Puerto Rico. Planning Board. ESTUDIO SOBRE MONUMENTOS HISTÓRICOS DE PUERTO RICO [Study of the historic monuments of Puerto Rico]. By Mario J. Buschiazzo, consultor. Santurce, P.R.: 1955. 74 p. Illus.

A preliminary inventory of monuments of historic and/or artistic value, including fortifications, a cemetary, individual buildings, and archaeological sites. Provided one of the building stones for Puerto Rico's highly significant preservation program.

ARCHITECTURAL HISTORIES, INVENTORIES, AND SURVEYS— ABROAD

Australia

253 Australian Council of National Trusts. HISTORIC BUILDINGS OF AUSTRALIA. 3 vols. Stanmore, New South Wales, and North Melbourne, Victoria: Cassell Australia, Ltd. Vol. I.: HISTORIC HOMESTEADS OF AUSTRALIA (1969) 288 p. Illus., folio; Vol. II.: HISTORIC PUBLIC BUILDINGS OF AUSTRALIA (1971) 306 p. Illus., folio; Vol. III.: HISTORIC HOUSES OF AUSTRALIA (1974) 302 p. Illus., folio.

Describe and illustrate the vast variety of elements comprising Australia's architectural patrimony. Texts and illustrations by a number of authors and photographers.

254 Cox, Philip, and Stacey, Wesley. HISTORIC TOWNS OF AUSTRALIA. Melbourne: Lansdowne, 1973. 247 p. Illus., bibliog.

States that the book was written to bring attention to some of the few remaining country towns in Australia which still have the majority of their nineteenth-century buildings intact. States the need to preserve total environments--trees, buildings, streetscapes, and townscapes--rather than merely isolated individual buildings. Includes contemporary and historical photographs to illustrate the text.

Description and Documentation

255   Leary, Frank, and Leary, Judith. COLONIAL HERITAGE: HISTORIC
       BUILDINGS OF NEW SOUTH WALES. Sydney: Angus and Robertson,
       1972. xii, 299 p. Illus.

       A photographic survey. Covers the vicinities of Sydney,
       Parramatta, Campbelltown, Windsor, Newcastle, and Bathurst;
       the Blue Mountains; and from Mittagong to Canberra.

Belgium

256   LE PATRIMOINE MONUMENTAL DE LA BELGIQUE [The monumental
       heritage of Belgium]. 4 vols. Liège, Soledi: 1971-- . Vol. 1:
       PROVINCE DE BRABANT: ARRONDISSEMENT DE LOUVAIN (1971)
       462 p.; Vol. 2: PROVINCE DE BRABANT: ARRONDISSEMENT DE
       NIVELLES (1974) 622 p.; Vol. 3: PROVINCE DE LIÈGE: ARRON-
       DISSEMENT DE LIÈGE; Ville de Liège (1974) 453 p.; Vol. 4:
       PROVINCE DE HAINAUT: ARRONDISSEMENT DE MONS (1975)
       626 p. Brussels: Ministère de la Culture Française. Illus., bibliog.,
       glossary.

       An ongoing monumental work which surveys the architectural
       heritage of Belgium. As illustrations, includes maps and
       plans as well as some color photographs, among the primarily
       black-and-white photographs. Includes illustrated glossaries
       identifying building types and architectural details of national
       usage.

Canada

257   Heritage Trust of Nova Scotia. FOUNDED UPON A ROCK: HISTORIC
       BUILDINGS OF HALIFAX AND VICINITY STANDING IN 1967. Halifax:
       1967. 119 p. Illus., paper.

       Begins with a message from the president of the Heritage Trust
       of Nova Scotia, in which he says: "Although all of the build-
       ings and structures included in this book were still standing on
       July 1, 1967, some will probably be gone by the time you
       read this . . . We hope that this book will help to show the
       citizens of Halifax, of Nova Scotia, indeed of Canada, that
       there is something here which must be preserved. Moreover,
       we hope that it will help to convince legislators at all levels
       that appropriate action must be taken immediately to stop and
       prevent further erosion of our physical heritage. And if we
       fail in some cases, at least there will be a pictorial record
       of what we once had--and could have kept."

258   Kalman, Harold D. THE RAILWAY HOTELS AND THE DEVELOPMENT
       OF THE CHATEAU STYLE IN CANADA. Studies in Architectural
       History No. 1. Victoria, B. C.: University of Victoria Maltwood
       Museum, 1968. 47 p. Illus. Paperbound.

74

From the Chateau Frontenac in Quebec City to the Empress
Hotel in Victoria Island, the hotels of the Canadian National
Railways and the Canadian Pacific Railway represent major
monuments in the development of a Canadian national architectural style.

259   Marsan, Jean-Claude. MONTRÉAL EN ÉVOLUTION: HISTORIQUE
DU DÉVELOPPEMENT DE L'ARCHITECTURE ET DE L'ENVIRONNEMENT
MONTRÉALAIS [Montreal in evolution: history of the development of
the architecture and the environment of Montreal]. Montreal: Fides,
1974. 423 p. Illus., bibliog., paper.

Examines the development of a unique urban setting, from the
first fortification to the most recent skyscrapers. Includes an
extensive selected bibliography and also a bibliographic essay
within the author's introduction.

260   Stewart, J. Douglas, and Wilson, Ian E. HERITAGE KINGSTON.
Kingston, Ontario: Agnes Etherington Art Centre, Queen's University,
1973. xii, 218 p. Illus., paper.

Reports that Kingston possesses what is possibly the most important group of early buildings in Canada, with the exception
of Quebec City and Montreal. Indicates that, despite strong
local citizen action for preservation, many of these buildings
have been destroyed to make way for "progress" in recent years.
Catalogs an exhibition held 3 June to 28 October 1973 at the
Agnes Etherington Art Centre, which, in Kingston's tercentenary
year, aimed at making a wider Canadian public aware of the
imperilled state of Kingston's heritage and theirs.

France

261   France. Direction de l'Architecture. LISTE DES IMMEUBLES PROTÉGÉS
AU TITRE DE LA LÉGISLATION SUR LES MONUMENTS HISTORIQUES
ET SUR LES SITES DANS LE DÉPARTMENT DE _____ [List of buildings
protected by virtue of legislation on historic monuments and sites in
the Department of _____]. Paris: Impr. nationale, n.d. Paperbound
pamphlets.

An ongoing series of pamphlets describing the protected historic monuments and sites in the various departments of France.

262   Lavedan, Pierre. POUR CONNAÎTRE LES MONUMENTS DE FRANCE
[To know the monuments of France]. With the collaboration of Simone
Goubet. Paris: B. Arthaud, 1971. 803 p. Illus., glossary, bibliog.

Starts with the materials and construction of French buildings,
and moves to decoration and architectural aesthetics. Moves

then, by period, from medieval to modern, with each period
subdivided by building type. Covers urbanism and monuments
along with architecture.

Great Britain

263   Allsopp, Bruce, and Clark, Ursula. HISTORIC ARCHITECTURE OF
       NORTHUMBERLAND AND NEWCASTLE UPON TYNE. London: Oriel
       Press, 1977. 124 p. Illus.

       Draws upon HISTORIC ARCHITECTURE OF NEWCASTLE-UPON-
       TYNE (1968) (see entry 122) and HISTORIC ARCHITECTURE OF
       NORTHUMBERLAND (1969). Concerned with both city and
       county. Primarily a photo album. Organized primarily by
       building types, towns and villages, and the city of Newcastle.

264   Collier, William. HISTORIC BUILDINGS: THE HISTORIC ARCHITECTURE
       OF THE THAMES VALLEY. Bourne End, Buckinghamshire: Spurbooks
       Limited, 1973. 137 p. Illus.

       A nine-century survey arranged by period: medieval, Tudor,
       Stuart, Queen Anne and Georgian, late Georgian, and
       Victorian.

265   Lincoln, E[dward]. F[rank]. THE HERITAGE OF KENT. The County
       Heritage Series. London: Oldbourne, 1966. 132 p. Illus.

       A history of Kent, with photographs of the natural and built
       landmarks of the county.

266   Mayo, Walter Longley Bourke, 8th Earl of, et al. THE THAMES VALLEY
       FROM CRICKLADE TO STAINES: A SURVEY OF ITS EXISTING STATE
       AND SOME SUGGESTIONS FOR ITS FUTURE PRESERVATION. London:
       University of London Press, 1929. xvi, 106 p. Illus.

       Very elegant presentation of the Thames Valley Branch of the
       Council for the Preservation of Rural England. Divided into
       two principal parts: (1) a "General Survey of Existing Con-
       ditions" and (2) "Recommendations." Considers subjects in-
       cluding towns and villages, bridges, roads, railways, bridle
       tracks, footpaths, and landscape.

267   Pevsner, Nikolaus, ed. THE BUILDINGS OF ENGLAND. 46 vols-- .
       Harmondsworth, Middlesex: Penguin Books, 1951-- .

       Twenty-five years of research are embodied in forty-six volumes
       covering every county in England. The volumes give full par-
       ticulars of the architectural features of all ecclesiastical, pub-
       lic, and domestic buildings of interest, of every period, in
       each town and village of the county concerned. Outlines

tours for the major towns, to guide the reader in finding the
streets and buildings of special interest. Detailed introductions
to each volume highlight the notable architectural features of
each county. Special sections on building materials and prehistory. A one-man national survey. Many of the volumes
have seen several editions.

268   SURVEY OF LONDON. Vol. 1-- , 1900-- . Vols. 1-24, London
Survey Committee and the London County Council; Vols. 25-32, London
County Council; Vol. 33-- , Greater London Council.

A fully documented and profusely illustrated survey. The first
volume covered THE PARISH OF BROMLEY-BY-BOW in 53 pages
and 36 plates. The 39th volume, 1977, under the general editor-
ship of F.H.W. Sheepard, covered THE GROSVENOR ESTATE
IN MAYFAIR in 236 pages and 56 plates.

Spain

269   Spain. Servicio de Información Artística, Arqueológica y Etnológica.
INVENTARIO DEL PATRIMONIO ARTÍSTICO Y ARQUEOLÓGICO DE
ESPAÑA [Inventory of the artistic and archaeological patrimony of
Spain]. By Carlos de Parrondo Acero. Colección Inventario de
Protección del Patrimonio Cultural Europeo, no. 3. Madrid: Comisaría
General del Patrimonio Artístico Nacional, 1973. 520 p.

A Spanish contribution to European Architectural Heritage
Year. An inventory of historic-artistic monuments and districts, picturesque places, and artistic gardens.

Chapter 5

GUIDEBOOKS

Although listed here as a separate chapter, guidebooks are intimately related to inventories and surveys and are an important element in the total concept of "Description and Documentation," as covered in the previous chapter. Because of their great number, the compiler has not included the state and local guidebooks issued in the AMERICAN GUIDE SERIES, produced during the 1930s by the Federal Writers' Project of the Works Progress Administration (WPA). A vast and complex project, the AMERICAN GUIDE SERIES resulted from the combined effort of approximately five thousand creative writers, researchers, clerical workers, and administrators. It drew upon the assistance of local architects, the American Institute of Architects, the Federal Art Project's Index of American Design, and the Historic American Buildings Survey. Several of the "American Guides" have recently been reissued.

EUROPE

270   Postal, Bernard, and Abramson, Samuel H.   THE LANDMARKS OF A
       PEOPLE: A GUIDE TO JEWISH SITES IN EUROPE.   New York: Hill
       and Wang, 1962.   xvi, 270 p.   Illus.

           Arranged by country and then by city and town within each
           country.   Describes historically important or architecturally
           unique synagogues, modern synagogues, historic cemeteries,
           places and street names that recall old Jewries, monuments
           and memorials to Jews, places and streets named for Jews,
           and other related landmarks.

GREAT BRITAIN

271   Dunbar, John G.   THE HISTORIC ARCHITECTURE OF SCOTLAND.
       London: B.T. Batsford Ltd., 1966.   268 p.   Illus., bibliog.

           Includes chapters on: "Castles, Towers and Palaces"; "Lairds'
           Houses"; "Country Mansions"; "Abbeys and Churches"; "Burgh

Architecture"; "Industrial Architecture"; and "Small Rural
Houses, Farms and Villages." Describes each of these categories and their subtypes in detail, from the architectural and
historical viewpoint. Indexes the building types by location
within Scotland.

272   Fedden, Robin, and Joekes, Rosemary. THE NATIONAL TRUST GUIDE.
      Rev. ed. London: Jonathan Cape, 1977. 608 p. Illus., glossary.

      Covers all of the important National Trust properties in Eng-
      land, Wales, and Northern Ireland. In each chapter, deals
      with a particular type of property, prefaced by an introductory
      essay followed by a gazetteer. Includes chapters on: "Houses";
      "Gardens and Landscape Parks"; "Follies, Monuments, Villages,
      Dovecotes, Chapels, and Buildings of Useful Intent"; "Medieval
      Buildings"; "Industrial Monuments"; "Archeological Sites"; and
      "Coast and Country." Published in the United States as THE
      NATIONAL TRUST GUIDE TO ENGLAND, WALES AND
      NORTHERN IRELAND (New York: Alfred A. Knopf, 1974.
      688 p.).

273   Fenwick, Hubert. SCOTLAND'S HISTORIC BUILDINGS. London:
      Robert Hale, 1974. 254 p. Illus., glossary.

      Includes chapters on: "Early Churches and Cathedrals"; "Abbeys
      and Later Churches"; "Castles and Towers"; "Palaces and Man-
      sions"; "Scottish Towns and Villages"; and "The Building of
      Edinburgh." Provides a list of buildings open to the public.

274   Lees-Milne, James. NATIONAL TRUST GUIDE: BUILDINGS. Foreword
      by Lord Esher. Illustrations by S.R. Badmin. London, New York,
      Toronto, Sydney: B.T. Batsford, 1948. viii, 184 p. Illus.

      A county-by-county and shire-by-shire guide to the properties
      of the National Trust as of the date of publication. (For a
      comparison of growth in just over ten years, see entry 62).
      Gives situation, conditions of admission, charges, and descrip-
      tion of the property.

275   Martin, Graham. HISTORIC CHURCHES OF THE THAMES VALLEY.
      Bourne End, Buckinghamshire: Spurbooks, 1973. 159 p. Illus., bibliog.

      From Staines to Windsor to Maidenhead to Marlow to Henley
      to Reading to Goring to Wallingford to Abingdon to Oxford.

276   National Trust for Places of Historic Interest or Natural Beauty. THE
      NATIONAL TRUST ATLAS, SHOWING PLACES OF HISTORIC, ARCHI-
      TECTURAL & SCENIC INTEREST IN ENGLAND, WALES AND NORTH-
      ERN IRELAND. London: 1964. Unpaged. Chiefly colored maps.

In the explanatory note, informs that this is an atlas, a guide
to situation, not a guide book. "It is so designed the traveller consulting it is able to discover at a glance what interesting
places lie within his reach." Consists of maps and corresponding gazetteers, with an index to the overall collection. Suggests supplementary publications for fuller information about
opening arrangements and descriptions of the properties: HIS-
TORIC HOUSES, CASTLES & GARDENS IN GREAT BRITAIN &
IRELAND (Index Publishers), MUSEUMS & GALLERIES IN
GREAT BRITAIN & IRELAND (Index Publishers), ANCIENT
MONUMENTS OPEN TO THE PUBLIC (Country Life Ltd.),
and ANCIENT MONUMENTS OF NORTHERN IRELAND (H.M.
Stationery Office, Belfast).

277   Ryan, Peter. THE NATIONAL TRUST AND THE NATIONAL TRUST
        FOR SCOTLAND: COMPLETE IN TEXT AND PICTURES. London:
        J.M. Dent & Sons, 1969. xxiv, 388 p. Illus.

        In pictures or text, or both, covers the whole of Britain,
        complete to the end of March 1969. Deals with every prop-
        erty of the National Trust in some degree, from a full entry
        down to a listing by name. Also published in a series of
        five separate volumes, each covering an area of Great
        Britain.

UNITED STATES

General

278   Barrington, Lewis. HISTORIC RESTORATIONS OF THE DAUGHTERS OF
        THE AMERICAN REVOLUTION. New York: Richard Smith, 1941.
        320 p. Illus.

        Published to mark the fiftieth anniversary of the National
        Society of the Daughters of the American Revolution. Presents
        photographs and textual descriptions of 210 historic restorations
        with which the organization is associated, often as the custo-
        dian of historic house museums in properties actually owned by
        city or state.

279   Boatner, Mark M. III. LANDMARKS OF THE AMERICAN REVOLUTION:
        A GUIDE TO LOCATING AND KNOWING WHAT HAPPENED AT THE
        SITES OF INDEPENDENCE. Harrisburg, Pa.: Stackpole Books, 1973.
        608 p. Bibliographical essay.

        Inventories sites in the United States and Canada in a book
        which the author calls "part travel guide, part regional his-
        tory, and part gazetteer."

Guidebooks

280   Broderick, Robert C. HISTORIC CHURCHES OF THE UNITED STATES.
       Drawings by Virginia Broderick. New York: Wilfred Funk, 1958.
       xxv, 262 p. Illus.

       A historical review of church buildings and congregations
       from the Spanish missions to the present era. In an appendix,
       lists notable churches, temples, cathedrals, and synagogues
       according to state.

281   Brown, Sheldon S. REMADE IN AMERICA: THE GRAND TOUR OF
       EUROPE AND ASIA WITHIN THE U.S.A. Salem, Oreg.: Old Time
       Bottle Publishing Co., 1972. 384 p. Illus.

       A photographic survey of evocative eclecticism shown side by
       side with the sources of inspiration.

282   Da Costa, Beverley, ed. GREAT HISTORIC PLACES. By the editors
       of AMERICAN HERITAGE. Introduction by Richard M. Ketchum. An
       American Heritage Guide. New York: American Heritage Publishing
       Co., 1973. 319 p. Illus.

       A state-by-state guide to more than a thousand historic sites,
       with description of the site and practical information for the
       visitor.

283   Haas, Irvin. AMERICA'S HISTORIC VILLAGES AND RESTORATIONS.
       New York: Arco Publishing Co., 1974. 150 p. Illus.

       In photographs and text, describes fifty preserved, restored,
       and reconstructed settlements. Arranged by region: New
       England, Middle Atlantic, South, and Midwest and West.

284   Hitchcock, Henry-Russell, and Seale, William. TEMPLES OF DEMOC-
       RACY: THE STATE CAPITOLS OF THE USA. New York and London:
       Harcourt Brace Jovanovich, 1976. 333 p. Illus., bibliog.

       A bicentennial year publication sponsored by the Victorian
       Society in America. Explores the practical and symbolic role
       of the state capitols in the fifty states, starting with their
       predecessors in the colonies. Includes projects along with
       built structures.

285   ILLUSTRATED GUIDE TO THE TREASURES OF AMERICA. Pleasantville,
       N.Y., and Montreal, Quebec: Reader's Digest Assoc., 1974. 624 p.
       Illus.

       Through nine regional tours of the United States, describes
       over five thousand national treasures, including "mills and
       meetinghouses, humble dwellings, bridges and dams, marvelous
       trains and automobiles, buildings made for commerce, great
       parks and gardens and places that are steeped in the history

of our land." Along with major monuments, buildings, sites, and museums, includes smaller museums, out-of-the-way historic houses, and special displays of artifacts and other objects. In an introductory chapter, describes the evolution of the fine arts, architecture, the mechanical arts, and the decorative arts in America.

286   Konikow, Robert B. DISCOVER HISTORIC AMERICA. Chicago: Rand McNally, 1973. 281 p. Illus.

A guide to more than twenty-eight hundred places of historic interest, arranged by seven regions: Northeast, Southeast, South Central, Great Lakes, Plains, Southwest, and Mountains and Pacific. Includes an introductory essay to each region, followed by maps, photographs, and descriptions of sites. Includes tables giving significant dates and other basic information about the fifty states and about the presidents of the United States. Provides a classified index to the sites described.

287   Murfin, James V., and the Office of Publication Staff. NATIONAL PARK SERVICE GUIDE TO THE HISTORIC PLACES OF THE AMERICAN REVOLUTION. Washington, D.C.: U.S. Department of the Interior, 1975. 135 p. Illus., bibliog., paper.

Bicentennial guide to locations associated with the American Revolution. Includes sites administered by the National Park Service as well as other sites not under the service's jurisdiction. Arranges national, state, and local historic sites by state, with a final category, "The Western Frontier." Gives names and addresses of organizations supplying travel, historic site, and bicentennial information following each geographic section. Gives a chronology of political and military events of the Revolution. In a reading list, includes books, folders, posters, and document reproductions concerning the Revolutionary War period, listed by source: Superintendant of Documents, Library of Congress, and National Archives.

288   Randall, Charles Edgar, and Clepper, Henry. FAMOUS AND HISTORIC TREES. Washington, D.C.: American Forestry Association, 1976. 90 p. Illus., paper.

Historic trees of the United States, including: trees no longer standing; trees associated with the development of the nation; trees associated with educators and educational institutions; trees associated with literature, music, and science; trees associated with churches and religion; trees esthetic, scenic, and unusual; trees famous because of unusual size or age.

289   U.S. National Park Service. THE PRESIDENTS, FROM THE INAUGURA-
        TION OF GEORGE WASHINGTON TO THE INAUGURATION OF
        GERALD R. FORD: HISTORIC PLACES COMMEMORATING THE CHIEF
        EXECUTIVES OF THE UNITED STATES. The National Survey of His-
        toric Sites and Buildings, vol. 20. Washington, D.C.: 1976. x, 598 p.
        Illus., bibliog.

        Describes presidential birthplaces, homes, memorials, libraries,
        and tombs in part 3; which follows part 1, "Historical Back-
        ground," and part 2, "Biographical Sketches."

290   Unrau, Harlan D. HERE WAS THE REVOLUTION: HISTORIC SITES OF
        THE WAR FOR AMERICAN INDEPENDENCE. Washington, D.C.:
        National Park Service, 1977. xii, 324 p. Illus., bibliog.

        An historical narrative illuminates the events that lead to
        national independence. What follows is a state-by-state
        guide to buildings and sites associated with the Revolutionary
        War--including not only places where events of the Revolution
        occurred, but also later memorials such as Mount Rushmore
        National Memorial in South Dakota. Includes publicly and
        privately owned buildings and sites and identifies those which
        are national historic landmarks or National Park Service areas.
        Does not include dates and hours of access to visitors or ad-
        mission costs.

291   Vanderbilt, Cornelius, Jr. THE LIVING PAST OF AMERICA: A
        PICTORIAL TREASURY OF OUR HISTORIC HOUSES AND VILLAGES
        THAT HAVE BEEN PRESERVED AND RESTORED. New York: Crown
        Publishers, 1955. xiv, 234 p. Illus.

        Presents the author's recollections of his father, General
        Cornelius Vanderbilt, comparing historic buildings in relation
        to history as the visible tips of icebergs in relation to the
        entire iceberg. An illustrated guide to preserved America
        with a "Directory of National Historic Preservations," by
        state, giving practical visitor information.

Statewide

292   Crocker, Mary Wallace. HISTORIC ARCHITECTURE IN MISSISSIPPI.
        Jackson: University and College Press of Mississippi, 1973. xiii,
        194 p.

        Describes representative historic buildings from various sections
        of the state, in photograph and text. Criteria for inclusion
        based on notable persons or events associated with the struc-
        tures, or significant design or construction.

293   Groff, Sibyl McC. NEW JERSEY'S HISTORIC HOUSES: A GUIDE TO
       HOMES OPEN TO THE PUBLIC. New York and S. Brunswick, N.J.:
       A.S. Barnes & Co.; London: Thomas Yoseloff, 1971. 247 p. Illus.

       A descriptive guide to the historic houses, villages and struc-
       tures in New Jersey to which the public is admitted. De-
       scribes not only the historic places, but also frequently their
       settings and nearby amenities.

294   Holmquist, June Drenning, and Brookins, Jean A. MINNESOTA'S
       MAJOR HISTORIC SITES: A GUIDE. Rev. ed. St. Paul: Minnesota
       Historical Society, 1972. xv, 191 p. Illus., bibliog., paper.

       Greatly revised version of original edition of 1963. Orga-
       nized by four major geographical divisions: the Twin Cities,
       Central, Southern, and Northern Minnesota. Covers every-
       thing from Indian petroglyphs to Sinclair Lewis's boyhood
       home. In final section, lists state monuments officially estab-
       lished by the Minnesota legislature.

295   O'Neal, William B. ARCHITECTURE IN VIRGINIA: AN OFFICIAL
       GUIDE TO FOUR CENTURIES OF BUILDING IN THE OLD DOMINION.
       New York: Walker & Co. for the Virginia Museum, 1968. 192 p.
       Illus., bibliog.

       A pocket-format guidebook which presents a choice of "fine
       examples of each type of structure that has played an impor-
       tant part in the development of building in the State." Six
       divisions correspond to six convenient geographical areas. The
       bibliography, by Frederick D. Nichols, contains a section of
       general works and a section for each of the six divisions.

296   Pepper, Adeline. TOURS OF HISTORIC NEW JERSEY. New Brunswick:
       Rutgers University Press, 1973. xii, 274 p. Illus.

       A guide to the natural and man-made landmarks of the state.

297   Society of Colonial Wars in the State of New Jersey. HISTORIC ROAD-
       SIDES IN NEW JERSEY: A CONDENSED DESCRIPTION OF THE PRINCI-
       PAL COLONIAL AND REVOLUTIONARY LANDMARKS IN NEW JERSEY,
       ARRANGED FOR THE CONVENIENCE OF STUDENTS AND MOTORISTS.
       Plainfield, N.J.: W.L. Glenney, 1928. 115 p. Illus., bibliog.

       A county-by-county excursion explores New Jersey's historic
       buildings and sites.

298   Strand, Janann. A GREENE & GREENE GUIDE. Sketches by Gregory
       Cloud. Pasadena, Calif.: G. Dahlstrom, 1974. ix, 112 p. Illus.,
       bibliog.

A guide to the work of the California architectural firm of
Greene & Greene (1893-1922). A compendium of information
on the architectural firm and on southern California architecture as well. Maps walking tours for Greene & Greene
houses, and illustrates many architectural details. Describes
the role of docents in the interpretation of the firm's major
work, the Gamble House in Pasadena.

City and Regional

299   American Association of University Women. Sacramento Branch.
       VANISHING VICTORIANS: A GUIDE TO THE HISTORIC HOMES OF
       SACRAMENTO: 1973. 124 p. Illus., paper.

       The work of the Historic Homes Committee of the Sacramento
       Branch of AAUW. Pictures homes possessing the dignity of
       age, which remind the viewer of a rich, but somewhat ne-
       glected historic heritage. Published in the hope that Sacramento
       will follow other communities in encouraging efforts to pre-
       serve what has survived. Divides the city into districts,
       wherein houses are described in photographs, drawings, and
       text. Provides separate illustrated folders for a walking tour,
       a bicycle tour, and an automobile tour.

300   American Institute of Architects. New Orleans Chapter. A GUIDE
       TO NEW ORLEANS ARCHITECTURE. New Orleans: 1974. xii,
       169 p. Paper.

       Describes the many architectural styles of New Orleans, in
       tours of eighteen separate areas.

301   American Institute of Architects. Washington Metropolitan Chapter. A
       GUIDE TO THE ARCHITECTURE OF WASHINGTON, D.C. Written
       and edited by Warren J. Cox et al. 2d ed. New York: McGraw-Hill,
       1974. 246 p. Bibliog.

       In handy pocket format, gives twenty walking and motoring
       tours of Washington and vicinity. Includes streetscapes along
       with monumental, and less monumental, buildings. Gives
       thumbnail descriptions accompanied by photographs and also
       by visitor information where appropriate. In an initial essay
       on "The Architecture of Washington, D.C.," by Francis D.
       Lethbridge, reviews the city's founding and its building his-
       tory. Contains an index of buildings and architects.

302   Brown, Elizabeth Mills. NEW HAVEN: A GUIDE TO ARCHITECTURE
       AND URBAN DESIGN. New Haven and London: Yale University
       Press, 1976. ix, 228 p. Illus., paper.

Published with the assistance of the New Haven Bicentennial
Commission and the New Haven Preservation Trust. Explores
New Haven's buildings and landmarks along fifteen distinct
itineraries. Describes and illustrates buildings, sites, and
natural features. Includes maps; a chronological table; an
index of architects, builders, planners, and artists; and a
general index.

303   Edmiston, Susan, and Cirino, Linda D. LITERARY NEW YORK: A
       HISTORY AND GUIDE. Boston: Houghton Mifflin Co., 1976. xix,
       409 p. Illus.

       Tours sites and districts associated with literature and with
       literary figures, primarily in Manhattan, but also including
       the other four boroughs.

304   Fine, Jo Renée, and Wolfe, Gerard R. THE SYNAGOGUES OF NEW
       YORK'S LOWER EAST SIDE. Introduction by Harry Golden. New
       York: New York University Press, 1978. x, 172 p. Illus., bibliog.

       New York's Jewish community dates from the mid-seventeenth
       century, and it is then that this survey begins. Indicates
       that the synagogue as a physical building is but one aspect of
       this sociological history, for which Wolfe produced the text
       and Fine the photographs.

305   Goldstone, Harmon, and Dalrymple, Martha. HISTORY PRESERVED: A
       GUIDE TO NEW YORK CITY LANDMARKS AND HISTORIC DISTRICTS.
       New York: Simon and Schuster, 1974. Reprint. New York: Schocken
       Books, 1976. 576 p. Illus., glossary, bibliog., paper.

       Explores officially designated landmark districts and landmark
       buildings, borough-by-borough and neighborhood-by-neighbor-
       hood. Gives the background for New York City's landmarks
       preservation law, and explains the workings of the Landmarks
       Preservation Commission. Defines the terms used by the
       commission to describe styles, and explains them in historical
       context. In chronological charts, lists individual landmarks
       that had been designated as of 14 March 1972.

306   Hodges, Allan A., ed. WASHINGTON ON FOOT: A CITY PLAN-
       NER'S GUIDE TO THE NATION'S CAPITAL. Washington, D.C.:
       National Capital Area Chapter, American Institute of Planners, 1976.
       208 p. Illus., paper.

       Pocket format. Published to coincide with the joint A.I.P.
       and American Society of Planning Officials National Planning
       Conference in Washington, D.C., 20-26 March 1976. With
       this audience in mind, highlights the city planning, archi-
       tectural, and historical aspects of the development of Wash-

Guidebooks

ington, D.C.; Old Town Alexandria, Virginia; and Historic
Annapolis, Maryland.

307 Marion, John Francis. BICENTENNIAL CITY: WALKING TOURS OF
HISTORIC PHILADELPHIA. Princeton, N.J.: Pyne Press, 1974. xiii,
210 p. Illus.

Divided into twelve walks. Primarily written descriptions of
historically significant sites and buildings. A brief essay on
suggested readings. Few illustrations.

308 Randall, A.L. NEWPORT: A TOUR GUIDE. Newport, R.I.: Catboat
Press, 1970. 120 p. Illus., bibliog., glossary, paper.

Organized into seven walks through historic Newport. Follows
Newport's architectural development, and informs the reader
about outstanding events and personages in the history of the
"several" Newports. For each tour, gives an introductory
narrative followed by photographs and descriptive captions
for individual buildings.

309 Rifkind, Carole, and Levine, Carol. MANSIONS, MILLS, AND MAIN
STREETS. New York: Schocken Books, 1975. viii, 248 p. Illus.

Through seven guided tours, covers the area within a fifty-
mile radius of New York City. Includes all kinds of structures, with emphasis on the local architectural types. Includes all manner of domestic, commercial, religious, and
industrial buildings, as well as such public spaces as parks,
village greens, cemeteries, and landscaped highways. Gives
details on visitor accessibility, where applicable.

310 Ritz, Richard E., ed. A GUIDE TO PORTLAND ARCHITECTURE.
Portland: Portland, Oregon, Chapter of the American Institute of
Architects, 1968. 74 p. Illus., paper.

Prepared at the time of the 100th national convention of the
American Institute of Architects, held for the first time in
Portland, in 1968. Aims to "guide the user to points of
interest and significant works, allowing the architecture to
speak for itself rather than to render architectural criticism."
Intended to be "helpful, in understanding the city and its
buildings, to place them in context with the geographical,
sociological and economic framework in which development
took place, and to draw some of the lines of architectural
connection necessary to understanding of stylistic development."

311 Scott, James Allen. DULUTH'S LEGACY. Vol. I: ARCHITECTURE.
Legacy Series. Photographs by John R. Ulven, Jr. Illustrations by
Robert T. Calton. Duluth, Minn.: City of Duluth through the Office
of the Department of Research and Planning, 1974. 165 p. Illus. Paper.

Traces the history and the development of Duluth. Provides
an illustrated guide to historically and architecturally significant structures, and digests basic data for almost one hundred
additional structures.

312   Teitelman, Edward, and Longstreth, Richard W. ARCHITECTURE IN
PHILADELPHIA. Cambridge: M.I.T. Press, 1974. xviii, 284 p.
Bibliog.

Begins with a brief historical review of architecture and planning in Philadelphia, and then tours the city, neighborhood-
by-neighborhood, describing it with photographs and captions.
Selected bibliography and sources. List of demolished buildings. Index of architects. Index of building types and styles.
Index of buildings and places.

313   White, Norval, and Willensky, Elliot. AIA GUIDE TO NEW YORK
CITY. Rev. ed. London: Collier Macmillan Publishers; New York:
Macmillan Publishing Co., 1978. xv, 653 p. Illus., glossary.

Prepared for the New York Chapter, American Institute of
Architects. First published in 1967. In the substantially enlarged edition of 1978, maintains the large and hefty "pocket"
format of the first edition. A guide to the buildings, structures, streets, landmarks, and parks of the five boroughs. Detailed coverage. In appendixes, describes population growth
from 1790 to 1970 and the geography, the geology, and the
infrastructure of the city. Also includes a calendar of parades
and street spectacles, a table of data on sixty-five bridges
and four tunnels, a guide to outdoor murals, a necrology of
lost landmarks, and other items.

314   Wolfe, Gerard R. NEW YORK, A GUIDE TO THE METROPOLIS:
WALKING TOURS OF ARCHITECTURE AND HISTORY. New York:
New York University Press, 1975. xiv, 434 p. Illus., bibliog., paper.

An outgrowth of "The Many Faces of Gotham," a course taught
by the author at New York University. Offers twenty walking
tours of New York City neighborhoods and historic districts.
Outlines each tour in a map, and provides information on
public transportation to the locality. Gives narrative descriptions featuring historical, architectural, and sociological information. Includes illustrations consisting of historical prints
as well as historical and contemporary photographs. Describes
buildings and sites, including those that have vanished, along
with contemporary landmarks and preserved historic buildings
and sites.

315   Wrenn, Tony P. WASHINGTON D.C.: WALKING TOURS. Edited
and produced by the Preservation Press, National Trust for Historic Pres-

ervation. Washington, D.C.: Parks and History Association, 1975.
128 p. Illus., paper.

A pocket format guide with detailed maps and descriptions
for exploring Washington on foot. Provides separate tours
for three major public areas and two residential areas: the
White House neighborhood, the Mall, the U.S. Capitol
area, Capitol Hill, and Kalorama.

PLAQUES AND MARKERS

316   New York Community Trust. THE HERITAGE OF NEW YORK:
       HISTORIC-LANDMARK PLAQUES OF THE NEW YORK COMMUNITY
       TRUST. New York: Fordham University Press, 1970. xxi, 402 p.
       Illus.

       The New York Community Trust, along with the Municipal
       Art Society of New York, was an early instrument in the re-
       cording of landmarks in New York City before the formation
       of the New York City Landmarks Preservation Commission.
       Indicates that since 1957 the Trust has placed plaques on
       landmarks in the city; since 1969 this has been done by the
       Landmarks Preservation Commission, with the Trust's assistance.
       Documents the first twelve years' work, with photographs of
       the buildings honored and of the plaques, themselves.

317   West Virginia Historic Commission. WEST VIRGINIA HIGHWAY
       MARKERS: HISTORIC, PREHISTORIC, SCENIC, GEOLOGICAL. Rev.
       ed. Beckley: 1967. 263 p. Paper.

       Lists highway markers alphabetically by name, and describes
       them in detail. In supplementary lists, arranged by county
       and by highway, refers the reader to the main alphabetical
       listing.

Chapter 6

DISTRICTS, ENSEMBLES, NEIGHBORHOODS, AND TOWNS

In recent years, preservation has changed its emphasis from a focus primarily on individual monuments and historic structures to a concern with the broader built environment. Aspects of this concern are discussed in the books listed in this chapter.

INTERNATIONAL POLICY AND PROGRAMS

318 CONGRESSO DI STORIA DELL'ARCHITETTURA [Congress of the history of architecture]. ACTS OF THE 14TH CONGRESS: BRESCIA, MANTOVA, AND CREMONA, 12-19 SEPTEMBER 1965. Part I. Contributi alla storia dell'architettura [Contributions to the history of architecture]. Part II. Restauro di monumenti e difesa di centri storici [The restoration of monuments and the protection of historic centers]. Rome: Centro di Studi per la Storia dell'Architettura, 1972. 412 p. Illus.

> The second part of the proceedings of this major three-city congress concerns restoration of monuments and, by extension, the protection of historic centers and the consequent vitalization of the contained buildings. Includes speakers and topics representing an international array, with a scope that includes the practical and technical along with the philosophical.

319 Council of Europe. DANGER AND PERILS: ANALYSIS OF FACTORS WHICH CONSTITUTE A DANGER TO GROUPS AND AREAS OF BUILDINGS OF HISTORICAL OR ARTISTIC INTEREST. By Pierre-Yves Ligen. Strasbourg, France: Council of Europe, Council for Cultural Cooperation, 1968. 46 p. Paper.

> The first part, speaks of galloping deterioration by the classic processes--the destructive action of time, of man, and of nature. In the second part, speaks of new dangers due to radical changes in the social environment--the revolution in human habitat, new forms of economic activity, and greater leisure.

320 _____. "Symposium A: Criteria and Methods for a Protective Inventory: Preservation and Development of Groups and Areas of Buildings of Historical and Artistic Interest. Barcelona, 17-19 May 1965. Report." Council of Europe, Council for Cultural Cooperation, n.d. ii, 49 p. Glossary. Mimeographed.

> The first of a series of symposiums. Sought to define criteria and methods for compiling an inventory of groups and areas of buildings of historical or artistic interest. Reports that the theme was chosen with the idea of emphasizing the overriding importance of the inventory, "without which no effective protection is conceivable." Provides a sample inventory card form as well as a glossary of comparative terminology in French, English, Spanish, German, Dutch, and Italian.

321 _____. "Symposium B: The Reviving of Monuments: Preservation and Development of Groups and Areas of Buildings of Historical or Artistic Interest. Vienna, 4-8 October 1965. Report." Council of Europe, Council for Cultural Cooperation, n.d. ii, 142 p. Mimeographed.

> Gives presentations by an international panel dealing with the problems and methods involved in finding and encouraging new uses for properties—such as country houses, chateaux, and villas—which are being abandoned by their occupants. Considers tourist implications, such as the Spanish paradores (hotels). Describes governmental action, such as the establishment in Italy of special legislation for the encouragement of the upkeep of the Venetian villas.

322 _____. SYMPOSIUM C: PRINCIPLES AND PRACTICE OF ACTIVE PRESERVATION AND REHABILITATION OF GROUPS AND AREAS OF BUILDINGS OF HISTORICAL OR ARTISTIC INTEREST: PRESERVATION AND REHABILITATION OF GROUPS AND AREAS OF BUILDINGS OF HISTORICAL OR ARTISTIC INTEREST. BATH, 3-7 OCTOBER 1966. REPORT. Strasbourg, France: Council of Europe, Council for Cultural Cooperation, 1967. 126 p. Paper.

> Talks, discussion summaries, and recommendations of "The Bath Symposium."

323 _____. SYMPOSIUM D: ACTIVE MAINTENANCE OF MONUMENTS, GROUPS AND AREAS OF BUILDINGS OF HISTORICAL OR ARTISTIC INTEREST WITHIN THE CONTEXT OF REGIONAL PLANNING: PRESERVATION AND REHABILITATION OF GROUPS AND AREAS OF BUILDINGS OF HISTORICAL OR ARTISTIC INTEREST. THE HAGUE, 22-27 MAY 1967. REPORT. Strasbourg, France: Council of Europe, Council for Cultural Cooperation, 1967. 107 p. Paper.

> Talks, discussion summaries, and recommendations of "The Hague Symposium."

324 _____. SYMPOSIUM E: POLICY FOR THE PRESERVATION AND
REHABILITATION: IMPLEMENTATION OF THE POLICY FOR THE
PRESERVATION AND REHABILITATION OF GROUPS AND AREAS OF
BUILDINGS OF HISTORICAL OR ARTISTIC INTEREST: PRESERVATION
AND REHABILITATION OF GROUPS AND AREAS OF BUILDINGS OF
HISTORICAL OR ARTISTIC INTEREST. AVIGNON, 30 SEPTEMBER-
5 OCTOBER 1968. REPORT. Strasbourg, France: Council of Europe,
Council for Cultural Cooperation, n.d. 117 p. Paper.

> Lectures, talks, discussion, and recommendations of the final
> of five symposiums held from 1965 to 1968.

325 International Council on Monuments and Sites. FIRST CONFERENCE
ON THE CONSERVATION, RESTORATION AND REVIVAL OF AREAS
AND GROUPS OF BUILDINGS OF HISTORIC INTEREST. CÁCERES,
SPAIN, 15-19.III.1967. Paris: 1968. 92 p. Paper.

> A conference to discuss the safeguarding of historic centers
> and of artistic sites, with participants from Europe, the
> Americas, Great Britain, Africa, and Asia. Gives statements
> of problems and solutions in the various areas represented by
> the participants, including: dangers which threaten the his-
> toric ensemble in the Americas, Eastern Europe, and Japan;
> legal, fiscal, and economic remedies in Western Europe; and
> town planning and the protection and revival of historic en-
> sembles.

326 _____. SECOND CONFERENCE ON THE CONSERVATION, RESTO-
RATION AND REVIVAL OF AREAS AND GROUPS OF BUILDINGS OF
HISTORIC INTEREST, TUNIS, 9-16.IV.1968. Paris: 1969. 194 p.
Paper.

> Reports of activity related to the conference theme in Tunisia,
> Egypt, Iran, Yugoslavia, Turkey, Spain, and France.

327 United Nations Educational, Scientific and Educational Organization.
THE CONSERVATION OF CITIES. Paris: UNESCO Press; London:
Croom Helm, 1975. 186 p. Illus.

> A series of reports by an international roster of contributors on
> problems of the conservation of historic cities and historic city
> centers. Discusses the many aspects of the problem of the
> choice between "urban renewal" and "urban retrieval." Gives
> resumes of legislation in Europe and the United States along
> with general concepts of town center conservation and specific
> examples of cities in danger or in the process of being saved.
> In an appendix, contains a summary of UNESCO Missions in
> the Conservation of Cultural Property.

328   _____. VENICE RESTORED. Paris: 1973. 95 p. Illus., paper.

In the first part, describes work done by private organizations
in the Federal Republic of Germany, Australia, the United
States, France, Italy, the United Kingdom, and Switzerland.
In the second part, describes urgently needed restoration work,
starting with "a general problem: stone and marble decay,"
and following by a catalog of individual structures and their
restoration needs.

329   United Nations Educational, Scientific and Cultural Organization.
Technical Mission for Advice and Assistance to Peru. CUZCO: RE-
CONSTRUCTION OF THE TOWN AND RESTORATION OF ITS MONU-
MENTS. By George Kubler. Museums and Monuments, no. 3. Paris:
1952. 39 p. Illus., paper.

Presents Cuzco as three cities--one Inca, the second Spanish
colonial, and the third modern. Gives the report of the
UNESCO mission of 1951, which visited Cuzco subsequent to
an earthquake there in 1950. Describes its findings, analyzes
them, and recommends a course of action. Gives a survey
including descriptions of religious architecture, major restorations, partial restorations, remodelings and repairs, demolitions
and replacements, and intact structures. Includes recommendations concerned with houses, streets, open spaces, and
traffic reform.

HISTORIC URBAN CENTERS

330   Aldous, Tony. GOODBYE, BRITAIN? Foreword by Sir John Betjeman.
London: Sidgwick & Jackson, 1975; New York: St. Martin's Press,
1976. 192 p. Illus.

By the former environmental correspondent to THE TIMES of
London. Explores the destruction-by-development of English
towns and cities, and makes a plea for conservation of the
built environment.

331   Brambilla, Roberto, and Longo, Gianni. FOR PEDESTRIANS ONLY:
PLANNING, DESIGN, AND MANAGEMENT OF TRAFFIC-FREE ZONES.
Foreword by Bernard Rudofsky. New York: Whitney Library of Design,
1977. 208 p. Illus., bibliog.

The result of a public information program on planning, design,
and management of traffic-free zones, carried out by the Institute for Environmental Action in association with the Columbia
University Center for Advanced Research in Urban and Environmental Affairs. Discusses the goals and implementation of
pedestrian zones. Presents twenty selected case studies in
European and North American cities. Describes a "compendium

of American malls." Gives a classified selected bibliography including: general readings, traffic management, economics, environment, pedestrian safety and behavior, legal aspects, and planning and design.

332   Browne, Kenneth. WEST END: RENEWAL OF A METROPOLITAN CENTRE. London: Architectural Press, 1971. 111 p. Illus.

Based on a series of articles reprinted from THE ARCHITECTURAL REVIEW. Attempts to examine London's West End in a special kind of way, to study its qualities and problems as urban landscape. States that the object of the book is "to encourage both a more sympathetic understanding of what exists and at the same time a more imaginative approach to conservation and renewal." Treats the West End, district-by-district, with special attention to the question of vehicular traffic, the riverside, the squares, and the character of the neighborhoods.

333   Brutzkus, Eliezer. PREREQUISITES FOR PRESERVATION OF HISTORIC URBAN QUARTERS. Jerusalem: Israel Ministry of Interior, Town and Country Planning Department, 1972. 42 p. Bibliog., paper.

Reviews principles and practices in the preservation of historic centers, drawing upon European and North African examples. Discusses the question of traffic control, and suggests that the preserved area must be treated as a "traffic impenetrable precinct destined primarily to pedestrian movement."

334   THE CONSERVATION OF GEORGIAN EDINBURGH: THE PROCEEDINGS AND OUTCOME OF A CONFERENCE ORGANIZED BY THE SCOTTISH CIVIC TRUST IN ASSOCIATION WITH THE EDINBURGH ARCHITECTURAL ASSOCIATION AND IN CONJUNCTION WITH THE CIVIC TRUST, LONDON. Edited by Sir Robert Matthew et al. Edinburgh: Edinburgh University Press, 1972. xv, 130 p. Illus.

Reports that the New Town of Edinburgh, dating from 1767, a unique example of Georgian town planning and distinguished architecture, showed signs of being subject to the usual ills and decline of historic city centers. Recounts the efforts to preserve, restore, and revitalize the New Town. The address by Count Sforza, Deputy Secretary of the Council of Europe, underscores the importance of such cultural monuments to all mankind.

335   Crosby, Theo. THE NECESSARY MONUMENT: ITS FUTURE IN THE CIVILIZED CITY. Greenwich, Conn.: New York Graphic Society; London: Studio Vista, 1970. 128 p. Illus., bibliog., paper.

Consideration of the monumental in the cityscape--Paris Opera, London's Tower Bridge, New York's Pennsylvania Station--and

of the need, also, for the comfortable, liveable scale provided by Georgian rows in London and brownstone rows in
New York. Reports that the question of identity is central:
"A good big monument is splendid, but much of the pleasure
of cities comes from small scale invention and complexity:
a doorway, a bay window, a spire, an element suddenly
seen and exploited in the context of the street."

336   Esher, Lionel Gordon Baliol Brett, 4th Viscount. YORK: A STUDY IN
CONSERVATION. Report to the Minister of Housing and Local Government and York City Council. London: Her Majesty's Stationery Office,
1968. 249 p. Illus., paper.

One of four reports on historic English towns, commissioned in
1966 by the Minister of Housing and Local Government and the
city and county councils concerned; the other three were for
Bath, Chester, and Chichester. Reports that the purpose of
the studies was to discover how to reconcile old towns with
the twentieth century without actually knocking them down,
realizing that they are a great cultural asset and (with the
growth of tourism) increasingly an economic asset as well.
Examines York's historic center in detail, reporting on its
existing state, and making proposals.

337   Fitch, James Marston, and Waite, Diana S. GRAND CENTRAL TER-
MINAL AND ROCKEFELLER CENTER: A HISTORIC-CRITICAL ESTIMATE
OF THEIR SIGNIFICANCE. Albany: New York State Parks and Recreation, Division for Historic Preservation, 1974. 42 p. Illus., bibliog.,
paper.

Speaks of these two complexes as "generators of urban energy,"
whose significance have little to do with architectural aesthetics in any conventional sense. Reports that endless manipu-
lation of these monumental engines can only lead to the irre-
versible weakening—or indeed the destruction—of their "truly
awesome power." Proposes that the protection and preservation
of the two complexes is literally vital to the city's life.

338   Hennawy, Mohsen ABD El-Kader, El. GIZA HISTORICAL CENTER:
A STUDY TO PRESERVE EGYPT'S ETERNAL ARCHITECTURAL HERITAGE
WITHIN THE LIVING URBAN ORGANISM. Washington, D.C.: Catholic
University of America Press, 1967. 128 p. Illus., bibliog., paper.

A dissertation presented toward the degree of Doctor of Architecture, concerned with the desert area surrounding the Nile
Valley, where lies the monumental heritage of Egypt's past and
where most of Egypt's contemporary urban centers, within the
expanding Cairo Metropolitan Center, are being developed.

339 González de Valcárcel, José Manuel. RESTAURACIÓN MONUMENTAL Y "PUESTA EN VALOR" DE LAS CIUDADES AMERICANAS/ARCHI-TECTURAL CONSERVATION AND ENHANCEMENT OF HISTORIC TOWNS IN AMERICA. Barcelona: Editorial Blume, 1977. 175 p. Illus., bibliog.

Written by the Spanish architect-restorer who had responsibility for the custody and restoration of the historically, culturally, and artistically rich zone of Toledo before becoming involved in related work in the Spanish New World. His "Pilot Plan of Quito," produced for the Organization of American States, provides much of the focus for this publication. The initial chapter, "Antecedentes/Background," reviews the history of preservation philosophy and activity on a broad basis. The text is bilingual, Spanish and English.

340 Gurrieri, Francesco. DAL RESTAURO DEI MONUMENTI AL RESTAURO DEL TERRITORIO [From the restoration of monuments to the restoration of territory]. Florence: CLUSF (Cooperativa Libraria Universitatis Studii Florentini), 1972(?). 115 p. Paper.

Treats of the reanimation of degraded city centers as an element in the restoration of monuments and historic territories. Summarizes and reviews major Italian and European confer-ences and declarations regarding the protection of the cultural patrimony.

341 Hargreaves, June M. HISTORIC BUILDINGS: PROBLEMS OF THEIR PRESERVATION. York, Engl.: York Civic Trust, 1965. 34 p. Illus., bibliog., paper.

A report resulting from a study to investigate the merits of preserving historic buildings and to discuss the various methods by which those buildings of worth can be preserved. Seen as a particular problem of current town planning which is in need of solution if some of "the finest treasures of our heritage are not soon to disappear in the swelling sea of speculation in urban redevelopment." Discusses the overall philosophy of townscape preservation, the preservation situation in Great Britain, and specific preservation questions that apply to the city of York.

342 Historic Towns and Cities Conference, York, England, April 1968. CONSERVATION AND DEVELOPMENT IN HISTORIC TOWNS AND CITIES. Edited by Pamela Ward. Newcastle-upon-Tyne: Oriel Press, 1968. x, 275 p. Illus.

A conference held in association with the Institute of Ad-vanced Architectural Study at the University of York. In-cludes contributions concerning economic and social aspects of conservation, the problem of traffic, management and

organization, historical research, the architecture of conservation, conservation policies in Europe and America, and
aspects of conservation policy.

343   Lottman, Herbert R. HOW CITIES ARE SAVED. New York: Universe
       Books, 1976. 255 p. Illus.

       Examines a number of Western European cities, along with
       Jerusalem and Tokyo, and demonstrates how they are rebuild-
       ing themselves, recreating neighborhoods, providing greater
       civic amenity, protecting landmarks, and improving the lives
       of their citizens.

344   LOTUS INTERNATIONAL (Quarterly Architectural Review), Milan,
       13 (December 1976): entire issue.

       This issue deals with the theme of historic city centers and
       urban renewal. Includes a discussion of "Berlin Old and New"
       by Gottfried Boehm, Vittorio Gregotti, Charles Moore, Alison
       Smithson, and Oswald Mathias Ungers. Presents several other
       articles, including discussions of renewal in Paris and in
       Oporto, Portugal. All articles in both English and Italian.

345   Papageorgiou, Alexander. CONTINUITY AND CHANGE: PRESER-
       VATION IN CITY PLANNING. Preface by Frederick Gutheim. New
       York, Washington, D.C., London: Praeger Publishers, 1971. 185 p.
       Illus., bibliog.

       Originally published in German as STADTKERNE IM KONFLIKT
       by the author, a professor in the Berlin Technical University's
       School of Landscape Design. An overview of historic centers
       of cities that crosses vast expanses of geography and time,
       from the Plaka of Athens to pedestrian malls in Paterson, New
       Jersey. Divided into four sections: historic urban centers,
       the significance of historic centers within the spatial cluster,
       the townscape, and the rehabilitation of historic urban centers.

346   Procter, Mary, and Matuszeski, Bill. GRITTY CITIES: A SECOND
       LOOK AT ALLENTOWN, BETHLEHEM, BRIDGEPORT, HOBOKEN,
       LANCASTER, NORWICH, PATERSON, READING, TRENTON, TROY,
       WATERBURY, WILMINGTON. Philadelphia: Temple University Press,
       1978. ix, 276 p. Illus., bibliog.

       A book of photographs and essays about a dozen northeastern
       cities with roots in the Industrial Revolution. Proposes that
       such cities do best when they grow and change by building
       on those things that gave them their character.

347   Rifkind, Carole. MAIN STREET: THE FACE OF URBAN AMERICA.
       New York: Harper & Row, 1977. xiii, 267 p. Illus., bibliog.

       This book, profusely illustrated with vintage photographs,
       describes the origins, the building up, the transformations,
       and the occasional preservation of Main Streets from Florida
       to Alaska.

HISTORIC DISTRICTS

348   Boston Redevelopment Authority. REVITALIZING OLDER HOUSES IN
       CHARLESTOWN. Washington, D.C.: U.S. Government Printing Office,
       1973. 28 p. Illus., paper.

       A booklet prepared by the Boston Redevelopment Authority's
       urban design staff, with the assistance of the Boston Landmarks
       Commission. Guidelines written and illustrated by George
       Stephen, with the assistance of Robert B. Rettig. Includes a
       preface addressed to the homeowners of Charlestown, in which
       Robert T. Kennedy, director of the Boston Redevelopment
       Authority, says that the booklet is "...a simple, clearly illus-
       trated guide to the rehabilitation of the characteristic--and
       even unique--architectural styles of Charlestown, along with
       a brief history that focuses on the growth and development of
       the last 150 years that produced this architecture." Goes on
       to say that the booklet "...is not intended as a rule book or
       as criticism of the important improvements that have been made
       thus far. It is simply meant to suggest--to provide information
       about what makes even the most unassuming building in Charles-
       town interesting, and to illustrate that some ways of remodeling
       may be more effective than others in retaining architectural
       character and thus enhance the value of a building."

349   Bureau of Governmental Research, New Orleans. PLAN AND PROGRAM
       FOR THE PRESERVATION OF THE VIEUX CARRE: HISTORIC DISTRICT
       DEMONSTRATION STUDY, CONDUCTED BY BUREAU OF GOVERN-
       MENTAL RESEARCH, NEW ORLEANS, FOR THE CITY OF NEW ORLEANS.
       Prepared under the supervision of Marcou, O'Leary and Associates,
       Washington, D.C. New Orleans: 1968. xiii, 170 p. Illus., paper.

       The Vieux Carre, the old French Quarter of New Orleans,
       and one of the best-known historic districts in the United
       States, includes all of the land within the original city estab-
       lished in 1718 as the capital of France's new American empire.
       Presents an in-depth report which has application not only to
       this major preserved district, but to historic districts elsewhere.

350   Tucson, Arizona. Department of Community Development, Planning
       Division. TUCSON'S HISTORIC DISTRICTS: CRITERIA FOR PRESER-
       VATION AND DEVELOPMENT. Tucson: 1972. 48 p. Illus., paper.

A study to provide the background and direction for the establishment of a historic district zoning ordinance to provide Tucson with the framework to preserve those areas in which its historic heritage remains. Presents redevelopment guidelines for new or remodeled structures to conform to the collective character of the buildings located within that district. Outlines the historic development of Tucson, and indicates the significant historic areas which still remain. Gives the Historic District Zoning Ordinance and recommendations for additional study and for application of the ordinance.

351 Codman, John. PRESERVATION OF HISTORIC DISTRICTS BY ARCHITECTURAL CONTROL. Chicago: American Society of Planning Officials, 1956. 32 p. Paper.

Starting with the first historic district legislation in the United States (Charleston, South Carolina, 1924), reviews such legislation to date, and describes in detail the procedure followed by the Beacon Hill Civic Association to secure passage by the Massachusetts legislature of the 1955 law which established the Beacon Hill historic district in Boston. A practical guide for those wishing to establish historic districts.

352 Ferro, Maximilian L. HOW TO LOVE AND CARE FOR YOUR OLD BUILDING IN NEW BEDFORD. New Bedford, Mass.: City of New Bedford, Office of Historic Preservation, 1977. 158 p. Illus., paper.

Prepared for the city of New Bedford under contract to the Society for the Preservation of New England Antiquities. Includes a plea for preservation; a short history of New Bedford; a guide to its architectural styles; and chapters on the maintenance, repair, and renovation of the local architecture. Gives direction for obtaining assistance from the Building Department, the Office of Historic Preservation, the Historical Commission, and other city services.

353 Griffin, Frances. OLD SALEM: AN ADVENTURE IN HISTORIC PRESERVATION. Winston-Salem, N.C.: Old Salem, Inc., 1970. 74 p. Illus., paper.

The history of zoning, restoration, and planning in this unique community of Moravian heritage. Includes North Carolina enabling act and Winston-Salem Historic Districts zoning ordinance in the appendix.

354 Lowell, Massachusetts. Division of Planning and Development. LOWELL: THE BUILDING BOOK. Prepared in association with Anderson Notter Associates. Lowell: 1977. 71 p. Paper.

Suggestions for property owners considering rehabilitation. Provides a guide to styles, design guidelines, and tips on the
care and maintenance of older buildings.

355   Maryland Historical Trust. ESTABLISHING AN HISTORIC DISTRICT:
A GUIDELINE FOR HISTORIC PRESERVATION. Prepared by Raymond,
Parish, Pine and Plavnick. Annapolis: 1973. 54 p. Illus., paper.

A report prepared as a part of the Comprehensive Plan for
Historic Preservation in Maryland, outlining the procedures
whereby local citizens might act to enhance an area of historical interest through the establishment of a historic district.
As an illustration, describes procedures used for the establishment of historic district in Chestertown, Maryland, in 1964.

356   Massachusetts Historical Commission. "Guidelines for Establishment of
Historic Districts." 1972(?). 27 leaves. Bibliog. Mimeographed.

Starts with a checklist of steps to establish a historic district,
continues to describe the history of historic district legislation
in the United States and to explain the purpose of historic
districts, and concludes with an elaboration of the steps outlined in the initial checklist. In appendixes, includes suggested guidelines for preliminary report; considerations for a
draft ordinance or by-law; a list of historic districts in Massachusetts, with their specific legislations; a bibliography; and
the text of the Historic Districts Act of Massachusetts.

357   National Trust for Historic Preservation. CONFERENCE OF LANDMARKS
COMMISSIONS REPRESENTATIVES: CITY HALL, CLEVELAND, OHIO,
OCTOBER, 1973. Transcript of proceedings. Washington, D.C.: n.d.
84 p. Paper.

The first in a series of such one-day conferences sponsored by
the National Trust in conjunction with its annual meetings.
Discusses legal and financial aspects. In appendixes, lists
conference participants and suggestions as to how the National
Trust might assist landmarks commissions.

358   _____. CONFERENCE OF LANDMARKS COMMISSIONS REPRESENTA-
TIVES: THE OLD CHURCH, PORTLAND, OREGON, OCTOBER, 1974.
Transcript of proceedings. Washington, D.C.: n.d. 83 p. Paper.

Presents discussion centering on design guidelines for rehabilitation and new construction, legislation and legal developments,
educational programs and liaison, and financial aspects.

359   _____. DIRECTORY OF LANDMARK AND HISTORIC DISTRICT COM-
MISSIONS. Washington, D.C.: Preservation Press, 1976. 80 p. Paper.

Prepared by the Landmarks Preservation Law Division of the
National Trust's Office of Preservation Services. Arranged by
locality within state, giving names, addresses, and telephone
numbers of landmark and historic commissions, with their chief
officers. In a second section, describes selected major commissions in detail.

360 _____. A GUIDE TO DELINEATING EDGES OF HISTORIC DISTRICTS.
Russell Wright, principal consultant. Washington, D.C.: Preservation
Press, 1976. 95 p. Illus., glossary, bibliog., paper.

Presents case studies of twenty historic districts, to examine
the impact of a historic district's boundaries on the maintenance
of its special ambience. Considers the question of going far
enough in delineating a district, without going too far.

361 New Haven Redevelopment Agency. EXTERIOR MAINTENANCE. New
Haven: 1961. 16 p. Illus., paper. Leaflet.

A leaflet addressed to the New Haven homeowner, urging
proper exterior maintenance and explaining some points on
painting, new siding, brick pointing, masonry upkeep, roofs,
gutters, and downspouts.

362 Old Island Restoration Commission. PRESERVATION GUIDE-BOOK FOR
THE OLD SECTION OF THE CITY OF KEY WEST. Key West, Fla.:
1975. 31 p. Illus., paper.

A guide for homeowners in preserving the traditional old Key
West character as they undertake to repair, renovate, or restore. Describes the characteristics of the various types of
domestic carpenter architecture which give the historic center
of this southernmost United States island its distinctive flavor.
Considers roofing, siding, windows, doors, porches, fences
and yards, and paint colors.

363 Urban Design Group. PRESERVATION AND REHABILITATION OF A
HISTORIC COMMERCIAL AREA: A DEMONSTRATION STUDY OF
THE WATERFRONT HISTORIC DISTRICT, NEW BEDFORD, MASS. Con-
ducted by the New Bedford Redevelopment Authority in cooperation
with the New Bedford City Planning Department and the Waterfront
Historic Area League. Prepared and designed by the Urban Design
Group. Newport, R.I.: 197(?). 132 p. Illus., paper.

Concerns New Bedford's waterfront commercial district, the
site of America's most important nineteenth-century whaling
center, and a surviving symbol of the city's character during
its most prosperous period; its significance is of a national,
rather than local, or even state, level. Presents the outcome
of a coalition of public and private groups seeking to produce
a workable method for the examination, protection, and re-

vitalization of the commercial area, which can serve as a model for other historic commercial areas.

NEIGHBORHOOD PRESERVATION

364   Ahlbrandt, Roger S., Jr.   FLEXIBLE CODE ENFORCEMENT: A KEY INGREDIENT IN NEIGHBORHOOD PRESERVATION PROGRAMMING. Washington, D.C.:   National Association of Housing and Redevelopment Officials, 1976.   93 p.   Paper.

Reports that the Housing and Community Development Act of 1974 focused the attention of many communities on neighborhood preservation.   Indicates that, in the course of this study, the author observed programs in Baltimore, Maryland; Memphis, Tennessee; Portland and Salem, Oregon; and Allegheny County, Pennsylvania.

365   Ahlbrandt, Roger S., Jr., and Brophy, Paul C.   NEIGHBORHOOD REVITALIZATION: THEORY AND PRACTICE.   Lexington, Mass.: Lexington Books, 1975.   xviii, 188 p.   Bibliog.

About the decline and revitalization of older neighborhoods. Provides a framework for understanding the process of decline and alternative policy options for revitalization.   Presents materials ranging from theory of the life cycle of neighborhoods to examples of preservation, stabilization, and revitalization (the terms are used interchangeably) in specific cities.

366   Dove, Donald.   PRESERVING THE URBAN ENVIRONMENT: HOW TO STOP DESTROYING CITIES.   Philadelphia: Dorrance & Co., 1976. 165 p.

Identifies the process of decay in cities, and offers suggestions for reversing the process.

367   Harris, Harry C.   "Neighborhood Conservation in New York City." New York: City of New York Housing and Redevelopment Board, June 1963.   37 leaves.   Maps.   Mimeographed.

Interim report of a program launched in 1959 as an experimental attempt to halt and reverse housing deterioration and to meet and ameliorate social problems affecting essentially sound though troubled neighborhoods.   Discusses seven Manhattan neighborhoods chosen for the venture: Chelsea, Bloomingdale, East Harlem, Carnegie Hill, Morningside, Hamilton-Grange, and Hudson.

368   Kidney, Walter C., and Ziegler, Arthur P., Jr.   ALLEGHENY.   Pittsburgh: Pittsburgh History and Landmarks Foundation, 1975.   80 p.   Illus.

Documents the development, decline, and renewal of Pitts-
burgh's North Side. Presents the result of the Allegheny Self-
Study Program, coordinated under the auspices of the Pittsburgh
History and Landmarks Foundation.

369   Kliment, Stephen A., ed. NEIGHBORHOOD CONSERVATION: A
        SOURCE BOOK. Neighborhood Conservation Conference, New York
        City, September 24-26, 1975. New York: Whitney Library of Design,
        n.d. 9, 37, 122, 37, 14 p. (various paginations).

        Discusses the role of the state in neighborhood conservation,
        and presents case studies of over forty localities. Discusses
        issues and options relating to political, legal, financial, social,
        and physical aspects.

370   McNulty, Robert H., and Kliment, Stephen A., eds. NEIGHBORHOOD
        CONSERVATION: A HANDBOOK OF METHODS AND TECHNIQUES.
        New York: Whitney Library of Design, 1976. 287 p. Illus., bibliog.

        A guide to the key administrative, legal, financial, social,
        and physical design issues governing the present and future of
        neighborhood conservation. Presents a narrative supplemented
        by case studies of forty-five American cities with a record of
        activity in neighborhood conservation, along with a detailed
        compendium of printed resources arranged by issue and subject
        matter. In a resource section, lists organizations and publi-
        cations.

371   Myers, Phyllis. NEIGHBORHOOD CONSERVATION AND THE ELDERLY.
        An Issue Report. Washington, D.C.: Conservation Foundation, 1978.
        72 p. Bibliog., paper.

        A report on the displacement effects on the elderly that result
        from historic districting and private renovation.

372   Myers, Phyllis, and Binder, Gordon. NEIGHBORHOOD CONSERVATION:
        LESSONS FROM THREE CITIES. An Issue Report. Washington, D.C.:
        Conservation Foundation, 1977. xii, 113 p. Paper.

        Draws on the experiences of Historic Annapolis (the historic
        district of Annapolis, Maryland); Mount Adams, Mount Auburn,
        and Over-the-Rhine, in Cincinnati; and Pioneer Square and
        Pike Place, in Seattle. Lists publications and interview
        sources for each.

373   New York City. City Planning Commission. NEIGHBORHOOD PRES-
        ERVATION IN NEW YORK CITY. New York: 1973. 148 p. Illus.,
        bibliog., paper.

Four chapters: "Neighborhood Transition," "Physical Deterioration," "Government Response," and "Policy Alternatives."
In the appendix, includes Executive Order No. 80 (May 23,
1973), "Creation of Neighborhood Preservation Program," and
describes five Neighborhood Preservation Areas: Bushwick and
Crown Heights in Brooklyn; Clinton and Washington Heights in
Manhattan; and West Tremont in the Bronx.

374   New York City. Department of City Planning. LITTLE ITALY
RISORGIMENTO: PROPOSALS FOR THE RESTORATION OF AN HIS-
TORIC COMMUNITY. New York: 1974. 55 p. Illus., paper.

Combining residential, commercial, and industrial functions,
Little Italy has "arrived" as historic center in lower Manhattan.
Indicates that proposals for pedestrian ways, preservation of
the character of the quarter, preservation and rehabilitation
of existing buildings, and sympathetic addition of needed new
buildings are all analogous to proposals for similar preservation
efforts in historic centers of ancient cities of the Old World;
the intent is not to embalm a district that was, but to inject
new vitality into a district that continues to have meaning.

375   _____. NEIGHBORHOOD ZONING: A PROPOSAL TO PRESERVE
KINGSBRIDGE. New York: Bronx Office, Department of City Planning,
1974. 22 p. Illus., paper.

Concerns a neighborhood of primarily one- and two-family
residences in which existing zoning would permit assemblages
for apartment house construction and resulting high density
development. Examines the necessity and consequences of a
zoning change to preserve the existing character of the neighborhood. In an area profile, considers land use, housing, and
population.

376   Old Town Restorations. BUILDING THE FUTURE FROM OUR PAST: A
REPORT ON THE SAINT PAUL HISTORIC HILL DISTRICT PLANNING
PROGRAM. St. Paul, Minn.: 1975. 136 p. Illus., glossary, paper.

Reports that in 1973, the Historic Hill District of St. Paul was
designated as the twenty-second historic district in the state
of Minnesota. Outlines a neighborhood revitalization program
for the district, designed to attract residents and businesses
back to the city through preservation planning. Contains historical background, an illustrated buildings inventory, programs,
traffic proposals, and implementation proposals.

377   Real Estate Research Corporation. NEIGHBORHOOD PRESERVATION:
LEGAL AND ADMINISTRATIVE DOCUMENTS. Prepared for the Office
of Policy Development and Research, U.S. Department of Housing and

Urban Development. Washington, D.C.: U.S. Government Printing Office, [1975]. 294 p. Illus., paper.

A companion document to NEIGHBORHOOD PRESERVATION: A CATALOG OF LOCAL PROGRAMS. Outlines and gives selected documents for programs in a number of geographically dispersed cities: code enforcement programs, comprehensive programs, focused public services programs, growth management and neighborhood control programs, historic preservation programs, management of abandonment programs, neighborhood services programs, and structural rehabilitation and financing programs. (See entry 380.)

378   Roggemann, Peter Joseph. "Community Organizations and Neighborhood Preservation: Housing Initiatives and Agency Response in New York City." Ph.D. dissertation, Rutgers University, 1976. 301 p. (DISSERTATION ABSTRACTS INTERNATIONAL, Vol. 37-A, Part 1, p. 657-- Urban and Regional Planning.)

A case study of the attempts of community organizations to sponsor a government program of housing and neighborhood preservation. Addresses the question of whether, and under what conditions, citizen groups can influence social policy as implemented by a government agency. Concerns the Bushwick neighborhood of Brooklyn, a multiethnic, low-wage, high-unemployment area with aging housing and public facilities, heavy service demands, and few political resources. Based on extensive field observations, interviews, survey data, and attendance at meetings and related events. Includes comparison with case studies of housing groups in two other New York neighborhoods which were more successful in obtaining assistance, despite their similar low status.

379   U.S. Department of Housing and Urban Development. NEIGHBORHOOD CONSERVATION & PROPERTY REHABILITATION . . . A BIBLIOGRAPHY. Washington, D.C.: 1969. 78 p. Paper.

Compiled by the HUD library. Primarily material published after 1965. Includes a section on films and one on training aids and courses.

380   U.S. Department of Housing and Urban Development. Office of Policy Development and Research. NEIGHBORHOOD PRESERVATION: A CATALOG OF LOCAL PROGRAMS. Washington, D.C.: 1975. 286 p. Glossary, paper.

A selection of one hundred locally initiated neighborhood preservation programs as a guide for local decision makers and community leaders. Complements NEIGHBORHOOD PRESERVATION: LEGAL AND ADMINISTRATIVE DOCUMENTS by the Real Estate Research Corporation (see entry 377).

381   Ziegler, Arthur P., Jr. HISTORIC PRESERVATION IN INNER CITY
       AREAS: A MANUAL OF PRACTICE. Rev. ed. Pittsburgh: Ober
       Park Associates, 1974. vi, 81 p. Illus.

       Drawing upon the experience of the Pittsburgh History and
       Landmarks Foundation, suggests means for establishing historic
       district programs as a means of bringing new health and life
       to inner city neighborhoods. From philosophy of preservation
       to the nuts and bolts of zoning and revolving funds.

URBAN HOMESTEADING

382   Hughes, James W., and Bleakly, Kenneth D., Jr. URBAN HOME-
       STEADING. New Brunswick, N.J.: Center for Urban Policy Research,
       Rutgers University, 1975. 276 p. Illus., bibliog.

       Uses Baltimore, Newark, Philadelphia, and Wilmington as the
       models for this detailed study of a means of countering urban
       housing abandonment.

383   U.S. Department of Housing and Urban Development. Office of Policy
       Development and Research. THE URBAN HOMESTEADING CATALOGUE.
       Prepared by Urban Systems Research and Engineering, Inc. Washington,
       D.C.: U.S. Government Printing Office, 1977. Vol. 1. vi, 260 p.
       Vol. 2. vi, 139 p. Vol. 3. v, 169 p. Paper.

       Volume 1: managing a program, financing rehabilitation,
       rehabilitating homesteads, resolving legal issues, homesteading
       outside the demonstration.

       Volume 2: selecting neighborhoods, selecting properties,
       attracting and selecting homesteaders.

       Volume 3: background and history of urban homesteading,
       demonstration program descriptions.

URBAN RENEWAL

384   Pace, Valerie Sue Halverson. "Society Hill, Philadelphia: Historic
       Preservation and Urban Renewal in Washington Square East." Ph.D.
       dissertation, University of Minnesota, 1976. 426 p. (DISSERTATION
       ABSTRACTS INTERNATIONAL, Vol. 37-A, Part 6, p. 3958-- Urban
       and Regional Planning.)

       Reports that, after World War II, Philadelphia experienced a
       major decline of its central city due to the deterioration of
       housing, the automobile, and increasing crime which resulted
       in a mass exodus of its population. Explains that the "Phila-
       delphia Renaissance," the press name given to the enactment
       of the city's physical development plan, sought to improve

the quality of life in the city by revitalizing the social, economic, physical, and aesthetic resources of the city. Indicates that the Society Hill neighborhood, a specific area of that plan, has been the scene of rehabilitation since the late 1950s. Studies the urban renewal process in Society Hill, examining the interrelationships of city planning, historic preservation, and center city revitalization.

385 U.S. Urban Renewal Administration. HISTORIC PRESERVATION THROUGH URBAN RENEWAL: HOW URBAN RENEWAL WORKS. Assembled and prepared by Margaret Carroll. Washington, D.C.: U.S. Government Printing Office, 1963. 28 p. Illus., paper.

Demonstrates how historic structures and sites are being retained and preserved through urban renewal. Covers a range of possibilities, from developing an entire project built around preservation to planning for individual structures to be retained and fitted in with new construction. Shows examples in Portsmouth, New Hampshire; Mobile, Alabama; Monterey, California; Bethlehem, Pennsylvania; Little Rock, Arkansas; York, Pennsylvania; San Francisco, California; Washington, D.C.; and Providence, Rhode Island.

386 Working Conference on Problems in Urban Renewal. REHABILITATION AND CONSERVATION ASPECTS OF URBAN RENEWAL. Proceedings of the Fourth Working Conference on Problems in Urban Renewal, sponsored by the Redevelopment Section of the National Association of Housing and Redevelopment Officials, in cooperation with the Department of Political Science and the Committee on the Regional Planning Course of the University of Wisconsin at the Wisconsin Center in Madison, April 5-8, 1959. Edited by William K. Brussat. Washington, D.C.: National Association of Housing and Redevelopment Officials, 1960. 60 p. Paper.

Among other aspects, discusses government incentives for rehabilitation, financing private rehabilitation, neighborhood organization for rehabilitation, and the role of colleges and universities in the urban renewal process.

Chapter 7

THE PHYSICAL FABRIC: MATERIALS AND TECHNOLOGY

The materials, tools, and technology of the construction of buildings and of the physical analysis and conservation of buildings are the concern of the books listed in this chapter.

BIBLIOGRAPHIES

387   ART AND ARCHAEOLOGY TECHNICAL ABSTRACTS. New York: Institute of Fine Arts, New York University, 1955-- . Semiannual.

> International coverage of articles, reports, new items, books, and other publications which deal specifically with the technical examination, investigation, analysis, restoration, preservation, and technical documentation of objects and monuments having historic or artistic significance. Coverage also of publications which, although not specifically dealing with historic or artistic objects, contain information or describe techniques that are more-or-less directly applicable to the study and treatment of art works or archaeological materials. Each volume covers one year and consists of two numbers, with a volume index in number 2. Continues ABSTRACTS OF TECHNICAL STUDIES IN ART AND ARCHAEOLOGY (1943-52). Formerly entitled ABSTRACTS OF THE TECHNICAL LITERATURE ON ARCHAEOLOGY AND THE FINE ARTS (1955-57) and IIC ABSTRACTS (1958-65).

388   Byrne, Richard O. "Conservation and Architectural Restoration Supply Sources and Brief Bibliography." Moncton, New Brunswick: Atlantic Conservation Centre, 1976. 40 p. Mimeographed.

> Includes sources for materials, tools, training, and other aspects. Lists professional organizations and journals.

389   Carlsson, Ingrid, and Holmstroem, Ingmar. CARE OF OLD BUILDINGS: AN ANNOTATED BIBLIOGRAPHY, PART I. Stockholm: National Swedish Institute for Building Research, 1975. 210 p. Paper.

Organized for either manual or computer retrieval. Consists of both old and new (to 1971) literature, mainly concerning technical questions. Approximately two thousand titles of books, reports, articles, and other items. Items written in a variety of languages, arranged chronologically, with annotations mostly in English, but in various other languages as well.

390   Ferguson, Eugene S. BIBLIOGRAPHY OF THE HISTORY OF TECHNOLOGY. Cambridge: M.I.T. Press and the Society for the History of Technology, 1968. xx, 347 p.

Declares its purpose as "to provide a reasonably comprehensive introduction to primary and secondary sources in the history of technology." Gives particular attention to specialized bibliographies and finding aids, to direct the user to the tools and resources of scholarship in this field.

391   Great Britain. Department of the Environment. Property Services Agency. "Preservation and Restoration of Buildings." Current Information on Maintenance. Part F. Library Bibliography 148F. London: Her Majesty's Stationery Office, June 1973. 47 p. Mimeographed.

Compiled by the library of the Property Services Agency. Preceeded by five related bibliographies: (A) "Cleaning Buildings," (B) "Design and Maintenance," (C) "Management and Economics," (D) "Building Services and Engineering," and (E) "Deterioration and Weathering of Materials." For part F, material assembled from the library's own collection and from those of learned societies and institutions whose concerns include preservation and restoration of buildings. In the choice of items included, emphasizes basic and current works. Entries arranged according to the repair of different parts of the building fabric, with a section on general works.

392   Harvey, John [Hooper], comp. "Conservation of Old Buildings: A Select Bibliography." TRANSACTIONS OF THE ANCIENT MONUMENTS SOCIETY, 16 (1968-69): 115-44.

A bibliography compiled, according to the compiler, for the use of architects and others directly concerned with the conservation and repair of individual buildings.

393   Entry deleted.

394   Isham, Norman Morrison. A GLOSSARY OF COLONIAL ARCHITECTURAL TERMS; WITH A BIBLIOGRAPHY OF BOOKS 1880-1930. 1939. Reprint.

With an essay on "The Dating of Old Houses" by Henry C. Mercer. Classic Guidebooks to the Visual Arts. Watkins Glen, N.Y.: American Life Foundation, 1968. 64 p. Illus., paper.

> Part of a series which issues limited editions of out-of-print introductory books for students of art, architecture, and antiques. Of interest to those who are in any way involved with aspects of construction technology of the American colonial period.

395   Stambolov, T., and Asperen de Boer, J.R.J. van. THE DETERIORATION AND CONSERVATION OF POROUS BUILDING MATERIALS IN MONUMENTS: A LITERATURE REVIEW. Rome: International Centre for the Study of the Preservation and Restoration of Cultural Property, 1972. 70 p. Bibliog., paper.

> Reviews a bibliography of three hundred and thirty-six items, within a systematic discussion of various forms of deterioration and various methods of preventing and combating same.

GENERAL WORKS

396   National Conservation Advisory Council. REPORT OF THE STUDY COMMITTEE ON ARCHITECTURAL CONSERVATION. Prepared for publication by Paula A. Degan. Washington, D.C.: 1977. 68 p. Paper.

> A project sponsored by the National Museum Act, administered by the Smithsonian Institution. Analyzes the need for architectural conservation services, and examines major areas of concern, including education and training, scientific support for architectural conservation, and the communication and coordination of conservation activities.

397   Peterson, Charles E., ed. BUILDING EARLY AMERICA: CONTRIBUTIONS TOWARD THE HISTORY OF A GREAT INDUSTRY. Radnor, Pa.: Chilton Book Co. for The Carpenters' Company of the City and County of Philadelphia, 1976. xvi, 407 p. Illus., paper.

> Reports that the bicentennial of The Carpenters' Company preceeded the American Bicentennial of 1976 by fifty-two years; BUILDING EARLY AMERICA is the product of a symposium held in Philadelphia in 1974 in connection with the company's 250th anniversary. Reports that among the participants in the conference were a substantial delegation from The Carpenters' Company of London, and a major portion of the program considered the American debt to the builders of Britain. In part

1, "Building History," contains twelve essays that range from "The King's Works: A Thousand Years of British Building" through "Building in the Age of Steam," "Roofing for Early America," "Early Nineteenth-Century Lighting," and "Building the Capitol." In part II, "Building Preservation," contains eight essays concerning preservation activities and programs in Canada, Great Britain, and New York state; the training of architects for conservation in Britain; and specific preservation projects at Independence Hall, the University of Virginia, and three British cathedrals--York Minster, Norwich, and St. Paul's.

HISTORIC MATERIALS, METHODS, AND TOOLS

398 Bealer, Alex W. OLD WAYS OF WORKING WOOD. Barre, Mass.: Barre Publishers, 1972. 231 p. Illus., bibliog.

Descriptions and drawings of all aspects of working wood, from felling a tree to splitting, sawing, hewing, boring, chiseling, shaping, planing, and turning.

399 _____. THE TOOLS THAT BUILT AMERICA. Barre, Mass.: Barre Publishers, 1976. vii, 212 p. Illus., bibliog.

Presents text illustrated by drawings and photographs of tools and of the products of those tools. Includes chapters on: "The Log Cabin and the Pioneer Jack-of-all-Trades," "The House and the Carpenter," "The Furniture Maker and the Cabinetmaker," and "Other Woodworkers." In the last, includes wheelwright, cartwright, coachmaker, cooper, shipwright, basketmaker, bellowsmaker, and gunstocker.

400 Hewett, Cecil Alec. THE DEVELOPMENT OF CARPENTRY, 1200-1700: AN ESSEX STUDY. New York: Augustus M. Kelley Publishers, 1969. 232 p. Illus., glossary.

In eight chapters, chronologically describes wooden construction in the English county of Essex, from the Carolingian Romanesque through the seventeenth century. In appendixes, describes the development of scarfing, the development of tying joints, and the development and decline of joist joints. Discusses dating of buildings by joints and other carpentry techniques.

401 Innocent, C[harles]. F[rederick]. THE DEVELOPMENT OF ENGLISH BUILDING CONSTRUCTION. Cambridge, Engl.: Cambridge University Press, 1916. Reprint. Introduction and bibliography by Sir Robert de Z. Hall. Newton Abbot, Engl.: David & Charles Reprints, 1971. 294 p. Illus. (Intro. and bibliog., 1971.)

An architectural history of "the lesser English house." Stresses
materials and methods.

402   McKee, Harley J. INTRODUCTION TO EARLY AMERICAN MASONRY:
       STONE, BRICK, MORTAR, AND PLASTER. National Trust/Columbia
       University Series on the Technology of Early American Building, no. 1.
       Washington, D.C.: National Trust for Historic Preservation, 1973. 92 p.
       Illus., bibliog., paper.

       Drawn from lectures given by the author at the School of
       Architecture, Columbia University, from 1967 to 1973. Con-
       siders historic American stone, brick, mortar, and plaster, in
       terms of their sources, composition, method of quarrying or
       manufacture, use in construction, deterioration, repair, and
       restoration.

403   Mercer, Henry C. ANCIENT CARPENTERS' TOOLS: TOGETHER WITH
       LUMBERMEN'S JOINERS' AND CABINET MAKERS' TOOLS IN USE IN
       THE EIGHTEENTH CENTURY. Foreword by Charles F. Hummel. 5th
       ed. Published for the Bucks County [Pennsylvania] Historical Society
       by Horizon Press, 1975. xii, 339 p. Illus., bibliog.

       Fifth edition of a work first published in 1929, to which
       addenda have been added by a number of contributors. De-
       scribes tools which are used for: felling, splitting and log
       sawing; moving and measuring; holding and gripping; surfacing,
       chopping and paring; shaping and fitting; fastening and un-
       fastening; and sharpening.

404   Nelson, Lee H. NAIL CHRONOLOGY AS AN AID TO DATING OLD
       BUILDINGS. Technical Leaflet, no. 48. Nashville: American Associ-
       ation for State and Local History, 1968. 12 p.

       Reprinted from HISTORY NEWS, November 1968. Describes
       the various nail types that are generally found in American
       buildings: hand wrought nails, cut nails, and wire nails--
       and a surprising variety with subtle differences within these
       major groups, which enable the use of nails as dating tools
       with some certainty.

405   Salaman, R.A. DICTIONARY OF TOOLS: USED IN THE WOOD-
       WORKING AND ALLIED TRADES, c. 1700-1970. Foreword by Joseph
       Needham. London: George Allen and Unwin, 1975. 545 p. Illus.,
       bibliog.

       Defines, describes, and illustrates the tools of not only the
       cabinetmaker, the carpenter, and the joiner--but also of the
       basketmaker, the bowlturner, the coffinmaker, the cooper,

the woodengraver, the millwright, the planemaker, the turner, the upholsterer, and many others.

406   Sloane, Eric. A MUSEUM OF EARLY AMERICAN TOOLS. New York: Wilfred Funk, 1964. xii, 108 p. Illus.

A sketchbook of early tools related to the felling of trees and preparation of lumber, agriculture, food preparation, transportation, and all manner of construction.

407   Weiss, Harry B., and Weiss, Grace M. EARLY BRICKMAKING IN NEW JERSEY. Trenton: New Jersey Agricultural Society, 1966. v, 85 p. Illus.

Contents: "Early Brickmaking," "Some Early Brick Structures of New Jersey," "Imported Bricks," "Brick Clays of New Jersey," "Some Early Brickmakers and Bricklayers of New Jersey," "The Art of Brickmaking," "Bricklaying." Lists brickmakers and bricklayers from 1679 to 1898.

DETERIORATION AND WEATHERING: MAINTENANCE AND RESTORATION

408   Braun, Hugh. THE RESTORATION OF OLD HOUSES. London: Faber and Faber, 1954. 192 p. Illus., glossary.

A practical guide to house restoration, with a focus on country houses in Britain. Chapters on surveys, structure, materials, shoring, foundations, rubble walls, masonry, brickwork, timber framing, roof timbering, roof coverings, and other topics.

409   Bullock, Orin M., Jr. THE RESTORATION MANUAL: AN ILLUS-TRATED GUIDE TO THE PRESERVATION AND RESTORATION OF OLD BUILDINGS. Written for the Committee on Historic Buildings of the American Institute of Architects. Foreword by Morris Ketchum, Jr. Norwalk, Conn.: Silvermine Publishers, 1966. 181 p. Illus., glossary, bibliog.

The result of the efforts of a subcommittee of the Committee on Historic Buildings. A manual of procedure intended for the use of architects who receive commissions to restore buildings. Includes chapters dealing with the development of programs, the selection of the period to be restored, historical research, archaeological research, architectural research, the execution of the restoration, specifications, and maintenance and interpretation of the restored structure. Although intended for the architect, also of value to owner and preservationist alike. In an appendix, contains articles on aspects of restoration by various authors that previously appeared in BUILDING RESEARCH, September--October 1964.

410   Chambers, J. Henry. CYCLICAL MAINTENANCE FOR HISTORIC
       BUILDINGS. Washington, D.C.: U.S. Government Printing Office,
       1976. 125 p. Illus., bibliog., paper.

       Prepared for the Interagency Historic Architectural Services
       Program, Office of Archaeology and Historic Preservation,
       National Park Service. Sets forth a systematic procedure for
       the preparation for maintenance, as well as the actual methods
       of maintenance. Discusses the training of maintenance staff,
       the contracting of outside services, the preparation of a
       maintenance manual, and the keeping of a maintenance log.
       Lists relevant organizations.

411   Harvey, William. THE PRESERVATION OF ST. PAUL'S CATHEDRAL &
       OTHER FAMOUS BUILDINGS: A TEXTBOOK ON THE NEW SCIENCE
       OF CONSERVATION, INCLUDING AN ANALYSIS OF MOVEMENTS
       IN HISTORICAL STRUCTURES PRIOR TO THEIR FALL. London: Archi-
       tectural Press, 1925. xiv, 153 p. Illus.

       "The conservation advocated in this book aims at the retention
       of the historic building, sound and whole, by means and meth-
       ods scientifically devised and inconspicuously applied to meet
       the needs of the case in the most complete manner possible.
       The science of conservation is of recent development, and has
       been evolved as a practical alternative to the demolition of
       ancient buildings or their disfigurement by extraneous patches
       and props . . . The book is written in popular form, to in-
       dicate how great arched buildings drift to their final collapse,
       and how optimistic custodians, unable to read the structural
       signs of approaching danger, permit them to do so and even
       assist in the process by injudicious repairs."

412   Insall, Donald W. THE CARE OF OLD BUILDINGS TODAY: A
       PRACTICAL GUIDE. London: Architectural Press, 1972; New York:
       Watson-Guptil, 1974. 197 p. Illus., bibliog.

       An enlarged version of "The Care of Old Buildings," written
       by Insall for ARCHITECTS' JOURNAL in 1957, on the occasion
       of the eightieth birthday of the Society for the Protection of
       Ancient Buildings. An amply illustrated, practical guide to
       building conservation problems and solutions; with a chapter
       on "Case-Histories in Conservation." Describes British organi-
       zations concerned with preservation, and reviews British pres-
       ervation legislation.

413   Johnson, Sidney M. DETERIORATION, MAINTENANCE, AND REPAIR
       OF STRUCTURES. New York: McGraw-Hill, 1965. x, 373 p. Illus.

       A practical and highly technical approach to the care of
       buildings and building materials. Considers materials, from
       timber, to concrete, to steel. Lists bibliographic references
       at end of each chapter.

414   Melville, Ian A., and Gordon, Ian A. THE REPAIR AND MAINTENANCE OF OLD HOUSES. London: Estates Gazette, 1973. xxi, 1,050 p. Illus., bibliog.

> Gives historic background of the English house from the Anglo-Saxons to the twentieth century, followed by detailed chapters on brick walls, stone walls, foundations, timber, shoring, roof coverings, dampness, internal and general matters, drainage, and the contract.

415   Powys, A[lbert].R[eginald]. REPAIR OF ANCIENT BUILDINGS. London and Toronto: J.M. Dent & Sons; New York: E.P. Dutton & Co., 1929. xv, 208 p. Illus., glossary.

> A philosophical and practical guide, specific to problems of ancient buildings in Britain, but applicable abroad as well. States, "It is the purpose of this book to suggest methods, in accordance with the principles of the Society for the Protection of Ancient Buildings, which may be employed in the repair of ancient buildings."

416   Richert, Roland Von S., and Vivian, R. Gordan, comps. RUINS STABILIZATION IN THE SOUTHWESTERN UNITED STATES. Publications in Archeology, No. 10. Washington, D.C.: National Park Service, 1974. xiii, 158 p. Illus., bibliog., paper.

> Ruins, historic and prehistoric, are subject to problems of deterioration resulting from weathering, structural faults, and human and animal disturbance. Materials used in the stabilization of ruins are discussed, as are the techniques and controls useful to stabilization. A chapter is devoted to the keeping of stabilizction records. "Publications in Archeology" is a continuation of "Archeological Research Series."

417   Sanpaolesi, Piero. DISCORSO SULLA METODOLOGIA GENERALE DE RESTAURO DEI MONUMENTI [Discourse on the general methodology of the restoration of monuments]. Florence: Editrice Edam, 1973. 451 p. Illus., bibliog., paper.

> Writings derived from the author's teaching of courses in restoration in the Faculty of Architecture at the University of Florence. Covers all aspects, from the philosophical to the highly technical, with attention to specific materials and their problems.

418   Simpson, John, and Horrobin, Peter J., eds. THE WEATHERING AND PERFORMANCE OF BUILDING MATERIALS. Aylesbury, Engl.: Medical and Technical Publishing Co., 1970. ix, 286 p. Illus.

> Presents chapters prepared by a team of specialists, most of whom lectured in a course titled "The Performance of the

External Surfaces of Buildings" at the University of Manchester
Institute of Science and Technology in 1970. Includes chapters on weathering and performance, concrete, clay products,
timber, metals, and plastics.

419   U.S. Department of the Army. Headquarters. HISTORIC PRESERVATION
MAINTENANCE PROCEDURES. Technical Manual TM 5-801-2 (February
1977). Washington, D.C.: 1977. iv, 55 p. (various paginations).
Illus., bibliog., paper.

Describes methods for preserving historic properties and their
original building materials through maintenance. In conjunction with TM-5-801-1, HISTORIC PRESERVATION: ADMINIS-
TRATIVE PROCEDURES, sets forth guidance to be used by the
Department of the Army in implementation of Executive Order
11593, "Protection and Enhancement of the Cultural Environment." Provides general information about the materials and
construction methods commonly found in older buildings. Es-
tablishes broad guidelines for maintenance procedures and
techniques which differ from those used in modern construction.

420   Waite, John G. THE STABILIZATION OF AN EIGHTEENTH-CENTURY
PLASTER CEILING AT PHILIPSE MANOR: A RESTORATION REPORT.
Albany: New York State Historic Trust, 1972. 37 p. Illus., bibliog.,
paper.

One of a series of reports dealing with the preservation and
restoration of historic buildings in New York state. Analyzes
the problem at hand within the broader context of the historic property, and describes the methodology of the analytical
diagnosis of the problem and the procedures followed in its
solution. States, "While the techniques described in this
report were developed for an eighteenth-century ceiling, the
same methods, with appropriate modifications, can be utilized
for ceilings of other periods as well.

421   White, R[alph].B[arton]. THE CHANGING APPEARANCE OF BUILDINGS.
London: Her Majesty's Stationery Office, 1967. v. 65 p. Illus.,
paper.

Published for the Ministry of Technology Building Research
Station, a discussion of the weathering of buildings, with
remedies for deterioration. Includes examples of fortuitously
changed appearance, as well.

SPECIFIC MATERIALS

422   International Council on Monuments and Sites. SYMPOSIUM ON THE
WEATHERING OF WOOD, LUDWIGSBURG, GERMANY, 8-11. VI.
1969. Paris: 1972. 259 p. Illus., bibliog., paper.

Papers on a variety of problems connected with the deterioration and preservation of wooden structures. Presentations in French summarized in English, and those in English summarized in French.

423 International Institute for Conservation of Historic and Artistic Works. NEW YORK CONFERENCE ON CONSERVATION OF STONE AND WOODEN OBJECTS, NEW YORK, 7-13 JUNE 1970. London: n.d. Part I: DECAY OF STONE. 134 p. Part II: WOOD DETERIORATION AND ITS PREVENTION. 136 p. Illus., paper. (Both parts bound as one, with separate pagination).

Presents contributions to the conference dealing with all aspects of the analysis, deterioration, and preservation of wooden and stone objects and buildings.

424 Nicholas, Darrel D., ed. WOOD DETERIORATION AND ITS PRE-VENTION BY PRESERVATION TREATMENTS. 2 vols. With the assistance of Wesley E. Loos. Syracuse Wood Science Series, no. 5. Syracuse: Syracuse University Press, 1973. Vol. I: DEGRADATION AND PROTECTION OF WOOD. 380 p. Vol. II: PRESERVATIVES AND PRESERVATIVE SYSTEMS. 402 p.

Presents chapters by various authors on aspects of wood deterioration and preservation from the development of wood technology, 2000 B.C.-A.D. 1550, to the present. Lists references at chapter ends.

425 Phillips, Morgan W., and Selwyn, Judith E. EPOXIES FOR WOOD REPAIRS IN HISTORIC BUILDINGS. Heritage Conservation and Recreation Service Publication No. 1. Washington, D.C.: U.S. Department of the Interior, 1978. vii, 67 p. Illus., bibliog., paper.

Considers two main subjects: (1) low-viscosity epoxy consolidants that can be soaked into rotted wood in order to restore its solidity and (2) epoxy pastes (patching compounds) for filling cracks and holes in woodwork. Presents the results of preliminary research and testing, teaches the basic technology involved, and provides suggested formulations and lists of suppliers.

426 PREMIER COLLOQUE INTERNATIONAL SUR LA DETERIORATION DES PIERRES EN OEUVRE/FIRST INTERNATIONAL SYMPOSIUM ON THE DETERIORATION OF BUILDING STONES: 11-16 SEPTEMBRE 1972. Chambéry: Imprimeries Réunies, 1973(?). 237 p. Illus.

Organized by the Centre de Recherches et d'Etudes Océano-graphiques. Papers by an international panel of experts on all aspects of the deterioration, conservation, and corrective intervention of building stone. In French or English, with summaries in the alternative language.

427 Shore, B[ertram].C[harles].G[lossop]. STONES OF BRITAIN: A
PICTORIAL GUIDE TO THOSE IN CHARGE OF VALUABLE BUILDINGS.
London: Leonard Hill, 1957. xii, 302 p. Illus.

> Addresses the geological--as distinct from the structural--reasons
> for the behavior of particular stones under certain conditions.
> Covers the composition and nature of various building stones,
> cement and mortar work, and problems of stone and their solu-
> tions. Profusely illustrated with photographic plates.

428 Thomas, James Cheston. RESTORING BRICK AND STONE: SOME DOS
AND DON'TS. Technical Leaflet, no. 81. Nashville: American
Association for State and Local History, 1975. 8 p. Illus., bibliog.

> Issued as part of HISTORY NEWS, January 1975. Gives guide-
> lines and cautions concerning a most sensitive area of building
> conservation and maintenance.

PROBLEMS OF MOISTURE

429 Corning Museum of Glass. THE CORNING FLOOD: MUSEUM UNDER
WATER. Corning, N.Y.: 1977. 60, xi p. Illus., paper.

> Reports that on 23 June 1972 the Corning Museum of Glass
> was flooded to a level of five feet four inches above the
> floor, possibly the greatest single catastrophe borne by an
> American museum. Presents the story of the restoration of
> the museum and its library, giving suggestions for planning
> for such disasters.

430 International Council on Monuments and Sites. CONFERENCE ON
THE PROBLEMS OF MOISTURE IN HISTORIC MONUMENTS, ROMA
11-14. X. 1967. Paris: 1969. 332 p. Bibliog., paper.

> Lists names and addresses of specialists and laboratories work-
> ing on problems of humidity. Papers in English or in French--
> some in both, or cross summarized.

431 Massari, Giovanni. HUMIDITY IN MONUMENTS. Rome: International
Centre for the Study of the Preservation and the Restoration of Cultural
Property, 1971. 47 p. Illus., paper.

> Reports that dampness, whether coming from contact with the
> liquid or the vaporous phase of water, is a major cause of
> problems in monuments and buildings. Briefly describes sev-
> eral case studies, their analyses, and cure.

Chapter 8

RENOVATION, RESTORATION, AND REUSE OF
EXISTING BUILDINGS

In the first part of this chapter are listed books that contain case studies, proposals, and reports which explore the vast potential for the use of structures
and sites which might otherwise be declared redundant and either be destroyed
or be permitted to decay. In the second part are books concerned with the
acquisition, renovation, and restoration of old houses for use as present-day
dwellings.

RECYCLING OLD BUILDINGS AND SITES

432   Architectural Heritage-Baltimore. FEASIBILITY STUDY FOR THE RESTO-
       RATION AND RENOVATION OF THE BALTIMORE CITY HALL.
       Baltimore: 1974. 103 p. Illus., paper.

          Describes the Baltimore City Hall, in use as Baltimore's munic-
          ipal headquarters since 1875, as "an architecturally important
          nineteenth century public building which has eminent merit
          for adaptation to the twentieth century." Studies prospects
          for this building's continued use, with chapters on: "Historical
          Background," "Investigative Research," "Program Development,"
          "Building Codes and Elevators," "Design," "Structural Systems,"
          "Mechanical Systems," "Electrical Systems," "Financial Evalu-
          ation," and "Project Structure and Schedules."

433   Bunnell, Gene. BUILT TO LAST: A HANDBOOK ON RECYCLING
       OLD BUILDINGS. Foreword by James Biddle. Preface by Michael
       S. Dukakis, Governor of the Commonwealth of Massachusetts. Washing-
       ton, D.C.: Preservation Press, 1977. 126 p. Illus., bibliog., paper.

          Case histories, with supporting tables of pertinent facts and
          figures, of over thirty completed and progressing rehabilitation
          and adaptive reuse projects in the Bay State. Prepared under
          the sponsorship of the Massachusetts Department of Community
          Affairs, Office of Local Assistance. In an appendix, lists
          information sources and funding sources.

434   Cantacuzino, Sherban.   NEW USES FOR OLD BUILDINGS.   London:
      Architectural Press, 1975.   xi, 264 p.   Illus.

      Divided into chapters representing different building types
      before conversion: churches and chapels; monastic and other
      religious establishments; fortifications, gates, and barracks;
      town houses, country houses, outhouses, and other ancillaries;
      schools; corn exchanges; barns and granaries; mills; maltings
      and breweries; warehouses and other industrial buildings; and
      pumping stations.   Gives primarily English examples, but there
      are also some from Europe and the United States.   Published
      to coincide with the Council of Europe's European Architec-
      tural Heritage Year, 1975.

435   Columbia University.   Center for Advanced Research in Urban and
      Environmental Affairs.   THE NEW YORK FEDERAL ARCHIVE BUILDING:
      A PROPOSAL FOR MIXED RE-USE.   Working Paper, no. 1.   New York:
      Columbia University (distributed by Jaap Rietman), 1976.   96 p.   Illus.

      Prepared for the New York Landmarks Conservancy.   Concerned
      with a vast and handsome warehouse dating from the end of
      the nineteenth century, which was about to be declared sur-
      plus property when the study was initiated.   Considers the
      physical condition of the building, its spatial and organiza-
      tional characteristics, its landmark qualities, its urban con-
      text, its possibilities for re-use, and the economic and legal
      implications of those possibilities.

436   Diamonstein, Barbaralee.   BUILDINGS REBORN: NEW USES, OLD
      PLACES.   New York: Harper & Row, 1978.   255 p.   Illus., bibliog.

      Case studies of every manner of proposed and completed adap-
      tation and renovation, drawn from a cross section of states.
      Includes photographs, history, and in some cases the cost of
      the project.   Arranged by city.

437   Getzels, Judith N.   RECYCLING PUBLIC BUILDINGS.   Planning
      Advisory Service Report, no. 319.   Chicago: American Society of
      Planning Officials, 1976.   34 p.   Illus., bibliog., paper.

      Techniques for renovation, remodeling, and reuse of schools
      and civic buildings.   Appendixes on state and federal pres-
      ervation programs and on the rental of surplus space.

438   Godfrey, Walter.   OUR BUILDING INHERITANCE: ARE WE TO USE
      OR LOSE IT?   London: Faber & Faber, 1944.   87 p.   Illus.

      In praise of the buildings of preindustrial England.   Urges
      their preservation and sympathetic conversion to comfortable
      modern use.

439   Great Britain. Department of the Environment. NEW LIFE FOR OLD
        BUILDINGS. Aspects of Conservation, no. I. Issued by the Depart-
        ment of the Environment, the Scottish Development Department, and
        the Welsh Office. London: Her Majesty's Stationery Office, 1971.
        50 p. Illus., paper.

        Describes twenty-two restoration and adaptive reuse case his-
        tories. Includes illustrations consisting of drawings and before-
        and-after photographs. First in a series of publications deal-
        ing with the preservation of the British building heritage in an
        age of change. Shows how, with skill and imagination, old
        buildings can be given new life for new purposes. Announces
        the proposed content of future booklets in the series as:
        "Other booklets to be issued later will show how the surround-
        ings of old buildings can be improved to enhance their charac-
        ter; and how, where there are gaps to be filled between old
        buildings, this can be done with new buildings which respect
        their neighbors."

440   Hardy Holzman Pfeiffer Associates. REUSING RAILROAD STATIONS.
        New York: Educational Facilities Laboratories, 1974. 78 p. Illus.,
        paper.

        A realistic appraisal of the potential for continued use and
        adaptive use of a numerous and highly endangered species
        of our architectural heritage. Includes historical overview;
        present state of the railroads; case studies of successful use;
        recommendations for action; and federal, state, local, and
        private participation.

441   Kidney, Walter C. WORKING PLACES: THE ADAPTIVE USE OF
        INDUSTRIAL BUILDINGS. Pittsburgh: Ober Park Associates, 1976.
        xii, 171 p. Illus.

        A handbook sponsored by the Society for Industrial Archeology,
        demonstrating case studies of adaptive use. In appendixes,
        deals with related laws and economics, and provides a list
        of suggested readings and audiovisual presentations.

442   Langenbach, Randolph. A FUTURE FROM THE PAST: THE CASE FOR
        CONSERVATION AND REUSE OF OLD BUILDINGS IN INDUSTRIAL
        COMMUNITIES. Edited by Gene Bunnell. Washington, D.C.: U.S.
        Government Printing Office, 1977. vi, 119 p. Illus.

        A joint publication of the U.S. Department of Housing and
        Urban Development and the Massachusetts Department of Com-
        munity Affairs. Focuses on economic advantages of preserva-
        tion, proposing imaginative methods of taxation to provide an
        incentive for preservation. Innovative approaches include
        "mothballing" portions of larger buildings until market demand
        develops. New England mill towns provide the examples:

Fall River, Massachusetts; Lawrence, Massachusetts; Lowell, Massachusetts; and Manchester, New Hampshire.

443 Shopsin, William C. SAVING LARGE ESTATES: CONSERVATION, HISTORIC PRESERVATION, ADAPTIVE RE-USE. Edited by Grania Bolton Marcus. N.p.: Society for the Preservation of Long Island Antiquities, 1977. vii, 199 p. Illus., bibliog.

Contains articles by a number of authors, some of which were previously published elsewhere, on the various aspects of conserving large buildings and land holdings. Addresses the problem most specifically within New York state--in Westchester County, Dutchess County, the Adirondack-Catskill area, and Long Island--but draws case studies and background from other states and from Great Britain. In a "Glossary of Agencies, Organizations and Programs," describes the agencies, organizations, programs, and funding sources mentioned in the volume, and gives sources for further detailed information.

444 Stanforth, Deirdre. RESTORED AMERICA. Photographs by Louis Reens. New York: Praeger Publishers, 1975. 245 p. Illus.

A photographic survey of restored houses and adaptive use conversions, showing interior, exterior, and streetscape views. Examples drawn from all over the United States. Presents adaptive use conversions to private, public, and commerical use, from a wide variety of original uses to an even wider variety of new uses.

445 Thomas, Selma, ed. REHABILITATION: AN ALTERNATIVE FOR HISTORIC INDUSTRIAL BUILDINGS. Washington, D.C.: Historic American Engineering Record, U.S. Department of the Interior, 1978. ix, 181 p. Illus., paper.

Explores the potential for rehabilitation, under the Tax Reform Act of 1976, of industrial buildings, sites, complexes, and districts. Examples drawn from Lynchburg, Virginia; Columbus, Georgia; and Spencer and Winston-Salem, North Carolina. Provides detailed financial analyses.

446 Thompson, Elisabeth Kendall, ed. RECYCLING BUILDINGS: RENOVATIONS, REMODELINGS, RESTORATIONS, AND REUSES. An Architectural Record Book. New York: McGraw-Hill, 1977. vii, 213 p. Illus.

By a former senior editor of ARCHITECTURAL RECORD. Presents a survey of articles drawn from that periodical. Gives solutions to many "new use" problems, covering every major building type from family homes to community and business buildings. Includes a chapter on "Restoration and Preservation

of Historic Buildings" and one on "Additions Designed for
Neighborhood Preservation."

447   Tulane University of Louisiana. School of Architecture. THE MINT.
       New Orleans: 1971. 98 p. Illus., paper.

       Proposes a major building of the architect William Strickland
       (1788-1854), no longer serving its original purpose, for a new
       role as an extension of the Louisiana State Museum. Con-
       tains plans for the building's restoration and adaptive reuse.

448   ULI-The Urban Land Institute. ADAPTIVE USE: DEVELOPMENT ECO-
       NOMICS, PROCESS, AND PROFILES. By Melvin A. Gamzon,
       Nathaniel M. Griffin, Thomas J. Martin, W. Paul O'Mara, Frank H.
       Spink, Jr., Joseph D. Steller, Jr., and Margaret A. Thomas. Washing-
       ton, D.C.: 1978. viii, 246 p. Illus., bibliog.

       Part 1: "Economics and Process"; part 2: "Case Studies"
       (15 major cases of adaptive re-use); part 3: "Profiles" (180
       cases, organized by building type). Presents a classified
       bibliography, including economic and legal aspects, conserva-
       tion technology, and specific project categories, in addition
       to general works.

449   Warner, Raynor M.; Groff, Sibyl McCormac; and Warner, Ranne P.;
       with Weiss, Sandi. BUSINESS AND PRESERVATION: A SURVEY OF
       BUSINESS CONSERVATION OF BUILDINGS AND NEIGHBORHOODS.
       Edited by Frank Stella. An INFORM Book. New York: INFORM, 1978.
       xii, 295 p. Illus., glossary, paper.

       Documents the involvement of business in recycling of build-
       ings, residential community revitalization, commercial redevel-
       opment, and general support of preservation efforts. A book
       designed to be a tool for "both businesses interested in build-
       ing reuse and neighborhood preservation, and preservation and
       community groups interested in soliciting business support for
       these causes." Includes seventy-one case studies illustrating
       the achievements of business in preservation. Lists an addi-
       tional seventy-one projects with short description in an appen-
       dix, to further demonstrate the scope and extent of activity.
       Examples selected for their variety, scale, and geographic
       location, as well as for the degree of company cooperation.

RENOVATING AND RESTORING OLD HOUSES

450   Brown, Charles Bernard. THE CONVERSION OF OLD BUILDINGS
       INTO NEW HOMES FOR OCCUPATION AND INVESTMENT. London:
       B.T. Batsford, 1955. xiv, 218 p. Illus.

One of many books published in Britain's postwar housing emergency, illustrating the means of utilizing the rich stock of standing buildings which awaited subdivision, renovation, conversion, and rehabilitation. Considers every practical detail.

451   Brownstone Revival Committee. HOME-BUYER'S GUIDE TO NEW YORK CITY BROWNSTONE NEIGHBORHOODS. 3d ed., rev. New York: 1977. 64 p. Illus., paper. Supplement, 1978. 24 p. Illus., paper.

Describes fifty-one brownstone neighborhoods and other reviving residential areas in the five boroughs of New York City and in Hoboken and Jersey City, New Jersey. Gives information on the character and amenities of each area, as well as information on its early history, history of its revival, availability of property, prices, mortgage possibilities, and so forth. Provides names and addresses of neighborhood representatives and organizations who can provide further information. Supplement profiles twenty more communities which emerged as revivals-in-progress.

452   Burden, Ernest. LIVING BARNS: HOW TO FIND AND RESTORE A BARN OF YOUR OWN. Boston: New York Graphic Society, 1977. 186 p. Illus., bibliog.

Recycling barns for human habitation. Chiefly photographs and ground plans of renovations, with a survey of American barn types.

453   Clifford, Dalton, and Enthoven, R.E. NEW HOMES FROM OLD BUILD-INGS. London: Country Life Ltd., 1954. 119 p. Illus.

Describes, in detail, conversions of every manner and size of domestic and nondomestic buildings into "new homes."

454   Congdon, Herbert Wheaton. EARLY AMERICAN HOMES FOR TODAY: A TREASURY OF DECORATIVE DETAILS AND RESTORATION PRO-CEDURES. Rutland, Vt.: Charles E. Tuttle, 1963. 236 p. Illus., glossary.

Declares, "This book is intended to be a help to the do-it-yourself man who has had the good fortune to come into the possession of one of New England's old homes." Discusses old-time construction methods and specific features such as eaves, gables, windows, doors, stairways, chimneys, and fire-places; and finishes with a treatise on the selection of fire-wood and the laying of open fires.

455   Edgerton, William H., et al. HOW TO RENOVATE A BROWNSTONE. Edited by J. Parker Sondheimer. New York: Halsey Publishing Co., 1970. xviii, 373 p. Paper.

A guide to all aspects--including architectural, legal, and
financial--of buying, renovating, and operating a New York
City "brownstone." In the appendixes, includes facsimiles of
many forms relating to legal, architectural, Building Department, and insurance matters. By contributors including New
Yorkers active in law, insurance, interior design, history,
real estate brokerage, management, financing, architecture,
and construction.

456   Greater Portland Landmarks. LIVING WITH OLD HOUSES. Portland,
Maine: Advisory Service of Greater Portland Landmarks, 1975. 105 p.
Glossary, bibliog., paper.

A guide to the preservation, restoration, renovation, and care
of old houses. Contains a primer of architectural styles in
Greater Portland and individual chapters by various authors on
such specific topics as: researching a house, lighting, floor
treatments, wallpaper, hardware, gardens, and other subjects.
Provides guidelines for moving old houses and advice on financing restoration work. Lists houses in Maine open to the
public and restoration organizations of the region.

457   Hawkins, R[eginald].R[obert]., and Abbe, C.H. NEW HOUSES FROM
OLD: A GUIDE TO THE PLANNING AND PRACTICE OF HOUSE
REMODELING. New York: McGraw-Hill, 1948. x, 558 p. Illus.,
bibliog.

Based on the authors' experience in remodeling frame houses
in New England and stone houses in Bucks County, Pennsylvania. Directed primarily to the homeowner, but does not
avoid becoming fairly technical when that is necessary.

458   Hooper, Charles Edward. RECLAIMING THE OLD HOUSE: ITS MODERN
PROBLEMS AND THEIR SOLUTIONS AS GOVERNED BY THE METHODS
OF ITS BUILDERS. New York: McBride, Nast & Co., 1913. 162 p.
Illus., glossary.

A pioneer work of its type in the United States. Incorporates
a great deal of information on local architectural variations,
historical conventions of paint, hardware, gardening, fencing
and enclosures, outbuildings, and other topics.

459   Jukes, Mary. NEW LIFE IN OLD HOUSES. Don Mills, Ontario:
Longmans Canada, 1966. 169 p. Illus.

A collection of articles which originally appeared in the
TORONTO GLOBE AND MAIL. Discusses every manner of
old building in Canada being used as a contemporary residence:
old farm houses, cottages, mansions, mills, barns, log houses,
coach-houses, rowhouses, and others.

460   McKenna, H. Dickson. A HOUSE IN THE CITY: A GUIDE TO
       BUYING AND RENOVATING OLD ROW HOUSES. New York: Van
       Nostrand Reinhold, 1971. 159 p. Illus., bibliog.

       A "brownstoners'" guide, containing a history of American
       row houses, current examples of renovation and preservation
       in a wide range of American cities, and practical advice
       to the buyer and renovator.

461   Stanforth, Deirdre, and Stamm, Martha. BUYING AND RENOVATING
       A HOUSE IN THE CITY: A PRACTICAL GUIDE. New York: Alfred
       A. Knopf, 1972. xiv, 400, xiv p. Illus.

       Extols the virtues and benefits of in-town town house living.
       Decribes the nuts and bolts of buying and renovating. Pre-
       sents a survey of neighborhood revival in inner-city districts
       of a number of eastern, southern, midwestern, and western
       cities.

462   Stephen, George. REMODELING OLD HOUSES: WITHOUT DESTROY-
       ING THEIR CHARACTER. New York: Knopf, 1973. xiii, 232, iii p.
       Illus., paper.

       Written by an architect, covers the full range of renovation--
       from restoration, to rehabilitation, to redesign. Gives advice
       from the practical to the aesthetic.

463   Wilkes, Joy, and Wilkes, Paul. YOU DON'T HAVE TO BE RICH TO
       OWN A BROWNSTONE. New York: Quadrangle/New York Times
       Book Co., 1973. xv, 139 p. Illus., bibliog.

       A compendium of useful, practical information on the city row
       house: how to fine one, finance its purchase, renovate it,
       and other aspects. Many case studies. A descriptive guide
       to New York City (and Hoboken, New Jersey) brownstone
       neighborhoods, detailing the availability of houses, price
       range and characteristics of the area, and names and addresses
       from whom to obtain further information for each area. In an
       additional appendix, describes residential historic districts in
       New York City.

464   Williams, Henry Lionel, and Williams, Ottalie K. OLD AMERICAN
       HOUSES AND HOW TO RESTORE THEM [1700-1850]. Garden City,
       N.Y.: Doubleday & Co., 1946. 239 p. Illus., glossary, bibliog.

       Gives information about the characteristics of early American
       houses, combined with practical advice to the homeowner.

Chapter 9

INTERPRETATION OF HISTORY THROUGH

BUILDINGS, OBJECTS, AND SITES

Promoting an understanding of history through the sensitive presentation of artifacts, structures, sites, and information is a major concern of those charged
with the administration of historic house museums, museum villages, and other
historic structures, sites, and complexes. The intricate nature of this aspect
of historic preservation can be seen in the wide variety of literature pertinent
to its execution.

CULTURAL AND SOCIAL HISTORY

465   Fitch, James Marston. AMERICAN BUILDING 1: THE HISTORICAL
       FORCES THAT SHAPED IT. Boston: Houghton Mifflin Co., 1966. ix,
       350 p. Illus.

       _____. AMERICAN BUILDING 2: THE ENVIRONMENTAL FORCES
       THAT SHAPE IT. Boston: Houghton Mifflin Co., 1972. xi, 349 p.
       Illus.

       Two volumes comprising the second edition revised and enlarged
       of a one-volume work originally published in 1948, AMERICAN
       BUILDING: THE FORCES THAT SHAPE IT. In the original edition
       the first seven chapters presented a chronological view of
       American building, while the final eleven chapters examined
       environmental considerations. The revised and enlarged version
       retains the format of the earlier one, expanding its two halves
       into two separate volumes. The author identifies building as,
       next to agriculture, America's largest production field. The
       great number of Americans directly involved in it (architects,
       engineers, manufacturers, carpenters, mortgage bankers, land-
       lords, etc.) have in common the identity of being "consumers
       of buildings" and "it is from this point of view, the consumer's,
       that building may be most fruitfully analyzed." (AMERICAN
       BUILDING 1) has been issued in paperback by Schocken Books,
       1973.)

466   Girouard, Mark. LIFE IN THE ENGLISH COUNTRY HOUSE: A
        SOCIAL AND ARCHITECTURAL HISTORY. New Haven: Yale Uni-
        versity Press, 1978. 344 p. Illus., bibliog.

        Reports that the English country house, the seat of political
        power, was a vast and highly organized domain with enormous
        staff; private, public, and service wings; and a never-ending
        stream of residents and sojourners. Describes its evolution and
        the conduct of upper-class life within, from the Middle Ages
        to the days approaching the Second World War.

467   _____. THE VICTORIAN COUNTRY HOUSE. Oxford: Clarendon
        Press, 1971. xxii, 218 p. Illus.

        Describes upper-class Victorian British country living in its
        architectural setting. Houses in England, Wales, Ireland,
        Scotland, and abroad--from Portugal to the Crimea--described
        in detail and cataloged. Biographical notes on major Victorian
        architects.

468   Glassie, Henry H. FOLK HOUSING IN MIDDLE VIRGINIA: A
        STRUCTURAL ANALYSIS OF HISTORIC ARTIFACTS. Knoxville: Uni-
        versity of Tennessee Press, 1975. xiv, 231 p. Illus., bibliog.

        An attempt at understanding people who left behind no literate
        legacy, obtaining information from the artifacts that they made.
        Along with a careful description and analytical interpretation
        of house plans, presents an explanation of the method used,
        "in order to see how the mute artifact can be made to speak."

469   Gould, Mary Earle. THE EARLY AMERICAN HOUSE: HOUSEHOLD
        LIFE IN AMERICA 1620-1850, WITH SPECIAL CHAPTERS ON THE CON-
        STRUCTION AND EVOLUTION OF OLD AMERICAN HOMES; FIRE-
        PLACES AND IRON UTENSILS; HEARTHSIDE AND BARNYARD ACTIV-
        ITIES. Rev. ed. Rutland, Vt.: Charles E. Tuttle Co., 1965. 152 p.
        Illus.

        Chapters: (I.) "Early One-room Houses and How They Grew,"
        (II.) "Chimneys and Fireplaces--Heart of the Home," (III.)
        "Antique Kitchenware and How It Was Used," (IV.) "Food
        and Drink in the Old Days," and (V.) "Everyday Life Through-
        out the Year." Includes photographs of exteriors, interiors,
        and artifacts.

470   Gowans, Alan. BUILDING CANADA: AN ARCHITECTURAL HISTORY
        OF CANADIAN LIFE. Toronto: Oxford University Press, 1966. xx,
        412 p. Illus., bibliographic notes at chapter ends.

A revised and enlarged edition of LOOKING AT ARCHITEC-
TURE IN CANADA, published in 1958. Calls itself a "popular" rather than a "scholarly" history of Canadian architecture,
explaining that "popular" means partly that it is addressed to
people with an intelligent interest in the subject but with no
special technical knowledge of architectural history, and partly
that the buildings represented are products of common, general,
"popular" taste in their time and place, rather than the works
of individual genius.

471 _____. IMAGES OF AMERICAN LIVING: FOUR CENTURIES OF
ARCHITECTURE AND FURNITURE AS CULTURAL EXPRESSION. Phila-
delphia and New York: J.B. Lippincott Co., 1964. xv, 498 p.
Illus., bibliographic notes at chapter ends.

The artifact as an expression of culture and history, examined
in the context of the broad patterns of development in American architecture and furniture. An attempt to read the artifact as a living and tangible record of the course of American
civilization.

472 Sloane, Eric. THE SEASONS OF AMERICA PAST. New York: Wilfred
Funk, 1958. 150 p. Illus.

Early American agriculture, crafts, transportation, toys, animal
husbandry, clothing, cookery, brewery, etc., seen against the
background of the changing seasons.

ENCYCLOPEDIAS OF ANTIQUES, DECORATIVE ARTS, AND FURNISHINGS

473 Aronson, Joseph. THE ENCYCLOPEDIA OF FURNITURE. New York:
Crown Publishers, 1938. vi, 202 p. Illus., bibliog.

A volume that has gone through numerous printings since it
first appeared in 1938. An alphabetical encylcopedia with
line drawing illustrations accompanying the text. Also includes
sections of photographic plates showing furniture of specific
periods and places and sections showing the chronological development of specific furniture types. Bibliography classified
by subject.

474 Boger, Louise Ade, and Boger, H. Batterson. THE DICTIONARY OF
ANTIQUES AND THE DECORATIVE ARTS: A BOOK OF REFERENCE
FOR GLASS, FURNITURE, CERAMICS, SILVER, PERIODS, STYLES,
TECHNICAL TERMS, &c. 2d ed., enl. New York: Charles Scribner's
Sons, 1967. ix, 662 p. Illus., bibliog.

Fully described in the subtitle--covers American, European, and Oriental decorative arts.

475   Bridgeman, Harriet, and Drury, Elizabeth, eds. THE ENCYCLOPEDIA OF VICTORIANA. Preface by Marcus Linell. New York: Macmillan Publishing Co., 1975. 368 p. Illus., glossaries, bibliog.

Includes articles by over a score of experts on furniture; photographs; clocks, watches, and barometers; pottery; porcelain; glass; sculpture; silver; metalwork; arms and militaria; jewelry; dress; textiles; wallpaper; juvenilia; and miscellany. Black-and-white photographs augmented by full-page color plates. Lists of manufacturers, retailers, and publishers. Lists of marks. Lists of houses with Victorian interiors, in Great Britain and the United States, which are open to the public.

476   Edwards, Ralph. THE SHORTER DICTIONARY OF ENGLISH FURNITURE: FROM THE MIDDLE AGES TO THE LATE GEORGIAN PERIOD. Rev. ed. London, New York, Sydney, and Toronto: Country Life, 1964. 684 p. Illus.

Based on a 1954 edition of three folio volumes which was, in turn, based on a first edition of 1924-25. English domestic furniture seen in the context of its development over a period of six centuries. Photographic illustrations. A final section on "Designers, Cabinetmakers, Etc."

477   ENCYCLOPEDIA OF ANTIQUES. Introduction by Wendell D. Garrett. Rosemary Klein, consultant editor. London: Phoebus Publishing Co., in cooperation with Octopus Books, 1971/1976; New York: Galahad Books, 1976. 480 p. Illus., bibliog.

Articles by a number of contributing experts. Major divisions: "Ceramics," "Furniture," "Glass," "Silver and Gold," and "Arts and Decoration." Many illustrations, including a high proportion of color photographs. In each subdivision, concludes with a world-wide list of museums where the class of objects can be seen to advantage and a list of further reading.

478   Fleming, John, and Honour, Hugh. DICTIONARY OF THE DECORATIVE ARTS. New York and London: Harper & Row, 1977. 895 p. Illus.

Concerned with " . . . furniture and furnishings-- i.e. movable objects other than paintings and sculpture-- in Europe from the Middle Ages onward and in North America from the Colonial Period to the present day." Includes four types of entries: definitions of stylistic and technical terms, accounts of materials and processes of working and embellishing them, biographies of leading craftsmen and designers, and brief histories of the more notable factories in which objects for house-

hold use and decoration have been made. Includes brief
bibliographies in some of the entries.

479   Gloag, John. A SHORT DICTIONARY OF FURNITURE: CONTAINING
       OVER 2,600 ENTRIES THAT INCLUDE TERMS AND NAMES USED IN
       BRITAIN AND THE UNITED STATES OF AMERICA. Rev. and enl.
       London: George Allen and Unwin, 1969. 813 p. Illus., bibliog.

       Originally published in 1952. In the first section, concerned
       with "The Description of Furniture," and in the second section,
       with "The Design of Furniture." In the third section, the
       major portion of the book, presents a dictionary of names and
       terms of furniture and various furnishing accessories made and
       used in England since A.D. 1100 and in North America since
       the mid-seventeenth century. In the final three sections,
       contains a short list of furniture makers in Britain and America;
       a short bibliography of relevant books and periodicals; and a
       series of tables giving an outline of the types of furniture,
       the materials and craftsmen employed, and the influences that
       have affected design and promoted styles and fashions during
       the last eight and one half centuries. Published in an abridged
       paperbound edition in 1966.

480   HOUSE AND GARDEN DICTIONARY OF DESIGN AND DECORATION.
       London and Glasgow: Collins London and Glasgow in association with
       Condé Nast Publications; New York: Viking Press (a Studio Book) in
       association with Condé Nast Publications, 1973. 538 p. Illus.

       From "Aalto, Alvar" to "Zucchi, Antonio"; from antiquity to
       the present; from dictionary definitions to short essays.

481   Phillips, Phoebe, ed.; Butler, Joseph; and Coombs, David, assoc. eds.
       THE COLLECTOR'S ENCYCLOPEDIA OF ANTIQUES. New York: Crown
       Publishers, 1973. 704 p. Illus., glossaries, bibliog.

       Includes contributions by sixteen experts in as many fields.
       Lavishly illustrated with black-and-white photographs and
       occasional drawings and full-page color plates. Includes
       chapters covering: furniture, glass, jewelry, metalwork,
       musical instruments, Netsuke and Inro, pewter, scientific
       instruments, silver, and toys and automata. Concludes chap-
       ters with bibliographies, lists of museum collections in Britain
       and the United States, glossaries, information on repairs and
       maintenance, and information on fakes and forgeries. In-
       cludes American, British, European, and Oriental objects.

482   Phipps, Frances. THE COLLECTOR'S COMPLETE DICTIONARY OF
       AMERICAN ANTIQUES. Garden City, N.Y.: Doubleday & Co., 1974.
       xv, 640 p. Illus.

Contents: "Historic Periods and Styles"; "Rooms--Their Place-
ment and Use"; "Crafts, Trades, and Useful Professions";
"Weights and Measures"; "Terms Used by Joiners and Cabinetmakers"; "Woods and Their Preferred Uses"; "Paints, Dyes,
Finishes, Varnishes"; "Cleaning, Polishing, and Repairing";
"Metals--Antique Formulae and Uses"; "Pottery, Porcelain,
and Minerals"; "Glass"; and "Furnishings Made Here or Imported for Use (including Apparel, Armorial Bearings, Jewelry,
and Textiles and Leather)."

483   THE RANDOM HOUSE COLLECTOR'S ENCYCLOPEDIA, VICTORIANA
       TO ART DECO. Introduction by Roy Strong. New York: Random
       House, 1974. 302 p. Illus., bibliog.

       An A-to-Z encyclopedia of furniture, furnishings, and jewelry,
       with photographic illustrations in color and black-and-white.
       Bibliography classified by subject. Continues THE RANDOM
       HOUSE ENCYCLOPEDIA OF ANTIQUES (see below).

484   THE RANDOM HOUSE ENCYCLOPEDIA OF ANTIQUES. Introduction
       by John Pope-Hennessy. New York: Random House, 1973. 398 p.
       Illus., bibliog.

       Devoted to the applied arts, with a cutoff date of 1875. An
       illustrated dictionary--from "Abacus" to "Zwischengoldglaeser"
       --followed by a selection of ceramic marks; silver date letters
       for London, Birmingham, Sheffield, and Edinburgh; and a
       classified bibliography that ranges from "Adam, Robert" to
       "Yi period." Continued by the RANDOM HOUSE COLLEC-
       TOR'S ENCYCLOPEDIA, VICTORIANA TO ART DECO (see
       above).

485   Stafford, Maureen, and Ware, Dora. AN ILLUSTRATED DICTIONARY
       OF ORNAMENT. Introduction by John Gloag. London: George Allen
       and Unwin, 1974. 246 p. Illus., bibliog.

       Entries by Dora Ware, illustrated by Maureen Stafford's draw-
       ings. Describes the ornament of architecture, furniture, ceram-
       ics, metalware, fabrics, books, and other items. In the "Se-
       lect Bibliography," includes principal works of the nineteenth
       and twentieth centuries.

PERIOD ARCHITECTURE, DECORATION, AND ARTIFACTS

486   Amery, Colin. PERIOD HOUSES AND THEIR DETAILS. London: Archi-
       tectural Press; New York: Whitney Library of Design (an imprint of
       Watson-Guptill Publications), 1974. 15 p. 212 plates.

       A reissue of drawings and photographs of English domestic

architecture which first appeared early in the twentieth century; first in THE ARCHITECTURAL REVIEW, as a series, "The Practical Exemplar of Architecture," and later as a series of portfolios published by the Architectural Press. Exteriors, doorways, gateways and ironwork, interiors, chimney pieces, and staircases, mostly of the seventeenth and eighteenth centuries.

487   Carpenter, Ralph E., Jr. THE ARTS AND CRAFTS OF NEWPORT, RHODE ISLAND, 1640-1820. Newport: Preservation Society of Newport County, 1954. xiii, 213 p. Illus., bibliog.

Furniture, painting, silversmithing, shell work, and other topics.

488   Fowler, John, and Cornforth, John. ENGLISH DECORATION IN THE EIGHTEENTH CENTURY. London: Barrie & Jenkins; Princeton, N.J.: Pyne Press, 1974. 288 p. Illus., bibliog.

The result of the authors' concern about the problems of preservation, restoration, and presentation of country houses. Aims to "relate fashions and practices in English decoration in the classical period to contemporary documents and to show how many of them grew out of social attitudes and changing patterns of behaviour." A sampling of the chapters: "The Concept of the Decorator," "The Uses of Houses and Their Arrangements," "The Practice of the Upholsterer," "Colour and the Painter's Craft," "The Treatment of Floors," "Lighting and Heating," and "Attitudes to Pictures and Picture Hanging." In the subject index, covers all manner of furnishings, materials, and decorative techniques. Relevant to the presentation and interpretation of not only English houses, but eighteenth-century American houses of English influence, as well.

489   Frangiamore, Catherine Lynn. WALLPAPERS IN HISTORIC PRESERVATION. Washington, D.C.: Technical Services Division, Office of Archaeology and Historic Preservation, National Park Service, U.S. Department of the Interior, 1977. v, 55 p. Illus., bibliog., paper.

Contents: "Historic Wallpaper Technology," "History of Wallpaper Styles and Their Use," "Wallpaper Within a Restoration Project." In the last includes: planning for wall treatments, research, uncovering and removing samples of old wallpaper, identifying samples, alternatives for wallpaper restoration. In appendixes, lists wallpaper reference collections, relevant preservation periodicals, and firms that reproduce wallpaper.

490   Grow, Lawrence. THE OLD HOUSE CATALOGUE. New York: Universe Books, 1976. 234 p. Illus., bibliog., paper.

Lists twenty-five hundred products, services, and suppliers for restoring, decorating, and furnishing the period house--from early American to 1930s modern. Supplemented in 1978 by THE SECOND OLD HOUSE CATALOG (see below).

491 _____. THE SECOND OLD HOUSE CATALOG. New York: Universe Books, 1978. 219 p. Illus., bibliog., paper.

A supplement, rather than a replacement, to the earlier publication (see above).

492 LATE VICTORIAN ARCHITECTURAL DETAILS: AN ABRIDGED FACSIMILE OF COMBINED BOOK OF SASH, DOORS, BLINDS, MOULDINGS, STAIR WORK, MANTELS, AND ALL KINDS OF INTERIOR AND EXTERIOR FINISH; A PATTERN BOOK FIRST PUBLISHED IN 1871 AND ENLARGED THROUGH MANY EDITIONS TO THIS FACSIMILE OF 1898. Library of Victorian Culture. Watkins Glen, N.Y.: American Life Foundation Study Institute, 1978. 300 p. Illus., paper.

An abridged facsimile of the 1898 COMBINED BOOK, which traces its ancestry to W.L. Churchill's UNIVERSAL MOULDING BOOK of 1871. Documents American domestic architectural details for the last quarter of the nineteenth century. Includes store doors, store fronts, verandahs, newel posts, brackets, storm windows, cut glass, wood ventilators, office and bank counters, pulpits, pews, pickets, shingles, portiere work, screen doors, and much more.

493 Myers, Denys Peter. GASLIGHTING IN AMERICA: A GUIDE FOR HISTORIC PRESERVATION. Washington, D.C.: U.S. Government Printing Office, 1978. 279 p. Illus., bibliog., paper.

Prepared by the Office of Archaeology and Historic Preservation, Heritage Conservation and Recreation Service, U.S. Department of the Interior. A report which focuses on the types and styles of gas fixtures which appeared in the rooms and on the streets of nineteenth- and early twentieth-century America. Arranged chronologically, illustrations drawn from dealers' catalogs, photographs, and contemporary graphics. In appendix, lists gas companies throughout the United States in order of the year they received their charters.

494 Noël Hume, Ivor. A GUIDE TO ARTIFACTS OF COLONIAL AMERICA. A Borzoi Book. New York: Alfred A. Knopf, 1970. xviii, 323 p. Illus.

Treats forty-three categories of artifacts, alphabetically arranged from "armor" to "wig curlers" (passing "bells," "bottles," "bricks," and "buckles" along the way). Includes photographs, drawings, and charts to elucidate the text. Written by the director of the department of archaeology at Colonial Williamsburg.

495 Nylander, Jane C. FABRICS FOR HISTORIC BUILDINGS. Washington, D.C.: Preservation Press, 1977. 64 p. Illus., glossary, bibliog., paper.

In the introductory section, deals with documentary research
prior to fabric selection, selecting reproduction fabrics, custom
reproduction work, and the construction and installation of
fabric furnishings. In the main section, presents a chronological catalog of documentary reproductions of fabrics used in
the United States between the eighteenth century and 1900,
including their current sources. In a separate section of the
catalog, describes nondocumentary and plain woven fabrics.
Concludes with a list of manufacturers and sources, with their
addresses.

496   THE OLD-HOUSE JOURNAL 1979 CATALOG: A BUYERS' GUIDE FOR
      HOUSES BUILT BEFORE 1920. Brooklyn, N.Y.: Old-House Journal,
      1979. 76 p. Illus., paper.

      A guide to 662 companies and 7,282 products and services of
      interest to the owners, restorers, or renovators of old houses.

497   Peterson, Harold L. AMERICANS AT HOME: FROM THE COLONISTS
      TO THE LATE VICTORIANS: A PICTORIAL SOURCE BOOK OF AMERI-
      CAN DOMESTIC INTERIORS WITH AN APPENDIX ON INNS AND
      TAVERNS. New York: Charles Scribner's Sons, 1971. xviii, 205
      plates and captions.

      Paintings, drawings, sketches, prints, and photographs of every
      manner and class of human habitation, from shacks and shanties
      to palatial dwellings. The vast array includes mining cabins,
      military quarters, and campsites. Kitchens are depicted in
      genre paintings and in idealized renderings. People are shown
      in a broad range of human activity.

498   Praz, Mario. AN ILLUSTRATED HISTORY OF FURNISHINGS FROM
      THE RENAISSANCE TO THE 20TH CENTURY. New York: George
      Braziller, 1964. 396 p. Illus.

      The drawings and paintings reproduced represent not only the
      settings and their furnishings, but usually their inhabitants, in
      scenes of daily life.

499   Wharton, Edith, and Codman, Ogden, Jr. THE DECORATION OF
      HOUSES. New York: C. Scribner's Sons, 1902. Reprint. Introductory
      notes to the reprint edition by John Barrington Bayley and William A.
      Coles. The Classical America Series in Art and Architecture. New
      York: W.W. Norton & Co., 1978. xlix, 204 p. Illus.

      A book originally written in 1897, recognized as the foundation
      stone of interior decoration as it is known today. Highly rele-
      vant for understanding the interior decor of the oppulent turn-
      of-the-century houses of the American rich. In this reprint of
      the 1902 edition, contains some new photographs which replace

original ones in the text. Also contains additional new illustrative material following the text in "A Portfolio of Pictures
of Interiors and Details Done According to the Canon of THE
DECORATION OF HOUSES."

500   Whitehill, Walter Muir; Garrett, Jane N.; and Garrett, Wendell D.
THE ARTS IN EARLY AMERICAN HISTORY: NEEDS AND OPPORTUNI-
TIES FOR STUDY. Chapel Hill: University of North Carolina Press,
1965. 170 p. Bibliog.

Published for the Institute of Early American History and
Culture, Williamsburg, Virginia. Includes an essay by Whitehill followed by a bibliography (pages 35-151) by the Garretts,
which covers: general works; architecture; topography; painting; sculpture and carving; graphic arts; medals, seals, and
heraldic devices; crafts; furniture; silver; pewter; other metals
and wooden ware; pottery; glass; lighting devices; wall decoration; folk art; textiles; and serial publications.

501   Winterthur Conference. TECHNOLOGICAL INNOVATION AND THE
DECORATIVE ARTS. Winterthur Conference, Report 1973. Edited by
Polly Anne Earl and Ian M.G. Quimby. Charlottesville: University
Press of Virginia for the Henry Francis du Pont Winterthur Museum,
Winterthur, Delaware, 1974. xiv, 373 p. Illus., paper.

Procedings of a conference which focused on an aspect of the
history of Anglo-American decorative arts: the close relationship between technological innovation during the eighteenth
and nineteenth centuries and the development of home furnishings. Presents papers by historians of science and technology
and museum curators of technology and decorative arts, covering a wide spectrum of materials, artifacts, and technological
development.

OLD KITCHENS

502   Bullock, Helen. THE WILLIAMSBURG ART OF COOKERY: OR,
ACCOMPLISH'D GENTLEWOMAN'S COMPANION: BEING A COLLEC-
TION OF UPWARDS OF FIVE HUNDRED OF THE MOST ANCIENT &
APPROV'D RECIPES IN VIRGINIA COOKERY. Williamsburg: Colonial
Williamsburg, 1972. 276 p. Illus., bibliog.

The subtitle continues as: Soups & Sauces, Flesh & Fish,
Breads, Garden Stuff, Pastry, Preserving, Confectionery, Cakes,
Puddings, Wines, Punches, &c. And Also A Table of favorite
Williamsburg Garden Herbs. To which is Added, An Account
of Virginia Hospitality; Treatises on the various Branches of
Cookery; an Account of Health Drinking; some Considerations
on the Observation of Christmas in Virginia, with traditional

Recipes for this Season; with the Author's Explanation of the Method of Collecting & Adapting these choice Recipes; and an alphabetical Index to the Whole.

This book, first issued in 1938, is perhaps the best known of American historical cookbooks. It is listed here as representative of a special genre of historic preservation publication which can be an important tool in the interpretation of historic periods. Based on extensive testing of recipes from published and manuscript cookbooks of the eighteenth and nineteenth centuries.

503   Franklin, Linda Campbell. AMERICA IN THE KITCHEN, FROM HEARTH TO COOKSTOVE: AN AMERICAN DOMESTIC HISTORY OF GADGETS AND UTENSILS MADE OR USED IN AMERICA FROM 1700 TO 1930. Florence, Ala.: House of Collectibles, 1976. xv, 271 p. Illus., bibliog.

An illustrated encyclopedia of kitchen items from "adapter rings" to "yellow ware." In appendixes, ranges from "Cleaning and Maintenance" to a "Guide to Historic Restorations, Collections, and Museums with Kitchen Utensils, Period Kitchens or Displays of Articles Covered in this Book."

504   Harrison, Molly. THE KITCHEN IN HISTORY. New York: Charles Scribner's Sons, 1972. 142 p. Illus., bibliog.

The kitchen as factory. The center of household operations seen primarily within the English context, but also some comment on eighteenth-century North America.

505   Lantz, Louise K. OLD AMERICAN KITCHENWARE 1725-1925. Camden, N.Y.: Thomas Nelson; Hanover, Pa.: Everybodys Press, 1970. 290 p. Illus., bibliog.

In the opening three chapters, describes the eighteenth-century kitchen, the Victorian kitchen, and the early twentieth-century kitchen. In the remaining ones, covers various types of kitchenware and other housekeeping equipment, as well as specific materials, such as soapstone, old aluminum, and pewter. In addition to photographic illustrations, includes reproductions of drawings and copy from old dealers' and manufacturers' catalogs.

506   Norwak, Mary. KITCHEN ANTIQUES. New York: Praeger Publishers, 1975. 135 p. Illus.

Contents: "The Fireplace and Cooking Equipment"; "Kitchen Furniture"; "The Dairy"; "The Laundry"; "Cleaning the House"; "Storage and Preservation"; "Moulds, Cutters and Serving Equipment"; "Labour-saving Devices"; "Convenience Foods

and Cleaning Materials"; "Billheads, Account Books and
Manuscript Recipes." Concludes with a list of kitchens,
houses, and museums to visit in Great Britain, Northern Ireland, and the United States.

HISTORIC HOUSES—GENERAL GUIDES

507 ARTISTIC HOUSES: BEING A SERIES OF INTERIOR VIEWS OF A
NUMBER OF THE MOST BEAUTIFUL AND CELEBRATED HOMES IN
THE UNITED STATES-WITH-A DESCRIPTION OF THE ART TREASURES
CONTAINED THEREIN. New York, 1883. Reprint. 4 vols. in 1.
New York: Benjamin Blom, 1971. 184 p. Illus.

With interior photographs and descriptions, catalogs the furnishings and arrangements of rooms in the late nineteenth century in distinguished homes and apartments of the American
rich.

508 Da Costa, Beverley, ed. HISTORIC HOUSES OF AMERICA OPEN TO
THE PUBLIC. By the editors of AMERICAN HERITAGE: THE MAGAZINE
OF HISTORY. Introduction by Marshall B. Davidson. An American
Heritage Guide. New York: American Heritage Publishing Co., 1971.
320 p. Illus.

Arranged alphabetically by state and by locality within state.
Describes historic districts as well as historic houses. Gives
visitor information for the houses.

509 Drury, John. THE HERITAGE OF EARLY AMERICAN HOUSES. Introduction by Vincent Price. New York: Coward-McCann; Waukesha,
Wis.: Country Beautiful, 1969. 298 p. Illus.

A tour of sixty-five preserved houses, arranged by region.
Historical and architectural commentary accompanied by numerous photographs.

510 Fitzpatrick, John Clement. SOME HISTORIC HOUSES, THEIR BUILDERS
AND THEIR PLACES IN HISTORY. New York: Macmillan Publishing
Co., 1939. x, 160 p. Illus.

Published under the auspices of the National Society of the
Colonial Dames of America. Surveys, from Maine to Oregon,
the houses then maintained by the member state societies. In
the narratives, includes the histories of the houses and their
inhabitants, architectural descriptions, and current circumstances.

511 Page, Marian. HISTORIC HOUSES RESTORED AND PRESERVED. New
York: Whitney Library of Design, 1976. 208 p. Illus., bibliog.

A collection of essays, some of which first appeared in IN-TERIORS magazine as part of a series on historic restorations. Describes British and American houses, grouped in sections headed: "Elizabethan England and Colonial America," "Palladian England and Federal America," "Regency England and Grecian America," and "The Romantic Era." Illustrates houses restored to a particular period; houses partly restored to an earlier period and partly adapted for modern use; houses preserved to reflect the successive generations, tastes, and styles that have given them their special character; houses that have come down almost intact—documents of their time, place, and culture.

512   Pratt, Richard. HOUSES, HISTORY AND PEOPLE. New York: M. Evans and Co., 1965. 240 p. Illus.

The histories of a number of well-known and not-so-well-known houses associated with the National Society of the Colonial Dames of America, described in text and photographs.

513   Zook, Nicholas. HOUSES OF NEW ENGLAND OPEN TO THE PUBLIC. Photographs by Katharine Knowles. Barre, Mass.: Barre Publishers, 1968. 126 p. Illus.

Guide to approximately three hundred homes in the six-state region. Describes the architectural features to be observed, and provides a directory of visitor information and historical data. Some houses described more fully than others, but basic historical data and practical information for the visitor uniformly given. A state-by-state arrangement, with an index by house name.

HISTORIC HOUSES—STATE GUIDES

514   Eberlein, Harold Donaldson, and Hubbard, Cortlandt V.D. HISTORIC HOUSES AND BUILDINGS OF DELAWARE. Dover, Del.: Public Archives Commission, 1963. 227 p. Illus.

Gives texts and photographs documenting the rich architectural heritage of this small state. Reports that, on the dividing line between North and South, and with colonists and settlers drawn from among the Swedes, Dutch, English, Scotch-Irish, Welsh, and French Huguenots, Delaware architecture carries the impact of diverse influences.

515   Motto, Sytha. OLD HOUSES OF NEW MEXICO AND THE PEOPLE WHO BUILT THEM. 2d ed. Albuquerque: Calvin Horn Publishers, 1973. x, 112 p. Illus.

Photographs and extensive narratives describing the houses, their histories, their builders, and their occupants.

516   National League of American Pen Women. Birmingham Branch. HIS-
TORIC HOMES OF ALABAMA AND THEIR TRADITIONS. Birmingham,
Ala.: Birmingham Publishing Co., 1935. xiii, 314 p. Illus.

The histories, families, and associations of fifty-six distinguished
Alabama homes described in separate essays by as many Alabama
Pen Women.

517   National Society of the Colonial Dames of America. Connecticut.
"Connecticut Houses: A List of Manuscript Histories of Connecticut
Houses." BULLETIN OF THE CONNECTICUT STATE LIBRARY, HARTFORD,
No. 17. Hartford: 1942. 47 p. Mimeographed.

Compiled by the Historic Buildings Committee of the Connecticut Society, Colonial Dames of America. Comprises a complete list of the 904 manuscript histories of early Connecticut
houses which had thus far been compiled and permanently
deposited in the Connecticut State Library by the committee,
all histories written and illustrated on special forms prepared
by the committee for this purpose. Arranged by town, giving
the name of the house, the names of the original owner and
the present owner, and the approximate date.

518   _____. OLD HOUSES OF CONNECTICUT: FROM MATERIAL COL-
LECTED BY THE COMMITTEE ON OLD HOUSES OF THE CONNECTI-
CUT SOCIETY OF THE COLONIAL DAMES OF AMERICA. Edited by
Bertha Chadwick Trowbridge. New Haven: Yale University Press,
1923. xxvii, 519 p.

A survey of sixty-four houses which grew out of the work of
a committee appointed by the Connecticut Society in 1900
for the purpose of preserving the records of the old colonial
houses of the state. A document to the history of historic
preservation in the United States and to the history of historic architecture surveying.

519   Richey, Elinor. REMAIN TO BE SEEN: HISTORIC CALIFORNIA HOUSES
OPEN TO THE PUBLIC. Berkeley: Howell-North Books, 1973. 180 p.
Illus., bibliog.

Eighteen major descriptions of historic residences, followed by
thumbnail sketches and visitor information for eighty-two more.

520 Rolleston, Sara Emerson. HISTORIC HOUSES AND INTERIORS IN SOUTHERN CONNECTICUT. New York: Hastings House, 1976. 208 p. Illus.

> Twenty-six houses stretching along the northern coast of Long Island Sound from Greenwich to Stonington. Some text, but predominantly photographs of interiors, furnishings, and artifacts, recording the domestic arts of coastal Connecticut from 1639 to 1919.

521 Zook, Nicholas. HOUSES OF NEW YORK OPEN TO THE PUBLIC. Barre, Mass.: Barre Publishers, 1969. 143 p. Illus.

> From New York City, to Long Island, to the Hudson, and beyond, a descriptive guide to the houses of New York state open to the public. In the narrative text, gives extended accounts of the lives of owners and the construction of houses--their architecture, their furnishings, and their histories. Followed by a listing of the properties, arranged alphabetically by location, with practical visitor information.

INDIVIDUAL HISTORIC HOUSES

522 Beale, Marie. DECATUR HOUSE AND ITS INHABITANTS. Washington, D.C.: National Trust for Historic Preservation, 1954. 156 p. Illus., bibliog.

> By Mrs. Truxton Beale, the last occupant of the Washington, D.C., mansion designed by Benjamin H. Latrobe, and the person who restored the house's facade to the original Latrobe design before donating the house to the National Trust. Recounts the mansion's long line of distinguished residents and visitors. (See entry 525.)

523 Blackburn, Roderic H. CHERRY HILL: THE HISTORY AND COLLECTIONS OF A VAN RENSSELAER FAMILY. Albany, N.Y.: Historic Cherry Hill, 1976. viii, 176 p. Illus., bibliog.

> Cherry Hill, overlooking the Hudson River just south of Albany, is a significant landmark in American cultural history, being one of the few eighteenth-century houses which have survived to the present day in the same family with a large portion of the possessions intact. It became a museum in 1963, established as a memorial to the Van Rensselaer family by its last owner, a fifth-generation descendant of its builder. This book is about the Van Rensselaer family, its home, and its possessions.

524   Bynum, William, comp. DRAYTON HALL: AN ANNOTATED BIBLIOG-
       RAPHY. Foreword by Dennis T. Lawson. Research on Historic Properties
       Occasional Papers, no. 2. Washington, D.C.: Preservation Press, 1978.
       vii, 67 p. Illus., paper.

       Concerns Drayton Hall, near Charleston, South Carolina, a
       recently acquired major property of the National Trust for
       Historic Preservation. Comprises one step in the Trust's re-
       search of the property. Has two major divisions: (1) "Mate-
       rials Having a Direct Reference to Drayton Hall or the Dray-
       ton Family" and (2) "Background Material." Includes books,
       magazines, journals, newspapers, and manuscripts.

525   National Trust for Historic Preservation. DECATUR HOUSE. Helen
       Duprey Bullock, sr.ed. Terry B. Morton, ed. Washington, D.C.:
       1968. 104 p. Illus.

       First published in HISTORIC PRESERVATION, volume 19, num-
       ber 3-4, July-December 1967. Presents various authors con-
       tributing chapters dealing with the architecture, the furnish-
       ings, and the personalities associated with this historic Wash-
       ington, D.C., house, owned and maintained as a historic
       house museum by the National Trust. In appendixes, deals
       with inventories, auction sale records, and estate appraisals.
       (See entry 522.)

526   Whitehill, William L. THE HERITAGE OF LONGWOOD. Jackson:
       University Press of Mississippi, 1975. ix, 110 p. Illus., bibliog.,
       paper.

       Reports that the octagonal Longwood Villa, near Natchez,
       Mississippi, inspired by Samuel Sloan's proposal for an "orien-
       tal villa" in his 1852 book, THE MODEL ARCHITECT, was
       under construction when one day in April 1861 work was
       abruptly halted. Explains that, with Civil War rolling over
       the South, the workmen dropped their tools to return to their
       homes, North and South, to rally to the cause; although work
       was later resumed, the house was never completed and stands
       today, with the paraphernalia of construction, as a shell, a
       wonderful example of a nineteenth-century architectural folly,
       and a frozen moment in time.

527   Wilshin, Francis. SAGAMORE HILL AND THE ROOSEVELT FAMILY.
       Historic Resource Study, Sagamore Hill National Historic Site. Denver:
       National Park Service, October 1972. ii, 149 p.

       Intimate glimpses of family life at Sagamore Hill, Oyster Bay,
       New York, the home of Theodore Roosevelt before, during,
       and after his presidency, are based on diaries, letters, deeds,
       newspaper accounts, and published works.

MUSEUM VILLAGES AND PRESERVED VILLAGES

528 Chamberlain, Samuel, and Flynt, Henry N. HISTORIC DEERFIELD:
HOUSES AND INTERIORS. New York: Hastings House, 1972. 188 p.
Chiefly illus.

Presents Samuel Chamberlain's photographs recording the buildings and artifacts of Old Deerfield, Massachusetts, one of the
earliest preserved and best preserved villages in the United
States. Photographs accompanied by extensive captions and
occasional additional text.

529 Gschwend, Max. BALLENBERG SCHWEIZERISCHES FREILICHTMUSEUM
FÜR LÄNDLICHE BAU- UND WOHNKULTUR: FÜHRER DURCH DAS
SCHWEIZERISCHE FREILICHTMUSEUM [Ballenberg Swiss open-air museum
of rural dwellings and life-styles: guide through the Swiss open-air
museum]. Schriften des Schweizerischen Freilichtmuseums Ballenberg
no. 1 [Publications of the Ballenberg Swiss open-air museum no. 1].
Brienz: Schweizerisches Freilichtmuseum Ballenberg, 1978. 100 p.
Illus.

Set in a 125-acre park near Brienz, the open-air museum at
Ballenberg will present a microcosm of Switzerland's rural
heritage. The guide describes the buildings accessible to the
public at the time of the museum's opening in May 1978.
Buildings are grouped primarily by regions within the Swiss
Cantons, but additional buildings and demonstrations are related to rural life in general. Among these are a charcoal
maker's hut and a demonstration of wood charring. The guide
is illustrated by photographs, by plan and section drawings,
and by a map of the park.

530 Henry Ford Museum Staff. GREENFIELD VILLAGE AND THE HENRY
FORD MUSEUM. New York: Crown Publishers, 1972. 247 p. Illus.

Reports that Greenfield Village presents a broad panorama of
American life from early settlers' cabins to the factory buildings of the Industrial Revolution. Indicates that the Henry
Ford Museum sharpens the focus upon that way of life by
presenting in chronological sequence the artifacts, tools, and
machinery used by it. The Village and the Museum, in
Dearborn, Michigan, described and illustrated in this collection of essays and photographs.

531 "The Restoration of Colonial Williamsburg in Virginia." ARCHITECTURAL
RECORD 78 (December 1935): 356-458.

An entire issue of the periodical, devoted to an authoritative
presentation of the restoration of Colonial Williamsburg. In-

cludes a sixty-page portfolio of photographs and short essays
by Fiske Kimball, William Graves Perry, Arthur A. Shurcliff,
and Mrs. Susan Higginson Nash.

532 SELECTED LIVING HISTORICAL FARMS, VILLAGES AND AGRICULTURAL
MUSEUMS IN THE UNITED STATES AND CANADA. Washington, D.C.:
Association for Living Historical Farms and Agricultural Museums, n. d.
63 p. Illus., paper.

Describes thirty-two farms and museums, from Massachusetts to
Hawaii. Gives visitor information, travel directions, and
addresses and telephone numbers for further information.

533 Whiffen, Marcus. THE EIGHTEENTH-CENTURY HOUSES OF WILLIAMS-
BURG: A STUDY OF ARCHITECTURE AND BUILDING IN THE COLO-
NIAL CAPITAL OF VIRGINIA. Williamsburg Architectural Studies,
vol. 2. Williamsburg: Colonial Williamsburg (distributed by Holt,
Rinehart, and Winston, New York), 1960. xx, 223 p. Illus.

In the first part, deals with building materials, building crafts
and craftsmen, craftmen's tools and books, general design of
Williamsburg houses, and construction and detail of Williamsburg houses. In the second part, discusses the houses one by
one, and illustrates them with photographs, plans, and elevations.

534 _____. THE PUBLIC BUILDINGS OF WILLIAMSBURG: COLONIAL
CAPITAL OF VIRGINIA. Williamsburg Architectural Studies, vol. I.
Williamsburg: Colonial Williamsburg, 1958. xvi, 269 p. Illus.,
bibliog.

A book about the buildings as they existed in the eighteenth
century, not a description of them as restored or reconstructed
in the twentieth. Tells how and why and through whom these
buildings came to be, relates them to the architecture of contemporary England, and shows how they influenced the architecture of the rest of Virginia.

535 Zook, Nicholas. MUSEUM VILLAGES, U.S.A. Barre, Mass.:
Barre Publishers, 1971. 136 p. Illus.

A profusely illustrated guide to more than 120 important museum
complexes in forty-two states. Presents villages as diverse as
Williamsburg, Virginia, and the Kuana Pueblo, New Mexico,
grouped by period and type. Includes a chapter on walking
tours in various historic districts and a directory of museum
villages arranged by state.

INTERPRETATION: THEORY AND PRACTICE

536   Alderson, William T., and Low, Shirley Payne. INTERPRETATION OF HISTORIC SITES. Nashville: American Association for State and Local History, 1976. 189 p. Illus., bibliographic essay, paper.

        Defines interpretation as "an attempt to create understanding." Discusses objectives for the interpretation of documentary sites, representative sites, and aesthetic sites. Covers such aspects as interpreting for school tours, the selection and training of interpreters, and the role of the interpreter with regard to security. Presents a case study in the preservation and interpretation of historic house. In an essay on suggested reading, a lead to the sparce literature of this field, includes mention of leaflets and other publications of the American Association for State and Local History.

537   Earle, Alice Morse. HOME LIFE IN COLONIAL DAYS. 1898. Reprint. Stockbridge, Mass.: Berkshire Traveller Press, 1974. 470 p. Illus., paper.

        A turn-of-the-century account describing daily home life; food and drink; making of cloth; travel, transportation, and taverns; Sunday in the colonies; flower gardens; and more.

538   _____. STAGE-COACH & TAVERN DAYS. 1900. Reprint. New York: Dover Publications, 1969. xvi, 449 p. Illus.

        Vehicles, paths and roads, inns, taverns, inn signs, food and drink--the traveler's life described.

539   Killan, Gerald. "Preserving Ontario's Heritage: A History of the Ontario Historical Society." Ph.D. dissertation, McMaster University, 1973. (DISSERTATION ABSTRACTS INTERNATIONAL, Vol. 35-A, Part 8, p. 5305-- History, Modern.)

        Seeks to relate the previously untold history of the Ontario Historical Society, from its earliest precursors in the mid-nineteenth century to the present time. Describes its programs to record, interpret, publicize, and preserve the heritage of this Canadian Province and its efforts to coordinate and encourage the work of local historical associations and museums. Illustrates how the society established itself as an educational and cultural force, and examines in detail its valuable role in historic preservation, a subject which the author considers to be largely ignored by historians.

540   Lynch, Kevin. WHAT TIME IS THIS PLACE? Cambridge: M.I.T. Press, 1972. viii, 277 p. Illus., bibliog.

A philosophical and speculative work which "deals with the evidence of time which is embodied in the physical world, how these signals fit (or fail to fit) our internal experience, and how that inside-to-outside relationship might become a life-enhancing one." Includes discussion ranging from historical preservation to the forms of transition, futurism, time signals, the aesthetics of time, biological rhythm, time perception, disaster, renewal, and revolution. Considers communities for living temporarily in different time zones.

541   Metropolitan Toronto and Region Conservation Authority. CONSERVA-
TION. Woodbridge, Ontario: 1967. 57 p. Illus., paper.

A decennial report of the authority's work, including an educational program at Black Creek Pioneer Village, where a log house and workshop have been built to accommodate a pioneer craft program in which students can participate in a variety of activities, including spinning, carding, candle making, and blacksmithing. Reports that the stress of this program is on man's dependence on his environment in nineteenth-century pioneer days.

542   Moore, George, et al. A REPORT: IOLANI PALACE RESTORATION
PROJECT. Honolulu: Friends of Iolani Palace, 1970. 214 p. Illus.,
paper.

Reports that the Iolani Palace, residence of the former monarchs of the Hawaiian Islands, is of major historic importance to the history of the state of Hawaii and to the United States. Prepared as a step toward the preservation, restoration, development, and operation of the palace as a unique "Living Restoration" dedicated to the public appreciation and contextual understanding of the latter days of the Hawaiian monarchy.

543   National Society of the Colonial Dames of America. Connecticut.
OLD INNS OF CONNECTICUT. Edited by Marian Dickinson Terry
from material collected by the Committee on Historic Buildings, National Society of the Colonial Dames of America in the State of Connecticut.
Hartford: Prospect Press, 1937. 253 p. Illus., bibliog.

Organized by region and/or road, documents the architecture and the daily life of old Connecticut inns and taverns. Descriptions: photographs of interiors, exteriors, and furnishings; drawings; reproductions of advertising broadsides; tickets to balls and assemblies; and a section on old inn signs.

544   Simmons, Terry Donald. "A Feasibility Study of the Recreation
and Tourism Potential of a Restored Historic Railway from Kearney
to Fort Kearney State Historical Park." Ph.D. dissertation, University of Utah, 1976. 168 p. (DISSERTATION ABSTRACTS IN-

TERNATIONAL, Vol. 37-A, Part 6, p. 3899--Recreation.)

Prepared to determine the feasibility of developing recreation and tourism attractions in conjunction with the restoration of a historic railway from Kearney to Fort Kearney State Historical Park in south central Nebraska. Determined the types of recreation and tourism attractions having the greatest potential for development primarily by interviewing knowledgeable persons in the Kearney area and state officials. Concludes that the restored railway should be developed to include the operation of a narrow-gauge steam train, a restored depot facility at Kearney, a small wildlife refuge, a staged Indian raid, and a Conestoga wagon ride; the proposed operation complementing the surrounding tourist accommodations and public recreation area as well as the other historical attractions in the vicinity.

545 Stotz, Charles Morse. POINT OF EMPIRE: CONFLICT AT THE FORKS OF THE OHIO. Pittsburgh: Historical Society of Western Pennsylvania, 1970. xv, 104 p. Illus., bibliog.; paper.

Reports that Point State Park, Pittsburgh, at the confluence of the Allegheny and the Monongahela Rivers, is a national historic landmark of the first order. Prepared by the architect and developer of the park, its reconstructions, and its museum. Presents a concise history of Pittsburgh's first half century, and demonstrates how the park and the Fort Pitt Museum serve to interpret that history.

546 Strong, Roy. RECREATING THE PAST: BRITISH HISTORY AND THE VICTORIAN PAINTER. London: Thames and Hudson; New York: Pierpont Morgan Library, 1978. 176 p. Illus.

Based on the author's 1974 Wall Lectures at the Pierpont Morgan Library. Scenes of daily life, along with representations of major historical events, as seen through Victorian British eyes. In an appendix, lists subjects from British history from the ancient Britons to the outbreak of the Napoleonic Wars exhibited at the Royal Academy, 1769-1904.

547 Tilden, Freeman. INTERPRETING OUR HERITAGE. Rev. ed. Chapel Hill: University of North Carolina Press, 1967. xviii, 120 p. Illus., paper.

Essentially conceived of as a manual for U.S. Park Service personnel. Concerned with interpretation in museums, parks, and historic sites. States that the chief aim of interpretation is not instruction, but provocation; and defines it, in this context, as "An educational activity which aims to reveal meanings and relationships through the use of original objects, by first hand experience, and by illustrative media, rather

than simply to communicate factual information." Presents
principles and guidelines for effective interpretation.

548   Weitzman, David. UNDERFOOT: AN EVERYDAY GUIDE TO EX-
       PLORING THE AMERICAN PAST. New York: Charles Scribner's Sons,
       1976. 192 p. Illus., bibliog.

       A guide to exploring and preserving the past on a personal
       level--such as one's family and one's town--through tape re-
       cording oral history; photography; inspection of graveyards,
       artifacts, buildings, and written records. Includes a chapter
       on historic buildings.

549   Williams, Hermann Warner, Jr. MIRROR TO THE AMERICAN PAST:
       A SURVEY OF AMERICAN GENRE PAINTING: 1750-1900. Greenwich,
       Conn.: New York Graphic Society, 1973. 248 p. Illus., bibliog.

       American life--urban and rural, simple and formal--depicted
       in a variety of costumes, settings, occupations, and attitudes.

MUSEUM ADMINISTRATION

550   Coleman, Laurence Vail. HISTORIC HOUSE MUSEUMS. Washington,
       D.C.: American Association of Museums, 1933. xii, 187 p. Illus.,
       bibliog.

       By the then director of the American Association of Museums.
       In the first chapter, presents a short history of American houses,
       with examples drawn from among those houses already dedicated
       to museum use. Remainder of the book constitutes a manual
       for people concerned with establishing or administering historic
       house museums. Explores the prospect of "museum resorts."
       In a directory, arranged by state, briefly describes four hund-
       red historic house museums.

551   Guldbeck, Per E. THE CARE OF HISTORICAL COLLECTIONS: A
       CONSERVATION HANDBOOK FOR THE NONSPECIALIST. Nashville:
       American Association for State and Local History, 1972. xvii, 160 p.
       Paper.

       In part I, "The Health and Safety of Collections," covers
       storage, security, fire protection, environment, and packing
       objects for shipment. In part II, "Preliminaries to Conserva-
       tion," treats of documentation of the artifact and the organi-
       zation and use of the workshop. In part III, "First Aid for
       Artifacts," covers paper, wood, leather, metals, textiles,
       ceramics, glass, bone, and stone, with lists of suggested
       reading following each category.

552   Lewis, Ralph H.   MANUAL FOR MUSEUMS.   Washington, D.C.:
      National Park Service, U.S. Department of the Interior, 1976.   xiii,
      412 p.   Illus., bibliog., paper.

      Based on the author's experience as a museum administrator
      and curator with many years of service in the National Park
      Service.   Discusses in detail acquisitions, care and conserva-
      tion, record keeping, interpretation, and exhibition.   In
      addition to the bibliographies at the end of such subsection,
      includes an appendix: A Bibliography of Park and Country-
      side Museums."

553   National Fire Protection Association.   Committee on Libraries, Museums,
      and Historic Buildings.   PROTECTING OUR HERITAGE: A DISCOURSE
      ON FIRE PROTECTION AND PREVENTION IN HISTORIC BUILDINGS
      AND LANDMARKS.   Edited by Joseph F. Jenkins.   2d ed.   Boston:
      1970.   v, 39 p.   Illus., paper.

      Published with the assistance of the American Association for
      State and Local History.   Offers practical advice on every
      level for the prevention of fire and the protection of build-
      ings, objects, personnel, and visitors.   Discusses the specific
      needs of older buildings subjected to wear and tear and visi-
      tation for which they were never intended.

554   Reibel, Daniel B.   REGISTRATION METHODS FOR THE SMALL MUSEUM.
      A Guide for Historical Collections.   Nashville: American Association
      for State and Local History, 1978.   160 p.   Illus., bibliog. note, paper.

      A practical manual of instruction for the acquisition, accession-
      ing, cataloging, and documentation of museum objects.   How
      to run a registry without a registrar.

Chapter 10

RELATED DISCIPLINES AND

SPECIALIZED PRESERVATION AREAS

In recent years, there have developed various specialized fields of archaeology whose areas of concern are closely related to those of historic preservation or whose practice can be put to the service of historic preservation. A sampling of their literatures is listed in this chapter. There has also been a proliferation of organizations and publications centering on specialized areas of early life, including farming, industry, and transportation. Publications related to these special areas are also listed in this chapter.

ANTHROPOLOGY

555   King, Thomas F.; Hickman, Patricia Parker; and Berg, Gary. ANTHRO-
       POLOGY IN HISTORIC PRESERVATION: CARING FOR CULTURE'S
       CLUTTER. Studies in Archeology. New York, San Francisco, London:
       Academic Press, 1977. xi, 344 p. Maps, bibliog.

       Argues for the centrality of basic anthropological thinking to
       historic preservation practice, outlines how historic preservation
       works and can be as an influence on government decision mak-
       ing, and suggests ways in which both archaeologists and socio-
       cultural anthropologists can work effectively within the his-
       toric preservation system. Outlines the history and current
       practice of historic preservation in the United States, and pro-
       vides the texts of major statutes, procedures, and associated
       memoranda, from the Antiquities Act of 1906 onward.

HISTORIC ARCHAEOLOGY

556   Deetz, James. IN SMALL THINGS FORGOTTEN: THE ARCHEOLOGY
       OF EARLY AMERICAN LIFE. Drawings by Charles Cann. Garden City,
       N.Y.: Anchor Press/Doubleday, 1977. 184 p. Illus.

Traces the development of the Anglo-American tradition in the years following 1620 by examining the "small things forgotten"--the artifacts of daily life left behind by the early Americans. Takes a special look at early black American culture through the excavation of a tiny community of freed slaves in Massachusetts, revealing the persistence of African culture in the New World.

557 _____. INVITATION TO ARCHAEOLOGY. Illustrations by Eric C. Engstrom. Garden City, N.Y.: The Natural History Press, for the American Museum of Natural History, 1967. x, 150 p. Illus. Bibliog.

An introduction to archaeology, describing its purpose and methods. The specific examples and illustrations used are primarily historical.

558 Dymond, D.P. ARCHAEOLOGY AND HISTORY: A PLEA FOR RECONCILIATION. London: Thames and Hudson, 1974. 192 p. Bibliog.

Discusses the archaeologist's method of interpreting physical evidence and the historian's method of interpreting verbal evidence, and the relationship between the two. Describes traditional concerns and achievements of both disciplines and proposes future opportunities for both. Appeals for a coordination of the physical and the documentary as a basis for study.

559 Hanson, Lee, and Hsu, Dick Ping. CASEMATES AND CANNONBALLS: ARCHEOLOGICAL INVESTIGATIONS AT FORT STANWIX, ROME, NEW YORK. Publications in Archeology, no. 14. Washington, D.C.: National Park Service, 1975. xii, 177 p. Illus., bibliog., paper.

Fort Stanwix played a key role in the American Revolution, serving as a plug to one of the two main invasion routes between Canada and the American colonies. Therefore, with a view toward the bicentennial of that event, the National Park Service began archeological investigations in July 1970, as a step toward its reconstruction. This report of those investigations is a companion publication to FORT STANWIX: HISTORY, HISTORIC FURNISHING, AND HISTORIC STRUCTURE REPORTS (see entry 172), published by the Park Service in the following year.

560 Hulan, Richard, and Lawrence, Stephen S. "A Guide to the Reading and Study of Historic Site Archaeology." Museum Brief, no. 5. Columbia: Museum of Anthropology, University of Missouri-Columbia, 1970. 127 p. Mimeographed.

A bibliography prepared for the Conference on Historic Site Archaeology. Begins each chapter with a bibliographic essay. Bulk of the listings selected primarily from materials relating

to the southeastern region of the United States. Includes
chapters dealing with: "General Historic Site Archaeology,"
"Techniques and Procedures," "Historic Sites," "Architecture,"
"Specific Materials," and "Specific Classes of Artifacts."

561   Robbins, Maurice, and Irving, Mary B. THE AMATEUR ARCHAEOLO-
       GISTS' HANDBOOK. 2d ed. New York: Thomas Y. Crowell Co.,
       1973. xiv, 288 p. Illus., glossary, bibliog.

       A revised edition, designed to keep amateur archaeologists
       abreast of the latest developments in the field, includes a new
       chapter, "Historical Archaeology." In addition to the theory
       and methodology of archaeology, includes directory information
       related to archaeological sites open to the public, archaeolog-
       ical societies and related organizations, archaeological museums
       and special collections, and antiquities laws.

562   South, Stanley. METHOD AND THEORY IN HISTORICAL ARCHEOL-
       OGY. Studies in Archeology. New York, San Francisco, London:
       Academic Press, 1977. xxiii, 345 p. Illus., bibliog.

       Theoretical foundations, methodology, quantitative analysis,
       and pattern recognition. Not for the lay person.

563   _____, ed. RESEARCH STRATEGIES IN HISTORICAL ARCHEOLOGY.
       Studies in Archeology. New York, San Francisco, London: Academic
       Press, 1977. xxviii, 345 p.

       Among the twelve chapters are "Artifacts and Status Differ-
       ences--A Comparison of Ceramics from Planter, Overseer, and
       Slave Sites on an Antebellum Plantation" by John Solomon
       Otto, and "Idiosyncratic Behavior in the Manufacture of Hand-
       wrought Nails" by Ronald C. Carlisle and Joel Gunn.

564   Wilson, David. THE NEW ARCHAEOLOGY. New York: Alfred A.
       Knopf, 1975. 349, xvi p. Bibliography.

       Describes the methods of an archaeology that applies computers,
       chemical analysis, and plant genetics to the data revealed by
       digging, in an attempt to apply the quantitative methods of
       the natural sciences to the science of archaeology, ". . .
       not only in obtaining answers, but also in asking questions;
       not only in assembling data for the archaeological record but
       also in deciding what data to assemble."

INDUSTRIAL ARCHAEOLOGY

565   Booth, Geoffrey. INDUSTRIAL ARCHAEOLOGY. Wayland Regional
       Studies: The Midlands. London: Wayland Publishers, 1973. 96 p.
       Illus., glossary, bibliog.

An archaeological guide to the Midlands, the cradle of the Industrial Revolution, giving background and suggesting places to visit in connection with coal, copper, iron, and lead; mining, drainage, smelting, nail making, chain making, needles and fishhooks, etc.; the gun trade, the toy trade, and factory production; textiles, leather, hosiery, fashions, lace, carpets, and footwear; silk, cotton, worsted, and flax; pottery and glass; food and brewing; and the town houses and country houses of the manufacturers.

566   Bracegirdle, Brian, ed. THE ARCHAEOLOGY OF THE INDUSTRIAL REVOLUTION. London: Heinemann, 1973; Rutherford, N.J.: Fairleigh Dickinson University Press, 1974. 207 p. Illus., bibliog.

Includes chapters on early industrial structures in Britain: "An Introduction to Industrial Archaeology" by Brian Bracegirdle, "Inland Waterways" by L.T.C. Rolt, "Railways" by Charles E. Lee, "Other Means of Communication" by A. Ridley, "Natural Sources of Power" by Rex Wailes, "Power from Steam" by Neil Cossons, "Electric Power" by Brian Bowers, "Coal and Other Fuels" by Will Slatcher and Brian Bracegirdle, "Iron and Steel" by W.K.V. Gale, and "Building for Industry" by Jennifer Tann. Concludes chapters with brief bibliographies. Fully illustrated with drawings in black and white and in color.

567   INDUSTRIAL ARCHAEOLOGISTS' GUIDE. Newton Abbot, Engl.: David & Charles, 1969-70. 128 p. Illus., bibliog., paper.

The introduction to the first issue notes, "The GUIDE will be revised at regular intervals . . ." Contents of the first issue include: "The National Record of Industrial Monuments," "Scientific and Technological Museums," "Museums in Great Britain with Science and Technology Collections," "On-Site Preservation," "Photography and Industrial Archaeology," "Local Societies Actively Concerned with Industrial Archaeology," and "Local Journals and Newsletters."

568   Pannell, J.P.M. THE TECHNIQUES OF INDUSTRIAL ARCHAEOLOGY. Edited by J. Kenneth Major. 2d ed. Newton Abbot, Engl.: David & Charles, 1974. 200 p. Illus., bibliog.

Addresses the basic needs and methodology of the beginner industrial archaeologist. Includes such chapters as: "Written, Printed and Verbal Sources," "Maps, Plans, and Pictures," "Surveying," "Measuring up Machines and Structures," "Keeping a Record," "Scope of Industrial Archaeology." In the final chapter, lists museums in Britain, under the following headings: "Aeroplanes and Aeronautics," "Agriculture and Rural Crafts," "Company Museums," "Engineering," "Folk Museums," "Industrial," "Metal Working," "Mining," "Rail-

ways," "Shipping," "Steam Power," "Textiles," "Transport,"
and "Watermills and Windmills."

569   Raistrick, Arthur. INDUSTRIAL ARCHAEOLOGY: AN HISTORICAL
       SURVEY. London: Eyre Methuen, 1972. xiii, 314 p. Illus., bibliog.

       Sixteen chapters in three parts: "The Materials and Field
       Evidence of Industrial Archaeology," "A View of Industrial
       Archaeology in Britain," and "The Place of Museums in In-
       dustrial Archaeology." In the final chapter, discusses pres-
       ervation, restoration, and recording.

570   Sande, Theodore Anton. INDUSTRIAL ARCHAEOLOGY: A NEW LOOK
       AT THE AMERICAN HERITAGE. Brattleboro, Vt.: Stephen Greene
       Press, 1976. Reprint. Middlesex, Engl., and New York: Penguin
       Books, 1978. vii, 152 p. Illus., bibliographical essay, paper.

       Intended as an introduction to American industrial archeology.
       Illustrates (with photographs, drawings, maps, and old engrav-
       ings) sites related to five categories of industrial activity:
       exploiting mineral resources, developing agricultural resources,
       producing energy, manufacturing,and transportation. Lists
       selected American industrial sites by state, and illustrates
       HAER (Historic American Engineering Record) inventory form.

571   Vogel, Robert M., ed. A REPORT OF THE MOHAWK-HUDSON AREA
       SURVEY: A SELECTIVE RECORDING SURVEY OF THE INDUSTRIAL
       ARCHEOLOGY OF THE MOHAWK AND HUDSON RIVER VALLEYS
       IN THE VICINITY OF TROY, NEW YORK, JUNE-SEPTEMBER 1969.
       Smithsonian Studies in History and Technology, no. 26. Washington,
       D.C.: Smithsonian Institution Press, 1973. viii, 210 p. Illus.

       The Historic American Engineering Record (HAER) was organized
       in 1969, within the National Park Service, to identify and re-
       cord, by graphic and verbal means, American structures of all
       periods having significance in the history of engineering. The
       Mohawk-Hudson Area Survey was its first undertaking. Co-
       sponsors of the survey with HAER were the Museum of History
       and Technology of the Smithsonian Institution, the American
       Society of Civil Engineers, and the New York State Office
       of Parks and Recreation. The first part of the report describes
       the survey, its rationale, its organization, and the mechanics
       of its conduct. The second part records the fifteen structures
       surveyed, by means of measured drawings, photographs, and
       historical accounts. The accounts are intended, in most cases,
       to be the starting point for further research.

SALVAGE ARCHAEOLOGY

572 Wendorf, Fred. A GUIDE FOR SALVAGE ARCHAEOLOGY. Santa Fe: Museum of New Mexico Press, 1962. 128 p. Bibliog., paper.

Describes salvage archaeology as a last-ditch means to protect cultural and scientific resources from needless destruction. Prepared in connection with an experimental training course in salvage archaeology concerned with river basin, pipeline, and highway projects. Includes brief discussions of the history and legal basis, problems of management, and operating procedures for each type of salvage project.

EARLY INDUSTRY AND EARLY INDUSTRIAL BUILDINGS

573 Reynold, John. WINDMILLS & WATERMILLS. Excursions into Architecture. New York and Washington, D.C.: Praeger Publishers, 1970. 196 p. Illus., glossary, bibliog.

A survey of the uses of water power and wind power in times past, with the buildings and contrivances that made this non-polluting energy use possible.

574 Sharp, Myron B., and Thomas, William B. A GUIDE TO THE OLD STONE BLAST FURNACES IN WESTERN PENNSYLVANIA. Pittsburgh: Historical Society of Western Pennsylvania, 1966. vii, 90 p. Illus., bibliog., paper.

A county-by-county guide. Gives historical and descriptive information as well as advice on reaching the sites and obtaining access.

575 Winter, John. INDUSTRIAL ARCHITECTURE: A SURVEY OF FACTORY BUILDING. London: Studio Vista, 1970. 128 p. Illus., bibliog.

A history of industrial buildings, including chapters on: the milling of corn, water power and textiles, steam power and textile mills, and the factory and the modern movement in architecture.

576 Zimiles, Martha, and Zimiles, Murray. EARLY AMERICAN MILLS. New York: Clarkson N. Potter, 1973. xii, 290 p. Glossary, bibliog.

The selection of buildings included in this survey, which covers New York state and New England, is based on aesthetic considerations. Discusses architectural and technical features. In part I, treats early mills; in part II, textile mills; in part III, miscellaneous industries; and in part IV, preservation.

SHIPS AND SHIPPING

577   Goldenberg, Joseph A. SHIPBUILDING IN COLONIAL AMERICA.
Charlottesville: University Press of Virginia, 1976. xiii, 306 p.
Illus., bibliog.

> A descriptive documentation of maritime building in early
> America, supported by numerous shipping tables. Published
> for the Mariners Museum, Newport News, Virginia.

578   Haas, Irvin. AMERICA'S HISTORIC SHIPS: REPLICAS AND RESTORA-
TIONS. New York: Arco Publishing Co., 1975. 127 p. Illus.

> A guide to historic ships and maritime museums.

579   National Trust for Historic Preservation. WOODEN SHIPBUILDING AND
SMALL CRAFT PRESERVATION. Washington, D.C.: Preservation Press,
1976. 100 p. Illus., bibliog., paper.

> Papers from the Symposium on the American Wooden Shipbuild-
> ing Industry sponsored by the Bath Marine Museum, 30 April -
> 2 May 1976, in Bath, Maine, and from the Second Annual
> Museum Conference on Small Craft sponsored by the Mariners
> Museum, 8-9 May 1976, in Newport News, Virginia. In-
> cludes papers dealing with "Preservation Philosophy," "Archae-
> ology and Historical Research," and "Techniques and Tools for
> Wooden Shipbuilding."

580   Rosebrock, Ellen Fletcher. COUNTING-HOUSE DAYS IN SOUTH
STREET: NEW YORK'S EARLY BRICK SEAPORT BUILDINGS. New York:
South Street Seaport Museum, 1975. 48 p. Illus., bibliog., paper.

> Documents daily life in the seaport mercantile world of
> nineteenth-century New York.

581   _____ . WALKING AROUND IN SOUTH STREET: DISCOVERIES
IN NEW YORK'S OLD SHIPPING DISTRICT. New York: South Street
Seaport Museum, 1974. 62 p. Illus., paper.

> A walking tour guide to the streets, buildings, piers, and ships
> of the South Street Seaport district of lower Manhattan.

582   Waite, John G., et al. A COMPILATION OF HISTORICAL AND
ARCHITECTURAL DATA ON THE NEW YORK STATE MARITIME MUSEUM
BLOCK IN NEW YORK CITY. New York: New York State Historic
Trust, 1972. 83 p. Illus.

> The second printing of a work first issued in 1969. A his-
> torical and architectural survey of Schermerhorn Row, one of
> the last complete rows of high-gabled commercial buildings

from a period when New York was a great sailing port. Reports that the "Row" was designated as a landmark by the New York City Landmarks Preservation Commission in 1968, and was acquired by the South Street Maritime Museum Association for development as the New York State Maritime Museum.

OTHER FORMS OF TRANSPORTATION

583   Auvil, Myrtle. COVERED BRIDGES OF WEST VIRGINIA: PAST AND PRESENT. 2d ed. Parsons, W.Va.: McClain Printing Co., 1973. 159 p. Illus.

Photographs, description, and historical episodes relating to the bridges. A plea for the preservation of those bridges that remain.

584   Bye, Ranulph. THE VANISHING DEPOT. Wynnewood, Pa.: Livingston Publishing Co., 1973. xiii, 113 p. Illus.

Reproduces a portfolio of the author's paintings of rail depots and depot life in Delaware, Maryland, New Jersey, Pennsylvania, New York, Connecticut, Rhode Island, Massachusetts, Vermont, and New Hampshire.

585   Drago, Harry Sinclair. CANAL DAYS IN AMERICA: THE HISTORY AND ROMANCE OF OLD TOWPATHS AND WATERWAYS. New York: Clarkson N. Potter, 1972. 311 p. Illus., bibliog.

Reports that the canal, once an important element in America's transportation system, was made obsolete by the steam locomotive. Presents the tenor of canal life, along with documentation of the various canals and canal systems.

586   Hahn, Thomas F. CHESAPEAKE AND OHIO CANAL: OLD PICTURE ALBUM. Shepherdstown, W.Va.: American Canal and Transportation Center, 1976. 104 p. Illus.

The Canal, since 1972, has been the Chesapeake and Ohio Canal National Historic Park. Illustrates its history, engineering, and architecture, in photographs dating from 1860 to recent times.

FARMS AND RURAL LIFE

587   Arthur, Eric, and Witney, Dudley. THE BARN: A VANISHING LANDMARK IN NORTH AMERICA. A.&W. Visual Library, 1972. 256 p. Bibliog., paper.

A documentation of every manner of barn indigenous to the
North American continent. Includes chapters on the New
World Dutch barn, the New World English barn, the Pennsylvania barn, and the circular and polygonal barn. Illustrates
the theme with photographs and drawings, as well as descriptions of rural life, barn construction, and barn use.

588 Bealer, Alex W., and Ellis, John O. THE LOG CABIN: HOMES OF
THE NORTH AMERICAN WILDERNESS. Barre, Mass.: Barre Publishing,
1978. 191 p. Illus., bibliog., paper.

Photographs by Ellis. Text and drawings by Bealer. In part
1, "The Log Cabin Tradition," discourses on the origins of
the tradition in North America, floor plans, outbuildings and
fences, construction methods, and log cabin living. In part
2, "The Log Cabin Preserved," shows " . . . some of the
best remaining examples of log cabins in the United States
and Canada." In an epilogue, describes the current log cabin
revival.

589 Blake, Verschoyle Benson, and Greenhill, Ralph. RURAL ONTARIO.
Toronto: University of Toronto Press, 1969. viii, 173 p. Illus.

A random survey of landscape and building types in rural
Ontario and country towns of Ontario.

590 Conrat, Maisie, and Conrat, Richard. THE AMERICAN FARM: A
PHOTOGRAPHIC HISTORY. Boston: Houghton Mifflin Co.; San
Francisco: California Historical Society, 1977. 256 p. Illus.

A photographic essay documenting a fast-disappearing way of
American life.

591 Halsted, Byron D. BARNS, SHEDS AND OUTBUILDINGS. 1881. Reprint. Brattleboro, Vt.: Stephen Greene Press, 1977. xii, 240 p.
Illus., bibliog.

The 1881 edition published by Orange Judd, New York, was
titled: BARNS PLANS AND OUTBUILDINGS. Includes
general barns, cattle barns, dairy barns, cattle shelters, sheep
barns and sheds, poultry houses, piggeries, carriage houses,
ice houses, dairy houses, spring houses, smoke houses, dog
kennels, bird houses, root cellars, and others. Includes a
bibliography which is newly added, citing publications from
1941 to 1976.

592 Hindle, Brooke, ed. AMERICA'S WOODEN AGE: ASPECTS OF ITS
EARLY TECHNOLOGY. Tarrytown, N.Y.: Sleepy Hollow Restorations,
1975. vii, 218 p. Illus., bibliog.

Contents: "The Span of the Wooden Age" by Brooke Hindle, "The Forest Society of New England" by Charles F. Carroll, "America's Rise to Woodworking Leadership" by Nathan Rosenberg, "Early Lumbering: A Pictorial Essay" by Charles E. Peterson, "Artisans in Wood: The Mathematical Instrument-Makers" by Silvio A. Bedini, "Colonial Watermills in the Wooden Age" by Charles Howell, and "Waterpower in the Century of the Steam Engine" by Louis C. Hunter.

593   Jordan, Terry G. TEXAS LOG BUILDINGS: A FOLK ARCHITECTURE. Austin and London: University of Texas Press, 1978. 230 p. Illus., glossary, bibliog.

Considers the log cabin's European origins and its diffusion to the New World, as a preliminary to the author's discussion of its position as a regional folk architecture of Texas. Examines construction of floors, roofs, and chimneys; methods of log preparation; the raising of log walls; corner notching (in its several variations); dwelling types and floor plans; and other topics. Provides a list of Texas restoration projects open to the public that include log structures and a list of replicas , or reconstructions of log buildings in Texas.

594   Shurtleff, Harold R[obert]. THE LOG CABIN MYTH: A STUDY OF THE EARLY DWELLINGS OF THE ENGLISH COLONISTS IN NORTH AMERICA. Edited with an introduction by Samuel Eliot Morison. Cambridge, Mass.: Harvard University Press, 1939. Reprint. Gloucester, Mass.: Peter Smith, 1967. xxi, 243 p. Illus.

A study of types of dwellings in the seventeenth-century colonies from Newfoundland to North Carolina, which explodes the popular myth of the log cabin as the house form of early English settlers on the North American continent.

595   Sloane, Eric. AMERICAN BARNS AND COVERED BRIDGES. New York: Wilfred Funk, 1954. 112 p. Illus.

Chapters on barns and bridges are preceded by chapters on the wood from which they were built and the tools with which they were built. Concludes with a state-by-state census of 1,617 covered bridges extant in the United States in the summer of 1954.

596   Weslager, C.A. THE LOG CABIN IN AMERICA: FROM PIONEER DAYS TO THE PRESENT. New Brunswick, N.J.: Rutgers University Press, 1969. xxv, 382 p. Bibliog.

From the Atlantic to the Pacific, including Alaska, examines the log cabin from a sociohistorical perspective, to give the general reader an understanding of the part it played in early

American family life, in the political arena, and in "promoting Americanization and hastening democracy." Presents the
ten chapters and conclusion in three sections: "Log Cabins
on the American Frontier," "Log Cabins in the Original
Colonies," and "Log Cabins in American Politics."

Chapter 11

NATURAL LANDSCAPE

Scenic and open space preservation are concerned with parklands, the natural environment, waterways, residential greenbelts, and rural settings. The interests of these areas of preservation frequently overlap with those of the environmental conservationists. The maintenance, restoration, and recreation of historic gardens and the reproduction of historic botanical specimens is becoming an increasingly important aspect of preservation, as the attempt is made to present historic buildings in their authentic historic settings. The works listed in this chapter reflect these varied concerns.

SCENIC AND OPEN SPACE PRESERVATION

597   Brett, [Hon.] Lionel [Gordon Baliol]. LANDSCAPE IN DISTRESS. London: Architectural Press, 1965. 159 p. Illus.

Covers the southeast region of Britain, chosen because of the effect of its great population growth on the natural scene. Presents detailed survey, recording postwar changes and the present state of the landscape of a typical sample of "green" countryside.

598   Cornish, Vaughan. THE SCENERY OF ENGLAND: A STUDY OF HARMONIOUS GROUPING IN TOWN AND COUNTRY. Foreword by the Earl of Crawford and Balcarres. London: Council for the Preservation of Rural England, 1932. 125 p. Illus., bibliog.

States in the foreword by the Earl of Crawford and Balcarres that the volume "presents us with a sequence and a whole picture gallery of English scenery." Goes on to say that the author's "scientific analysis of the sentiment aroused by the different influences of scenery--visual, temperamental, aesthetic--shows how every phase of Nature can exercise its impact upon the mind." In appendixes, describes the aims and objectives of the Council for the Preservation of Rural England and powers and duties of local authorities, and lists constituent bodies and affiliated bodies of the council.

599   Council for the Preservation of Rural England. Lancashire Branch.
        BUILDING IN LANCASHIRE. Edited by C. Gustave Agate. Foreword
        by the Right Hon. the Earl of Derby. Preston: 1937. 96 p. Illus.,
        bibliog., paper.

        In the chapter on "The Preservation of Old Buildings," states:
        "The principle which underlies the treatment of old buildings
        is commonsense. Like all other things which serve human
        needs they should be preserved, altered, or as a last resort
        destroyed according to whether they fulfil these needs or not.
        When there is a question as to which course is best, it is
        proper to remember that the decision should depend on our
        desire to secure a right development of England, and this
        development is not the making of a new country where no
        old traditions remain, but the building up of a better country
        in which the good things of the past stand as in a great es-
        tate which we should not spoil but improve."

600   Council for the Preservation of Rural England. Sheffield and Peak
        District Committee. Peak District Advisory Panel. HOUSING IN THE
        PEAK DISTRICT. Foreword by E. Guy Dawber. Sheffield: 1934.
        72 p. Illus., paper.

        Alert to the danger of the disfigurement of the beautiful Eng-
        lish countryside, sets forth criteria for planning, siting, design,
        and materials--with emphasis on the smaller house--to encour-
        age harmonious development that preserves the landscape.

601   Dunham, Allison. PRESERVATION OF OPEN SPACE AREAS: A STUDY
        OF THE NON-GOVERNMENTAL ROLE. Welfare Council of Metro-
        politan Chicago Publication, no. 1014. Chicago: The Council, 1966.
        101 p. Paper.

        The result of collaboration between the Midwest Open Land
        Association and the Welfare Council of Metropolitan Chicago.
        Explores all aspects of private initiative in the area of open
        space preservation. Discusses legal, financial, and tax aspects.

602   French and Pickering Creeks Conservation Trust. PROCEEDINGS OF
        THE CONFERENCE ON VOLUNTARY PRESERVATION OF OPEN SPACE.
        Pottstown, Pa.: 1975. viii, 102 p. Illus., paper.

        A conference held in Bucktown, Pennsylvania, on 9 March 1974.
        Includes several presentations concerned with easements: "Ease-
        ments as a Way of Land Preservation," "Easements in the Pres-
        ervation of Historic Sites," "Experiences in the Use of Ease-
        ments," and "Legal and Tax Aspects of Voluntary Easements."

603   National Trust for Historic Preservation. CONFERENCE ON CON-
        SERVING THE HISTORIC AND CULTURAL LANDSCAPE, DENVER,
        COLORADO, MAY 2-3, 1975. Washington, D.C.: Preservation Press,
        n.d. 41 p. Paper.

Selected papers from the conference dealing with: criteria
for defining the historic and cultural landscape, the economics
of open space preservation, protection and enhancement of
historic waterfronts, and applying the natural resources inventory process to the historic and cultural landscape.

604   New York City. City Planning Commission. PRESERVATION OF
NATURAL FEATURES AND SCENIC VIEWS OF NEW YORK CITY.
New York: 1974. 58 p. Illus., paper.

A revised report, modified by the Planning Commission after
public hearings, based upon a report prepared by Clarke and
Rapuano, Inc., and Haines Lundberg and Waehler. A study
concerned with the establishment of "Special Natural Area
Districts" and "Special Scenic View Districts." Describes the
first instance of the former as proposed for a section of Staten
Island, the first of the latter as adopted for Brooklyn Heights
on 24 October 1974. Reports that the "view" to be protected
is: "the panoramic view of the lower Manhattan skyline which
includes such landmarks as the Brooklyn Bridge archway, the
South Street Seaport and the Whitehall Ferry Terminal, and
the vistas of the Statue of Liberty and Governor's Island," as
seen from the Brooklyn Heights Promenade. Explains that the
"natural features" protected relate to topography, ecology,
geology, aquantic features, and the habitation of native flora
and fauna, which are to be protected against development
and/or site alteration. Discusses recently developed conservation techniques in the United States and organizations for the
conservation of natural areas in New York City. Gives texts
of the scenic view zoning and the proposed natural area zoning.

605   Niering, William A. NATURE IN THE METROPOLIS: CONSERVATION
IN THE TRI-STATE NEW YORK METROPOLITAN REGION. New York:
Regional Plan Association, 1960. 64 p. Illus., paper.

Prepared for the Park, Recreation, and Open Space Project of
the New York City metropolitan area in the states of Connecticut, New Jersey, and New York. Suggests practical means
of meeting the growing need for open space for the people of
a twenty-two county region. Reports that the projected ex-
plosion of the region's population makes all the more crucial
the race for open space and the effort to preserve the open
country: shorelines; beaches and dunes; salt marshes; bays
and ponds; and the upland--woodlands, farmlands, and wet-
lands. Describes existing private and public conservation in
the region.

606   Olson, George T. PRESERVATION OF RESERVOIR SITES. Regional
Studies Monograph No. 1. Chapel Hill: Center for Urban and Regional

Studies, Institute for Research in Social Science, University of North Carolina, 1964. 82 p. Illus., bibliog., paper.

Reports that water resources development policy in a situation of extensive and increasing urbanization is a field of research that is as yet greatly unexplored. Breaks ground in an area related to environmental concerns as well as to landscape preservation and preservation planning.

607   Regional Science Research Institute. THE PRESERVATION OF OPEN SPACE IN THE NEW JERSEY PINELANDS. RSRI Discussion Paper Series, no. 73. Philadelphia: 1974. 90 p. Illus., bibliog., paper.

The Pine Barrens is an area located in the heart of megalopolis and in the most urbanized state in the nation, but still maintaining an average population density of only sixteen persons per square mile. A collection of papers, originally presented at the 1973 convention of the Middle States Division, Association of American Geographers, held in Philadelphia, focusing on resolving the problem of an emerging conflict of interest between those who seek to preserve the "wilderness refuge" aspect of the area and those who are interested in its potential for commercial facilities and suburban housing.

608   Roosevelt, Nicholas. CONSERVATION: NOW OR NEVER. New York: Dodd, Mead & Co., 1970. 238 p.

Addresses the problem of saving scenic resources. Reviews the changing concepts of conservation since the early twentieth century. Gives case histories of the forces working for and against conservation, and discusses the sometimes conflicting roles of government agencies. Presents a concept of scenery as a natural resource which is to be enjoyed without being consumed, and describes some successful efforts in the cause of saving natural scenery. Concludes with a chapter on future needs and prospects.

609   Toulan, Nohad Abdellatif. "Public and Private Costs of Open Space Preservation: with Particular Reference to the Philadelphia Metropolitan Area." Ph.D. dissertation, University of Pennsylvania, 1965. 222 p. (DISSERTATION ABSTRACTS INTERNATIONAL, Vol. 27-A, Part 10, p. 3530--Sociology, Regional and City Planning.)

Reports that the preservation of open space in metropolitan areas raises physical, legal, social, and economic questions. Addresses here the economic question, and within that question limits itself to the cost elements. Bases investigation on a natural open space system which is water-oriented and consists of several categories: acquifers, aquifer recharge areas, forests, marshes, flood plains, and steep slopes. Sees limited development as possible in all but the marshes and the flood plains.

610   U.S. National Park Service. PRESERVING A HERITAGE: FINAL RE-
PORT TO THE PRESIDENT AND THE CONGRESS OF THE NATIONAL
PARKS CENTENNIAL COMMISSION, WASHINGTON, D.C. Washing-
ton, D.C.: 1973. xii, 196 p. Illus., bibliog.

> Reports that the establishment of Yellowstone National Park
> in 1872 began a worldwide national park movement. Presents
> the report of the commission founded in honor of the centen-
> nial of that event, describing current national park activity
> at home and abroad, and presenting recommendations and
> guidelines for preservation and use as the dynamic principles
> underlying the National Park System.

611   Vermont. Division of Historic Sites. HISTORIC PRESERVATION
THROUGH LAND USE LEGISLATION. Montpelier: State of Vermont,
Agency of Development and Community Affairs, 1973. 24 leaves,
plus plates and maps. Text of "Vermont Land Use and Development
Act" (16 p.) in pocket. Paper.

> An early report following the U.S. Senate's Federal Land Use
> Policy and Planning Assistance Act of 1972, which was presaged
> by the state of Vermont's passing enabling land use legislation
> in 1969. Reports that a focus in developing a land use pro-
> gram for Vermont was based on the concept that " . . . the
> historic environment and natural environment are inseparable,
> and since historic resource conservation is essential to total
> environmental planning, the historic preservation agency be-
> comes an environmental as well as a cultural agency."

612   Zube, Ervin H., et al., eds. LANDSCAPE ASSESSMENT: VALUES,
PERCEPTIONS AND RESOURCES. Community Development Series, no.
11. Stroudsburg, Pa.: Dowden, Hutchinson & Ross (distributed by
Halsted Press, New York), 1975. xii, 367 p. Illus., bibliog.

> A collection of essays by various authors, of which the most
> relevant to historic preservation are "The Historic American
> Landscape" by John B. Jackson and "Qualitative Landscape
> Values: the Historical Perspective" by Roderick Nash.

HISTORIC GARDENS AND GARDEN HISTORY

613   Anderson, Frank J. AN ILLUSTRATED HISTORY OF THE HERBALS.
New York: Columbia University Press, 1977. xiv, 270 p. Illus.
Glossary, bibliog.

> Illustrated books concerned with plants having medicinal prop-
> erties are traced from the DE MATERIA MEDICA of Dioscorides
> (1st century A.D.) to the RERUM MEDICARUM of Francisco
> Hernandez (16th century A.D.)--from the Greco-Roman world
> to the world of New Spain.

614   Betts, Edwin Morris. THOMAS JEFFERSON'S GARDEN BOOK 1766-
        1824: WITH RELEVANT EXTRACTS FROM HIS OTHER WRITINGS.
        Philadelphia: American Philosophical Society, 1944. xiv, 704 p.
        Illus., bibliog.

        A commentary on the GARDEN BOOK, which is in the pos-
        session of the Massachusetts Historical Society. In appendix
        VII, presents: "Books and Pamphlets on Agriculture, Garden-
        ing, and Botany in the Library of Thomas Jefferson."

615   DUMBARTON OAKS COLLOQUIUM ON THE HISTORY OF LANDSCAPE
        ARCHITECTURE. 4 vols. Vol. 1: THE ITALIAN GARDEN. David R.
        Coffin, ed. Washington, D.C.: 1972. xi, 114 p. Illus.; Vol. 2:
        THE PICTURESQUE GARDEN AND ITS INFLUENCE OUTSIDE THE
        BRITISH ISLES. Nikolaus Pevsner, ed. Washington, D.C.: 1974.
        vii, 121 p. Illus.; Vol. 3: THE FRENCH FORMAL GARDEN.
        Elisabeth B. Macdougall and F. Hamilton Hazlehurst, eds. Washington,
        D.C.: 1974. vi, 87 p. Illus.; Vol. 4: THE ISLAMIC GARDEN.
        Elisabeth B. Macdougall and Richard Ettinghausen, eds. Washington,
        D.C.: 1976. 135 p. xxxv plates. Illus.

        In each volume, contains several scholarly essays on aspects
        of garden history; together they form a corpus of material on
        the primary sources of historical landscape architecture in
        much of the world.

616   Favretti, Rudy J., and De Wolf, Gordon P. COLONIAL GARDENS.
        Barre, Mass.: Barre Publishers, 1972. 163 p. Illus., bibliog.

        Discusses design and location of the colonial garden and the
        creation or restoration of colonial gardens. Gives recommenda-
        tions for research and archaeology. Discusses relevant plant
        materials of all kinds--"before 1700" and "1700 to 1776."

617   Favretti, Rudy J., and Favretti, Joy P[utnam]. FOR EVERY HOUSE A
        GARDEN: A GUIDE FOR REPRODUCING PERIOD GARDENS. Chester,
        Conn.: Pequot Press, 1977. 137 p. Illus., paper.

        Guide for the layperson to reproduce or restore period gardens.
        Includes information on garden structures. Includes chapters on:
        "Farmstead Gardens, 1607-1940," "Gardens of City Merchants
        and Country Gentlemen, 1620-1860," "Gardens of Prosperity,
        1860-1900," "Gardens of Craftsmen and Workmen, 1620-1900,"
        and "Authentic Plants, 1620-1900."

618   _____. LANDSCAPES AND GARDENS FOR HISTORIC BUILDINGS:
        A HANDBOOK FOR REPRODUCING AND CREATING AUTHENTIC
        LANDSCAPE SETTINGS. Nashville: American Association for State
        and Local History, 1978. 202 p. Illus., bibliog., paper.

Reviews American landscape design from the colonial period
to the early twentieth century, including cemeteries and the
settings for public buildings and spaces. Sets forth a procedure for the development of a restoration plan, from the
analysis of site through recording, researching, and documentation, to the development of a philosophy and, ultimately, a
plan of action. Provides an extensive list of authentic plants
for period landscape settings and discusses styles and trends in
their use and availability throughout the various periods. Outlines procedures for maintaining the restored landscape.

619   Fitch, James M., and Rockwell, F.F. TREASURY OF AMERICAN
       GARDENS. New York: Harper & Brothers, 1956. 175 p. Illus.

       A book which presents to the reader a panorama of American
       gardens, old and modern, large and small, which show "how
       gardening in the United States had its beginnings, what shaped
       those beginnings, and the changes that have taken place up
       to the present." Organized primarily by geographical region,
       with an initial section dealing with the earliest American gar-
       dens and a final section dealing with special garden forms.

620   Gothein, Marie Luise. A HISTORY OF GARDEN ART. Edited by
       Walter P. Wright. Translated from the German by Mrs. Archer-Hind.
       New York: E.P. Dutton & Co., 1928. Reprint. New York: Hacker
       Art Books, 1966. Vol. I., xxiv, 459 p.; Vol. II., xv, 486 p. Illus.,
       bibliog.

       A reprint of the 1928 translation of Gothein's classic and
       monumental GESCHICHTE DER GARTENKUNST, first published
       in 1913, with a second edition in 1925. Practically every
       region of the world and every period of history is examined
       in a historical and social context. To the original work
       the editor of the English language version has added two
       supplementary chapters, one on modern English garden art
       and one on American garden art.

621   Hyams, Edward. A HISTORY OF GARDENS AND GARDENING. New
       York and Washington, D.C.: Praeger Publishers, 1971. ix, 345 p.
       Illus., bibliog.

       Profusely illustrated text on gardens and plant materials through-
       out history and geography.

622   International Council on Monuments and Sites. "Proceedings of the
       First International Symposium of the Conservation and Restoration of
       Gardens of Historic Interest. Fountainebleu, France, 13-18. IX. 1971."
       250 p. Mimeographed.

Reports, in French and/or English, ranging from the general
purpose and background of the symposium, to problems specific to various participating countries, to specific major gardens.
Gives closing observations and recommendations, including the
resolve to draw up an initial inventory, country by country,
of all historic gardens in existence.

623   "Whose Time Is This Place: The Emerging Science of Garden Pres-
       ervation." LANDSCAPE ARCHITECTURE 66 (May 1976): entire issue.

       Selected papers from the International Conference on the Pres-
       ervation of Historic Gardens and Landscapes, held in the Dis-
       trict of Columbia on April 16-18, 1975, under the sponsor-
       ship of the American Horticultural Society, Dumbarton Oaks,
       and the National Trust for Historic Preservation. The title
       article, by Grady Clay, is followed by "Pollen as Botanical
       Evidence of the Past" by G.W. Dimbleby, "From Vesuvius'
       Dust: Pompeii Emerges as a City of Gardens and Vineyards"
       by Wilhelmina Jashemski, "Great Garden at Hanover Returns
       to Original Design" by Gerda Gollwitzer, "Sourcebook for
       Plant Documentation" by Gordon P. DeWolf, "Shifting Mean-
       ings in a Swiss Garden Landscape" by H.R. Heyer, "Het Loo--
       The Dutch Treat: English Queen Influences Restoration of
       Netherlands Estate" by J.B. Baron van Asbeck, "Following
       Washington Down the Garden Path" by Robert B. Fisher,
       "Historical Archaeology in Garden Restoration" by Audrey
       Noël Hume, "Record-Keeping for Botanical Gardens" by
       Richard A. Brown, "Fitting Species and Cultivars to the Land-
       scape" by J.C. McDaniel, "Photogrammetry's Use in Fixing
       Scenes" by Perry Borchers, and "Preservation Requires Tact,
       Modesty and Honesty Among Designers" by James Marston
       Fitch.

624   Williams, Dorothy Hunt. HISTORIC VIRGINIA GARDENS: PRES-
       ERVATIONS BY THE GARDEN CLUB OF VIRGINIA. Charlottesville:
       University Press of Virginia, 1975. xvi, 350 p. Illus., bibliog.

       Published for the Garden Club of Virginia. Detailed verbal,
       photographic, and graphic descriptions of twenty-three projects
       undertaken by the club in about a half century. Includes
       gardens representing the full range of American garden design
       before the advent of the industrial age. Reports that, since
       the club's first restoration at Kenmore in 1929, attitudes to-
       ward archaeological research and historic authenticity have
       changed considerably, but, as the author states, "Although
       the methods of preservation have changed . . . the motives
       have remained the same: to save the past for the enlighten-
       ment of the future."

Chapter 12

LOSSES

This chapter, in part a necrology, contains within it books dedicated to the hopeful mission of preventing the future unnecessary damage, decay, demolition, and disappearance of the material evidences of mankind's artistic, cultural, and historic patrimony.

LOST OR ENDANGERED LANDMARKS

625   Amery, Colin, and Cruickshank, Dan. THE RAPE OF BRITAIN. London: Paul Elek, 1975. 192 p. Illus.

A thirty town city-by-city guide to the erosion and destruction of Britain's historic fabric caused by unstopped decay, willful destruction, and development. In a chapter on "How to Stop It," calls attention to the Civic Amenities Act of 1967 and the Town and Country Amenities Act of 1974, and lists organizations and publications helpful for citizen action.

626   Booker, Christopher, and Green, Candida Lycett. GOODBYE LONDON: AN ILLUSTRATED GUIDE TO THREATENED BUILDINGS. London: Fontana/Collins, 1973. 160 p. Illus., paper.

"An area-by-area guide to several hundred redevelopment schemes with pictures of existing buildings threatened. Includes a directory of the chief developers, architects, and planners involved; a brief guide to planning legislation; and some recommendations as to how the citizen can involve himself in what happens."

627   Cornforth, John. COUNTRY HOUSES IN BRITAIN: CAN THEY SURVIVE? An independent report commissioned by the British Tourist Authority and published for them in 1974 by COUNTRY LIFE. 130 p. Paper.

Discusses the uniqueness of the English country house in relation to its counterparts abroad, reviews the private and governmental role in its upkeep and preservation, and considers future needs.

628   Fay, Stephen, and Knightley, Phillip. THE DEATH OF VENICE.
        London: André Deutsch; New York: Praeger Publishers, 1976. 190 p.
        Illus.

        A lively chronicle of the patterns of decay in Venice and of
        the complicated international crusade to save that city since
        the disastrous floods of 1966. Anecdotal, while informative
        and detailed.

629   Greiff, Constance M., ed. LOST AMERICA: FROM THE ATLANTIC
        TO THE MISSISSIPPI. Foreword by James Biddle. Princeton, N.J.:
        Pyne Press, 1971. x, 244 p. Illus.

        Contains photographs, contemporary paintings and drawings,
        and reconstruction drawings displaying the wealth of built
        environment that has been lost because of natural disaster,
        gradual decay, or willful demolition. Not only honors and
        recalls a lost cultural heritage, but also calls attention to
        the increasing number of preservationists and their changing
        role. (See also below.)

630   _____. LOST AMERICA: FROM THE MISSISSIPPI TO THE PACIFIC.
        Foreword by James Biddle. Princeton, N.J.: Pyne Press, 1972. x,
        243 p. Illus.

        The sad saga continues. (See above.)

631   Hobhouse, Hermione. LOST LONDON: A CENTURY OF DEMOLITION
        AND DECAY. London: Macmillan Publishing Co., 1971. 250 p.
        Chiefly illus.

        In the introduction, describes at length the need for historic
        preservation in London--to prevent it from becoming another
        Manhattan, devouring itself, and becoming a city of the very
        rich and the very poor. Highlights this need with a survey
        of lost and threatened structures.

632   Howells, John Mead. LOST EXAMPLES OF COLONIAL ARCHITECTURE:
        BUILDINGS THAT HAVE DISAPPEARED OR BEEN SO ALTERED AS TO
        BE DENATURED. Introduction by Fiske Kimball. New York: W. Helburn,
        1931. Reprint. New York: Dover Publications, 1963. 244 p. Chief-
        ly illus.

        In an introduction by Fiske Kimball, describes the author's
        "seven years of loving labor" in bringing together the photo-
        graphs which constitute this volume. Draws the architecture
        and architectural details illustrated from every class of public
        and private building throughout the eastern seaboard.

633   Lagarde, Pierre de. GUIDE DES CHEFS-D'OEUVRE EN PERIL [Guide
      to endangered masterpieces]. Preface by Wladimir d'Ormesson. Paris:
      Jean-Jacques Pauvert, 1967. xxxii, 266 p. Illus.

      Describes, region by region, the endangered castles, churches,
      convents, villages, mills, archaeological sites, and other
      landmarks of France. Gives names and addresses of various
      national organizations concerned with aspects of preservation,
      with the suggestion that these organizations be enlisted to
      aid in saving the endangered species included in this guide-
      book.

634   _____. GUIDE DES CHEFS-D'OEUVRE EN PERIL: PARIS ET L'ILE-
      DE-FRANCE [Guide to endangered masterpieces: Paris and the Ile-
      de-France]. Paris: Jean-Jacques Pauvert, 1969. 156 p. Illus.

      Covers Paris and the Ile-de-France in this pocket guide to
      endangered architecture.

635   Lowe, David. LOST CHICAGO. Boston: Houghton Mifflin Co., 1975.
      xii, 241 p. Illus.

      In this celebration of the Chicago that was, presents the
      author's hopes that "Perhaps, by showing the splendor which
      has been lost, I might, in some small way, help to preserve
      the splendor not yet departed." Includes extensive text and
      numerous interior and exterior photographs.

636   Morton, Terry B., ed. "I FEEL I SHOULD WARN YOU...": HISTORIC
      PRESERVATION CARTOONS. With an essay by Draper Hill. Washing-
      ton, D.C.: Preservation Press, 1975. xxv, 86 p. Chiefly illus.

      Presents cartoons, almost all of which first appeared in PRES-
      ERVATION NEWS, the monthly newspaper of the National
      Trust for Historic Preservation. Records the eternal struggle
      between preservationist and bulldozer, and comments on this
      situation with all the poignancy, humor, and irony of the
      cartoonist's craft; the earliest example is a woodblock by
      Charles Stanley Reinhart, from HARPER'S WEEKLY of 28 Octo-
      ber 1871, ironically titled, "The March of Modern Improve-
      ment." In part I, gives general preservation cartoons, and
      in part II, gives preservation-related cartoons. In part III,
      shows cartoons addressing specific preservation issues, and in-
      cludes text describing the history of each case illustrated.

637   Robinson, William F. ABANDONED NEW ENGLAND: ITS HIDDEN
      RUINS AND WHERE TO FIND THEM. Boston: New York Graphic
      Society, 1976. xi, 211 p. Illus., bibliog.

      Describes such relics as roads, canals, farms, schools, churches,
      mills, tanneries, springs, resorts, mines, kilns, schooners, rope-

walks, and railroads. In an appendix, lists sites by state
and town, with driving instructions.

638   Silver, Nathan. LOST NEW YORK. Boston: Houghton Mifflin, 1967.
       Reprint. New York: Schocken Books, 1971. xiii, 242 p. Illus.,
       paper.

       An outgrowth of 1964 exhibition at Columbia University
       School of Architecture. Presents photographs and drawings
       from a variety of archival and library sources. A plea for
       preservation, illustrates gems still standing as well as those
       that have disappeared.

639   Strong, Roy, et al. THE DESTRUCTION OF THE COUNTRY HOUSE,
       1875-1975. London: Thames & Hudson, 1974. 192 p. Illus.

       The outgrowth of an exhibition on the theme, held at London's
       Victoria and Albert Museum in 1973, as the museum's con-
       tribution to European Architectural Heritage Year. Includes
       innumerable photographs of vanished houses interspersed with
       essays by a number of contributors on various aspects of the
       country house and historic preservation. Concludes with a
       county-by-county listing of houses destroyed in England, Scot-
       land, and Wales in the past hundred years, with the date of
       destruction when known.

640   Zorzi, Alvise. VENEZIA SCOMPARSA [Vanished Venice]. 2 vols.
       Milan: Electa Editrice, 1972(?). Vol. 1: STORIA DI UNA SECOLARE
       DEGRADAZIONE [History of secular degradation]; Vol. 2: REPERTORIO
       DEGLI EDIFICI VENEZIANI DISTRUTTI, ALTERATI O MANOMESSI
       [Repertory of Venetian buildings destroyed, altered or manhandled].
       Milan: Electa, 1972? 288 p., 367 p. Illus., bibliog.

       In the first volume, gives a chronology of destruction in Venice
       from the beginnings to 1966; in the second volume, a descrip-
       tive and illustrated listing of all manner of destruction and
       spoilation, by category of structure. Includes a chronological
       bibliography, 1486-1971.

PICTORIAL HISTORIES AND GENERAL NOSTALGIA

641   Black, Mary. OLD NEW YORK IN EARLY PHOTOGRAPHS: 1853-
       1901. New York: Dover Publications, 1973. xvi, 228 p. Illus.,
       paper.

       Presents 196 rare photographs from the collection of the New-
       York Historical Society, with descriptive captions, in an album
       prepared by the society's curator of painting and sculpture.
       Explores Manhattan Island in a northward trek from the Battery
       to Spuyten Duyvil.

642 Bush, Graham. OLD LONDON: PHOTOGRAPHED BY HENRY DIXON AND ALFRED & JOHN BOOL FOR THE SOCIETY FOR PHOTOGRAPHING RELICS OF OLD LONDON. London: Academy Editions; New York: St. Martin's Press, 1975. 173 p. Chiefly illus.

Published in the society's centenary year, contains photographs by three nineteenth-century photographers showing London interiors and exteriors--many, unfortunately, carrying demolition dates. Annotations by Graham Bush.

643 d'Iberville-Moreau, Luc. LOST MONTREAL. Toronto: Oxford University Press, 1975. 183 p. Illus.

A record in photograph and text of nineteenth-century Montreal. In the preface, states, " . . . the title and approach of the book imply the loss of a particular environment that was made humane and aesthetically pleasing by its architecture and green spaces. It also implies a loss that goes far beyond the destruction of individual monuments. It is part of our history that we have destroyed and continue to destroy."

644 Gillon, Edmund V., Jr. A NEW ENGLAND TOWN IN EARLY PHOTO-GRAPHS: 149 ILLUSTRATIONS OF SOUTHBRIDGE, MASSACHUSETTS, 1878-1930. Introduction and captions by Arthur J. Kavanagh. New York: Dover Publications, 1976. 170 p. Illus., paper.

Presents Gillon's selection of photographs from four collections augmented by loans from a number of individuals, to provide a remarkable memory of small-town America from the 1870s up into the 1930s. Traces the evolution of Southbridge from a small green town to a bustling factory town, and records the succession of ethnic groups who have peopled the place.

645 Paher, Stanley W. DEATH VALLEY GHOST TOWNS. Las Vegas: Nevada Publications, 1973. 48 p. Illus., bibliog.

Presents nostalgic photographs illustrating descriptions of towns with such colorful names as Borate, Calico, Chloride Cliff, Furnace, Old Stovepipe Well, Scotty's Castle, Skidoo, and Wildrose Spring.

646 Singleton, Esther, ed. HISTORIC LANDMARKS OF AMERICA: AS SEEN AND DESCRIBED BY FAMOUS WRITERS. New York: Dodd, Mead & Co., 1907. xiv, 305 p. Illus.

A collection of forty-two accounts, including Hernando Cortes on Mexico, Washington Irving on The Bermudas, Daniel Webster on Bunker Hill, Lord Cornwallis on Yorktown, John Knox on The Plains of Abraham, and so forth.

647   Sirkis, Nancy. REFLECTIONS OF 1776: THE COLONIES REVISITED.
        Text by Ellwood Parry. A Studio Book. New York: Viking Press,
        1974. 217 p. Illus., bibliog.

        Presents the author's photographs giving a view of "the remnants
        of colonial America as they would have looked in 1776."
        Shows architecture and artifacts in an atmosphere untouched
        by later centuries. Includes three chapters, "New England,"
        "The Middle Colonies," and "Tidewater Towns and Southern
        Plantations." Includes a text by Ellwood Parry complementing
        the primarily visual presentation.

648   Wheeler, Thomas C., ed. A VANISHING AMERICA: THE LIFE AND
        TIMES OF THE SMALL TOWN. New York, Chicago, San Francisco:
        Holt, Rinehart and Winston, 1964. 191 p. Illus.

        Presents twelve authors describing life in twelve regional towns
        from Vermont to Washington, evoking the most minute details
        of a nineteenth-century and early twentieth-century way of
        life that has all but disappeared.

649   Wilson, Everett B. VANISHING AMERICA. New York: A.S. Barnes
        & Co.; London: Thomas Yoseloff, 1961. 187 p. Illus.

        Includes four chapters: "Our Changing Farms," "Our Changing
        Homes," "Our Changing Towns," and "Our Changing Trans-
        portation." Photographs and descriptions of everything from
        haystacks, to washboards, to buttonhooks, to shaving mugs,
        to watch fobs, to peddler wagons, to covered bridges, to
        upper berths and street cars.

650   Younger, William Lee. OLD BROOKLYN IN EARLY PHOTOGRAPHS:
        1865-1929. New York: Dover Publications, 1978. ix, 163 p. Illus.,
        paper.

        Contains 157 prints from the collection of the Long Island
        Historical Society which cover the Waterfront; Williamsburg;
        Downtown Brooklyn and Adjacent Areas; Brooklyn Heights,
        Park Slope, and Other Residential Areas; Flatbush; Southwest
        Brooklyn; Coney Island; and Prospect Park, Greenwood Ceme-
        tary, and Other Areas. A celebration of Brooklyn's urban
        leadership in "the rejuvenation of many of its old neighbor-
        hoods and the subsequent influx of a new generation of city
        dwellers."

THE RAVAGES OF WAR

651   Burr, Nelson R., comp. SAFEGUARDING OUR CULTURAL HERITAGE:
        A BIBLIOGRAPHY ON THE PROTECTION OF MUSEUMS, WORKS OF

ART, MONUMENTS, ARCHIVES AND LIBRARIES IN TIME OF WAR.
Washington, D.C.: U.S. Library of Congress, 1952. 117 p. Paper.

International and multilingual. Provides substantial annotations
to books, pamphlets, articles, and other sources.

652   Howard, R.T. RUINED AND REBUILT: THE STORY OF COVENTRY
       CATHEDRAL 1939-1962. Coventry, Engl.: Council of Coventry Cathed-
       ral, 1962. xii, 132 p. Illus.

       Coventry Cathedral was all but destroyed in an air raid in
       1940. Rebuilt in a modern architectural idiom incorporating
       the ruins of the ancient edifice, and reconsecrated in 1962, it
       provides a dramatic statement of destruction, resurrection, and
       reconciliation. By the Provost of Coventry, 1933-1958. (See
       also entry 657.)

653   Italy. Direzione Generale delle Antichità e Belle Arti. LA RICOSTRU-
       ZIONE DEL PATRIMONIO ARTISTICO ITALIANO [The reconstruction of
       the Italian artistic patrimony]. Rome: Libreria dello Stato, 1950. 221
       p. Illus., paper.

       A postwar report on the restoration of war-damaged monuments,
       the reorganization of museums and galleries, and the restora-
       tion of works of art. Includes a section describing the activ-
       ity of the Istituto Centrale del Restauro.

654   Kent, William. THE LOST TREASURES OF LONDON. London: Phoenix
       House, 1947. x, 150 p. Illus.

       A record of the destruction of London's treasured monuments
       suffered in the German air raids of World War II. In addition
       to the details of loss, also gives historical background and
       descriptions prior to damage.

655   LaFarge, Henry, ed. LOST TREASURES OF EUROPE: 427 PHOTOGRAPHS.
       New York: Pantheon Books, 1946. 39 p., 352 p. of illus.

       From Aachen to Xanten, describes the degree of war damage
       or destruction. Gives photographs showing the monuments in
       the predamage state, with occasional additional photographs
       showing the damaged state.

656   Noblecourt, André. PROTECTION OF CULTURAL PROPERTY IN THE
       EVENT OF ARMED CONFLICT. Museums and Monuments, no. 8.
       Paris: UNESCO, 1958. xix, 346 p. Illus., bibliog., paper.

       Translated from the author's original French text of August
       1956. In part I, discusses "Protection--an International Duty:
       The Hague Convention of 1954." In part II, discusses the

variety of risks to cultural property, including those directly
due to military operations and those due to other natural,
environmental, and man-caused hazards. In part III, comments
on protection and its techniques. In part IV, offers action
plans and documentation regarding organization of protection
on the international and the national level. In part V, deals
with the construction and equipment of museum buildings and
buildings to shelter cultural properties in time of danger.

657   Spence, Basil. PHOENIX AT COVENTRY: THE BUILDING OF A
      CATHEDRAL. Foreword by Cuthbert Coventry, the Bishop of Coventry.
      London: Geoffrey Bles, 1969. xvii, 141 p. Illus.

      The architect's story of the rebuilding of war-destroyed Cov-
      entry Cathedral. (See also entry 652.)

658   Visscher, Charles de. INTERNATIONAL PROTECTION OF WORKS OF
      ART AND HISTORIC MONUMENTS. U.S. Department of State Publi-
      cation No. 3590. Washington, D.C.: U.S. Government Printing Office,
      1949. pp. 821-71.

      Reprinted from DOCUMENTS AND STATE PAPERS, June 1949.
      A collection of essays which first appeared in the REVUE DE
      DROIT INTERNATIONAL ET DE LÉGISLATION. By a professor
      of international law at the University of Louvain and a judge
      on the International Court of Justice. Reviews the history of
      war plundering and postwar disposition of taken cultural proper-
      ties. Part I "Historic Monuments and Works of Art in Time of
      War and in the Treaties of Peace," and part II, "The Protection
      of National Artistic and Historic Possessions; the Need for In-
      ternational Regulation." In an appendix, gives drafts of decla-
      rations and conventions regarding international cooperation in
      the protection of artistic and historic properties.

659   Williams, Sharon A. THE INTERNATIONAL AND NATIONAL PRO-
      TECTION OF MOVABLE CULTURAL PROPERTY: A COMPARATIVE
      STUDY. Dobbs Ferry, N.Y.: Oceana Publications, 1978. 302 p.

      Analysis and comparison of past and current laws for peace-
      time and war. In appendixes, includes the texts of various
      resolutions, rules, regulations, treaties, conventions, and other
      documents.

Chapter 13

PERIODICALS

This chapter lists magazines and journals, newsletters, newspapers, and bulletins that are most relevant to historic preservation. They are divided into two groups: those periodicals that are statewide in coverage and those that are broader in coverage. Further sources of information related to historic preservation can be found in periodicals concerned with Americana, antiques, archeology, architecture, architectural history, art history, arts management, decorative arts, history, landscape architecture, law, and planning. Up-to-date information on periodicals can be gotten from such directories as the AYER DIRECTORY OF PUBLICATIONS, ULRICH'S INTERNATIONAL PERIODICALS DIRECTORY, and the ENCYCLOPEDIA OF ASSOCIATIONS. Information regarding statewide publications can be obtained from the state historic preservation officer in each of the states and territories. Current names and addresses of the officers can be obtained from the National Trust for Historic Preservation and from the Heritage Conservation and Recreation Service of the U.S. Department of the Interior.

GENERAL PUBLICATIONS

660   ADVISORY COUNCIL ON HISTORIC PRESERVATION BRIEFS. Washington, D.C.: Advisory Council on Historic Preservation. Monthly.

661   ADVISORY COUNCIL ON HISTORIC PRESERVATION COMPLIANCE ISSUE. Washington, D.C.: Advisory Council on Historic Preservation. Quarterly.

662   ADVISORY COUNCIL ON HISTORIC PRESERVATION REPORT-SPECIAL ISSUE. Washington, D.C.: Advisory Council on Historic Preservation, Quarterly.

663   AMERICAN CANALS. Shepherdstown, W.Va.: American Canal Society. Quarterly.

Periodicals

664   AMERICAN HERITAGE. New York: American Heritage Publishing Co.
       Bimonthly.

665   AMERICAN PRESERVATION. Little Rock, Ark.: American Preservation.
       Bimonthly.

666   AMERICAS. Washington, D.C.: Organization of American States.
       Monthly.

667   ANCIENT MONUMENTS SOCIETY NEWSLETTER. London: Ancient
       Monuments Society. Semiannual.

668   ANCIENT MONUMENTS SOCIETY TRANSACTIONS. London: Ancient
       Monuments Society. Annual.

669   APT BULLETIN. Ottawa: Association for Preservation Technology.
       Quarterly.

670   APT COMMUNIQUE. Ottawa: Association for Preservation Technology.
       Bimonthly.

671   ARCHITECTURAL PRESERVATION FORUM. Philadelphia: Committee on
       Architectural Preservation, Society of Architectural Historians. Irregular.

672   ASSOCIATION FOR INDUSTRIAL ARCHAEOLOGY BULLETIN. Iron
       Bridge, Telford, Engl.: Association for Industrial Archaeology. Bimonthly.

673   BACK TO THE CITY NEWSREPORT. New York: Back to the City, Inc.
       Quarterly.

674   BROWNSTONER. New York: Brownstone Revival Committee. 5/yr.

675   BULLETIN DE LA COMMISSION ROYALE DES MONUMENTS ET DES
       SITES [Bulletin of the Royal Commission of Monuments and Sites].
       Brussels: Royal Commission of Monuments and Sites. Annual or Semi-
       annual.

676   CANADIAN HISTORIC SITES/LIEUX HISTORIQUES CANADIENS. Ottawa:
       Parks Canada. Irregular.

677   CASTILLOS DE ESPAÑA [Castles of Spain]. Madrid: Asociacion
       Española de Amigos de los Castillos. Quarterly.

678   CCI. Ottawa: Canadian Conservation Institute. Annual.

679   CHRONICLE OF THE EARLY AMERICAN INDUSTRIES ASSOCIATION. Ambridge, Pa.: Early American Industries Association. Quarterly.

680   CIVIC TRUST NEWS. London: Civic Trust. Bimonthly.

681   CLASSICAL AMERICA. Long Island City, N.Y.: Classical America, Inc. Irregular.

682   COMMITTEE FOR THE PRESERVATION OF ARCHITECTURAL RECORDS NEWSLETTER. New York: Committee for the Preservation of Architectural Records. Quarterly.

683   CONSERVATION PROGRESS. London: Civic Trust. Quarterly.

684   CONSERVE NEIGHBORHOODS. Washington, D.C.: National Trust for Historic Preservation. 5/yr.

685   CONVERSATION. Ottawa: Heritage Canada. Quarterly.

686   COUNCIL FOR THE PROTECTION OF RURAL ENGLAND QUARTERLY BULLETIN. London: Council for the Protection of Rural England.

687   COUNCIL FOR THE PROTECTION OF RURAL ENGLAND REPORT. London: Council for the Protection of Rural England. Annual.

688   DEUTSCHE KUNST UND DENKMALPFLEGE [German art and monument protection]. Munich: Deutscher Kunstverlag. Semiannual.

689   EARLY AMERICAN LIFE. Gettysburg, Pa.: Early American Society. Bimonthly.

690   GEORGIAN GROUP NEWS. London: Georgian Group. Monthly.

691   HEIMATSCHUTZ [Homeland Protection]. Zurich: Schweizer Heimatschutz. Quarterly.

692   HERITAGE CANADA. Ottawa: Heritage Canada. Bimonthly.

693   HISTORIC PRESERVATION. Washington, D.C.: National Trust for Historic Preservation. Bimonthly.

Periodicals

694   ICCROM CHRONIQUE/NEWSLETTER. Rome: International Centre for the Study of the Preservation and the Restoration of Cultural Property. Annual.

695   ICOMOS BULLETIN. Paris: International Council on Monuments and Sites. Irregular.

696   ICOMOS NEWSLETTER/NOUVELLES DE L'ICOMOS. Paris: International Council on Monuments and Sites. Irregular.

697   INTERNATIONAL CASTLES INSTITUTE BULLETIN. Rapperswil, Switzerland: International Castles Institute. Irregular.

698   IUCN BULLETIN. Morges, Switzerland: International Union for Conservation of Nature and Natural Resources. Monthly.

699   JOURNAL OF THE AMERICAN INSTITUTE FOR CONSERVATION. Washington, D.C.: American Institute for Conservation of Historic and Artistic Works. Semiannual.

700   JOURNAL OF THE SOCIETY OF ARCHITECTURAL HISTORIANS. Philadelphia: Society of Architectural Historians. Quarterly.

701   LANDMARK AND HISTORIC DISTRICT COMMISSIONS NEWSLETTER. Washington, D.C.: National Trust for Historic Preservation. Bimonthly.

702   LANDMARKS.' Washington, D.C.: League for Urban Land Conservation. Irregular.

703   THE LIVABLE CITY. New York: Municipal Art Society. Quarterly.

704   LIVING HISTORICAL FARMS BULLETIN. Washington, D.C.: Association for Living Historical Farms and Agricultural Museums. 6/yr.

705   MEMO: NEWSLETTER PRESERVATION ALUMNI COLUMBIA UNIVERSITY. New York: Preservation Alumni of Columbia University, Graduate School of Architecture and Planning, Columbia University. Irregular.

706   LES MONUMENTS HISTORIQUES DE LA FRANCE [The historic monuments of France]. Paris: Caisse Nationale des Monuments Historiques. Bimonthly.

707   MONUMENTUM. Louvain, Belgium: International Council on Monu-
       ments and Sites. Semiannual.

708   MUSEUM. Paris: International Council of Museums. Quarterly.

709   MUSEUM NEWS. Washington, D.C.: American Association of Museums.
       Bimonthly.

710   NATIONAL PARKS AND CONSERVATION MAGAZINE. Washington,
       D.C.: National Parks and Conservation Association. Monthly.

711   NATIONAL PARK SERVICE NEWSLETTER. Washington, D.C.: National
       Park Service. Monthly.

712   NATIONAL TRUST. London: National Trust. Irregular.

713   NATIONAL TRUST OF AUSTRALIA BULLETIN. Sydney: National Trust
       of Australia. 5/yr.

714   NATIONAL TRUST YEARBOOK. London: National Trust.

715   NEIGHBORHOOD CONSERVATION AND REINVESTMENT. Washington,
       D.C.: Preservation Reports, Inc. 22/yr.

716   NEIGHBORHOOD PRESERVATION. Washington, D.C.: Urban Rein-
       vestment Task Force. Quarterly.

717   NINETEENTH CENTURY. Philadelphia: Victorian Society in America.
       Quarterly.

718   ÖSTERREICHISCHE ZEITSCHRIFT FÜR KUNST UND DENKMALPFLEGE
       [Austrian Journal for Art and Monument Protection]. Vienna:
       Österreichisches Bundesdenkmalamt. 5/year.

719   OLD-HOUSE JOURNAL. Brooklyn, N.Y.: Old-House Journal.
       Monthly.

720   OLD MILL NEWS. Wiscasset, Maine: Society for the Preservation of
       Old Mills. Quarterly.

721   OLD-TIME NEW ENGLAND. Boston: Society for the Preservation of
       New England Antiquities. Quarterly.

Periodicals

722   PARKS. Washington, D.C.: National Park Service. Quarterly.

723   PRESERVATION ACTION ALERT! Washington, D.C.: Preservation
       Action. Irregular.

724   PRESERVATION BULLETIN. New York: Program in Historic Pres-
       ervation, Graduate School of Architecture and Planning, Columbia
       University. Semiannual.

725   PRESERVATION LEAGUE OF NEW YORK STATE TECHNICAL SERIES.
       Albany: Preservation League of New York State. Bimonthly.

726   PRESERVATION NEWS. Washington, D.C.: National Trust for
       Historic Preservation. Monthly.

727   PRESERVATION NOTES. Setauket, N.Y.: Society for the Preserva-
       tion of Long Island Antiquities. Irregular.

728   PUBLIC WORKS HISTORICAL SOCIETY NEWSLETTER. Chicago:
       Public Works Historical Society. Quarterly.

729   RESTAURO [Restoration]. Naples: Edizioni Scientifiche Italiane.
       Bimonthly.

730   SOCIETY FOR INDUSTRIAL ARCHEOLOGY NEWSLETTER. Washing-
       ton, D.C.: Society for Industrial Archeology. Bimonthly.

731   SOCIETY OF ARCHITECTURAL HISTORIANS NEWSLETTER. Philadelphia:
       Society of Architectural Historians. 5/yr.

732   STUDIES IN CONSERVATION. London: (IIC) International Institute
       for Conservation of Historic and Artistic Works. Quarterly.

733   TECHNOLOGY & CONSERVATION. Boston: Technology Organiza-
       tion, Inc. Quarterly.

734   VICTORIAN SOCIETY IN AMERICA BULLETIN. Philadelphia: Vic-
       torian Society in America. 10/yr.

735   VIELLES MAISONS FRANÇAISES [Old French Houses]. Paris: Associ-
       ation Reconnue d'Utilité Publique. Quarterly.

736   WINTERTHUR PORTFOLIO. Winterthur, Del.: Henry Francis duPont
Winterthur Museum. Quarterly.

737   YORK INSTITUTE OF ARCHITECTURAL STUDY BULLETIN. Micklegate,
York, Engl.: York Institute of Architectural Study. Annual.

STATEWIDE PUBLICATIONS

Alabama

738   PRESERVATION REPORT. Montgomery: Alabama Historical Commission.
Bimonthly.

Alaska

739   ALASKA HISTORY NEWS. Anchorage: Alaska Historical Society.
Bimonthly.

Arizona

740   ARIZONA PRESERVATION NEWS. Phoenix: Arizona State Historic
Preservation Office. Monthly.

California

741   CALIFORNIANS FOR PRESERVATION ACTION NEWSLETTER. Sacramento: Californians for Preservation Action. Quarterly.

Connecticut

742   PRESERVATION/CONNECTICUT. New Haven: Connecticut Trust for
Historic Preservation. 3/yr.

District of Columbia

743   DON'T TEAR IT DOWN. Washington, D.C.: Don't Tear It Down.
Bimonthly.

Georgia

744   THE RAMBLER. Atlanta: Georgia Trust for Historic Preservation.
Quarterly.

Periodicals

Hawaii

745   HISTORIC HAWAII NEWS. Honolulu: Historic Hawaii Foundation. Monthly.

Illinois

746   LANDMARKS PRESERVATION COUNCIL NEWS. Chicago: Landmarks Preservation Council. 8/yr.

Indiana

747   INDIANA PRESERVATION. Indianapolis: Historic Landmarks Foundation of Indiana. Quarterly.

Iowa

748   THE BRACKET. Iowa City: Iowa State Historical Department. Irregular.

Kentucky

749   HERITAGE NEWS. Frankfort: Kentucky Heritage Commission. Quarterly.

Louisiana

750   PRÉSERVATION. New Orleans: Louisiana Landmarks Society. Quarterly.

Maine

751   CITIZENS FOR HISTORIC PRESERVATION NEWSLETTER. Bath: Citizens for Historic Preservation. Quarterly.

Maryland

752   SWAP: SOME WORDS ABOUT PRESERVATION. Annapolis: Maryland Historical Trust. Monthly.

Massachusetts

753   MASSACHUSETTS HISTORICAL COMMISSION NEWSLETTER.   Boston:
Massachusetts Historical Commission.   Quarterly.

Minnesota

754   THE MINNESOTA HISTORY INTERPRETER.   St. Paul: Minnesota
Historical Society.   Quarterly.

Mississippi

755   MISSISSIPPI HISTORY NEWSLETTER.   Jackson: Mississippi Department
of Archives and History.   Monthly.

Missouri

756   MISSOURI PRESERVATION NEWS.   Jefferson City: Missouri Heritage
Trust, Inc.   Quarterly.

Nebraska

757   THE CORNER STONE.   Lincoln: Nebraska State Historical   Society.
Bimonthly.

Nevada

758   H P & A.   Carson City: Nevada Division of Historic Preservation
and Archeology.   Quarterly.

New Hampshire

759   HISTORICAL NEW HAMPSHIRE.   Concord: New Hampshire Historical
Society.   Quarterly.

New Jersey

760   NEW JERSEY HISTORICAL COMMISSION NEWSLETTER.   Trenton:
New Jersey Historical Commission.   10/yr.

New York

761   PRESERVATION LEAGUE OF NEW YORK STATE NEWSLETTER.
       Albany: Preservation League of New York State.   Bimonthly.

North Carolina

762   NORTH CAROLINA PRESERVATIONIST.   Raleigh: Historic Preservation
       Society of North Carolina, Inc.   Quarterly.

North Dakota

763   PRAIRIE COMMUNITY DESIGN CENTER NEWSLETTER.   Fargo: Prairie
       Community Design Center.   Quarterly.

Oklahoma

764   OUTLOOK IN HISTORIC CONSERVATION.   Oklahoma City: Oklahoma
       Historic Preservation Office.   Bimonthly.

Oregon

765   HISTORIC PRESERVATION LEAGUE OF OREGON.   Portland: Historic
       Preservation League of Oregon.   Irregular.

Rhode Island

766   RHODE ISLAND HISTORICAL PRESERVATION COMMISSION NEWS-
       LETTER.   Providence: Rhode Island Historical Preservation Commission.
       Bimonthly.

South Carolina

767   NEW SOUTH CAROLINA STATE GAZETTE.   Columbia: Confederation
       of South Carolina Local Historical Societies.   Quarterly.

South Dakota

768   HISTORICAL PRESERVATION CENTER NEWSLETTER.   Vermillion: His-
       torical Preservation Center, Alumni House, University of South Dakota.
       Irregular.

Tennessee

769   THE COURIER. Nashville: Tennessee Historical Commission. 3/yr. Quarterly.

Texas

770   THE MEDALLION. Austin: Texas Historical Commission. Bimonthly.

771   TEXAS HERITAGE COUNCIL NEWSLETTER. Austin: Heritage Council of Texas Historical Foundation. Monthly.

Utah

772   UTAH HERITAGE FOUNDATION NEWSLETTER. Salt Lake City: Utah Heritage Foundation. Monthly.

Vermont

773   POSSIBILITIES. Burlington: Historic Preservation Graduate Curriculum, History Department, University of Vermont. Quarterly.

Virginia

774   NOTES ON VIRGINIA. Richmond: Virginia Historic Landmarks Commission. Quarterly.

Washington

775   WASHINGTON LANDMARKS. Seattle: Washington Trust for Historic Preservation. Irregular.

Wisconsin

776   NATIONAL REGISTER OF HISTORIC PLACES IN WISCONSIN NEWSLETTER. Madison: State Historical Society of Wisconsin. Bimonthly.

Trust Territory of the Pacific Islands

777   MICRONESIAN PRESERVATION. Saipan, Mariana Islands: Trust Territory Historic Preservation Office. Quarterly.

Chapter 14

A CHECKLIST OF HISTORIC

AMERICAN BUILDINGS SURVEY PUBLICATIONS

This chapter contains a listing of books, leaflets, drawings, and other publications of the Historic American Buildings Survey (HABS) and publications by others which are based primarily on the survey's records. Items which have been given fuller treatment elsewhere in this volume include cross references. The HABS archives in the Division of Prints and Photographs of the Library of Congress contain more than thirty-four thousand measured drawings, forty-four thousand photographs, and thirteen thousand pages of documentation for more than sixteen thousand historic buildings. The public is encouraged to make wide use of HABS records, which may be used without restriction, although the courtesy of a credit line is requested.

NATIONAL CATALOGS (OLD SERIES)

778   Historic American Buildings Survey. CATALOG OF THE MEASURED DRAWINGS AND PHOTOGRAPHS OF THE SURVEY IN THE LIBRARY OF CONGRESS, MARCH 1, 1941. Washington, D.C.: U.S. Government Printing Office, 1941.

779   _____. CATALOG SUPPLEMENT, CATALOG OF THE MEASURED DRAWINGS AND PHOTOGRAPHS OF THE SURVEY IN THE LIBRARY OF CONGRESS, COMPRISING ADDITIONS SINCE MARCH 1, 1941. Washington, D.C.: U.S. Government Printing Office, 1959.

780   _____. A CHECK LIST OF SUBJECTS, ADDITIONS TO THE SURVEY MATERIAL DEPOSITED IN THE LIBRARY OF CONGRESS SINCE PUBLICATION OF THE HABS SUPPLEMENT, JANUARY 1959-JANUARY 1963. Washington, D.C.: National Park Service, 1963.

STATE AND REGIONAL CATALOGS (NEW SERIES)

District of Columbia

781   Schwartz, Nancy B. DISTRICT OF COLUMBIA CATALOG. Charlottesville: University Press of Virginia for the Columbia Historical Society,
n.d.

Illinois

782   Rudd, William J., comp. CHICAGO AND NEARBY ILLINOIS AREAS.
Park Forest, Ill.: Prairie School Press, 1966.

Indiana

783   Thompson, William P., comp. INDIANA CATALOG. Washington,
D.C.: National Park Service, 1971.

Maine

784   Myers, Denys Peter, comp. MAINE CATALOG. Augusta: Maine
State Museum, 1974.

Maryland

785   Historic American Buildings Survey. RECORDS OF HISTORIC MARY-
LAND BUILDINGS. Philadelphia: HABS 1964, revised 1969.

Massachusetts

786   Poppeliers, John C., ed. MASSACHUSETTS CATALOG. Boston:
Secretary of the Commonwealth, 1965.

Michigan

787   McKee, Harley J., comp. MICHIGAN CATALOG. Lansing: Historical Society of Michigan and Michigan Society of Architects, 1967.

New Hampshire

788   "New Hampshire Catalog, Historic American Buildings Survey, Records
in the Library of Congress." HISTORICAL NEW HAMPSHIRE 18 (Oct.
1963): 1-17.

Gives a supplementary list in the October 1967 issue of the same magazine.

New Jersey

789   Bassett, William B., comp. NEW JERSEY CATALOG. Edited by John C. Poppeliers. Newark: New Jersey Historical Society, n.d.

Pennsylvania

790   Webster, Richard, comp. PHILADELPHIA PRESERVED. Philadelphia: Temple University Press, 1976.

Rhode Island

791   Overby, Osmund, comp. RHODE ISLAND CATALOG. Washington, D.C.: HABS, 1972.

South Carolina

792   McKee, Harley J., comp. RECORDS OF BUILDINGS IN CHARLESTON AND THE SOUTH CAROLINA LOW COUNTRY. Philadelphia: HABS, 1965.

Texas

793   Goeldner, Paul, comp. TEXAS CATALOG. San Antonio: Trinity University Press, 1974.

Utah

794   Goeldner, Paul, comp. UTAH CATALOG. Salt Lake City: Utah Heritage Foundation, 1969.

Virginia

795   Virginia Historic Landmarks Commission, and Historic American Buildings Survey, comps. VIRGINIA CATALOG. Charlottesville: University Press of Virginia, 1976.

Wisconsin

796   Bailey, Worth, ed. WISCONSIN ARCHITECTURE. Richard W.E.
Perrin, narrator. Washington, D.C.: HABS, 1965.

DOCUMENTARY PUBLICATIONS

797   GEORGETOWN HISTORIC WATERFRONT, WASHINGTON, D.C.:
A REVIEW OF CANAL AND RIVERSIDE ARCHITECTURE. Washington,
D.C.: U.S. Commission of Fine Arts and the Office of Archeology
and Historic Preservation, National Park Service, 1968.

798   HISTORY OF A 19TH-CENTURY URBAN COMPLEX ON THE SITE OF
FT. STANWIX. Albany: New York State Historic Trust, 1972.

HABS SELECTION SERIES

799   1. HISTORIC ARCHITECTURE OF THE VIRGIN ISLANDS. Philadelphia:
HABS, 1966.

800   2. GEORGETOWN COMMERCIAL ARCHITECTURE, M-STREET. Washington, D.C.: U.S. Commission of Fine Arts and HABS, 1967.

801   3. GEORGETOWN COMMERCIAL ARCHITECTURE, WISCONSIN
AVENUE. Washington, D.C.: U.S. Commission of Fine Arts and HABS,
1967.

802   4. GEORGETOWN ARCHITECTURE, THE WATERFRONT. Washington,
D.C.: U.S. Commission of Fine Arts and HABS, 1968.

803   5. GEORGETOWN RESIDENTIAL ARCHITECTURE, NORTHEAST.
Washington, D.C.: U.S. Commission of Fine Arts and HABS, 1969.

804   6. GEORGETOWN ARCHITECTURE, NORTHWEST. Washington, D.C.:
U.S. Commission of Fine Arts, 1970.

805   7. NEW YORK CITY ARCHITECTURE. Washington, D.C.: HABS,
1969.

806   8. WASHINGTON, D.C. ARCHITECTURE, MARKET SQUARE. Washington, D.C.: Urban Design and Development Corporation and HABS, 1969.

807   9. NEW HAVEN ARCHITECTURE. Washington, D.C.: HABS, 1970.

808   10. GEORGETOWN ARCHITECTURE. Washington, D.C.: U.S. Commission of Fine Arts and HABS, 1970.

809   11. THE NEW ENGLAND TEXTILE MILL SURVEY. Washington, D.C.: HABS, 1971.

810   12. THE ARCHITECTURE OF CLEVELAND: TWELVE BUILDINGS, 1836–1912. Cleveland: Western Reserve Historical Society and HABS, 1973.

811   15. Nelson, Lee H. AN ARCHITECTURAL STUDY OF FORT McHENRY. Philadelphia: National Park Service, 1961.

SELECTIONS OF MEASURED DRAWINGS

812   Historic American Buildings Survey. MEASURED DRAWINGS OF NORTHERN ILLINOIS ARCHITECTURE. 3 vols. Sponsored by the National Park Service, the Illinois State Historical Library, and the Illinois Relief Commission, 1934–37.

813   _____. THE ROBIE HOUSE. Palos Park, Ill.: Prairie School Press, 1968.

814   MEASURED DRAWINGS OF NATIONAL TRUST PROPERTIES. Washington, D.C.: National Trust for Historic Preservation.

       Sets of drawings for Belle Grove (Virginia), Casa Amesti (California), Clivedon (Pennsylvania), Decatur House (Washington, D.C.), Lyndhurst (New York), Pope-Leighey House (Virginia), and Shadows-on-the-Teche (Louisiana).

GENERAL PUBLICATIONS

815   Brumbaugh, Thomas B., et al., eds. ARCHITECTURE OF MIDDLE TENNESSEE. Nashville: Vanderbilt University Press, 1974.

816   DOCUMENTING A LEGACY. Washington, D.C.: U.S. Government Printing Office, 1973.

       (See entry 174)

817   HISTORIC AMERICAN BUILDINGS SURVEY. Washington, D.C.: HABS, 1973. Leaflet.

818   HISTORIC BUILDINGS OF MASSACHUSETTS. Scribner's Historic
Buildings Series. New York: Charles Scribner's Sons, 1976.

819   Kidney, Walter C. HISTORIC BUILDINGS OF OHIO. Preface by
James C. Massey. Pittsburgh: Ober Park Associates, 1972.

820   McKee, Harley J., comp. RECORDING HISTORIC BUILDINGS.
Washington, D.C.: HABS, 1970.

       (See entry 180)

821   Maddex, Diane. HISTORIC BUILDINGS OF WASHINGTON, D.C.
Foreword by Arthur Cotton Moore. Pittsburgh: Ober Park Associotes,
1973.

       (See entry 249)

822   Massey, James C. THE ARCHITECTURAL SURVEY. Preservation Leaflet Series. Washington, D.C.: National Trust for Historic Preservation,
1974.

       (See entry 181)

823   Poppeliers, John C., ed. SHAKER BUILT: A CATALOG OF THE
SHAKER ARCHITECTURAL RECORDS FROM THE HISTORIC AMERICAN
BUILDINGS SURVEY. Washington, D.C.: National Park Service,
1974.

       (See entry 188)

824   Poppeliers, John C.; Chambers, S. Allen; and Schwartz, Nancy B.,
comps. WHAT STYLE IS IT? Washington, D.C.: Preservation Press,
1977.

825   PRESERVATION THROUGH DOCUMENTATION. Washington, D.C.:
U.S. Government Printing Office, 1968.

       (See entry 175)

826   Ramirez, Constance Werner. THE HISTORIC ARCHITECTURE AND
URBAN DESIGN OF NANTUCKET. Washington, D.C.: Smithsonian
Institution, 1970.

827   Regnery, Dorothy F. AN ENDURING HERITAGE. Stanford: Stanford
University Press, 1976.

Appendix

DEVELOPING THE HISTORIC PRESERVATION LIBRARY

Historic preservation is a multidisciplinary field of study with a rapidly expanding body of literature supporting it. Although preservationists review the literature of a wide range of related professions, there are also many publications specifically on preservation activities. Examples of these activities are establishing a historic district, interpreting a historic site, amending building codes, starting a neighborhood preservation organization, restoring a period room, or planning for the continued use of a locally significant building. To complete such projects preservationists rely on many types of information resources including pictorial resources, audiovisual presentations, governmental and legal records, and architectural records, as well as monographs and serials.

The reasons for acquiring publications on preservation range from the general purpose of having information on cultural heritage available for the public to the more specific purpose of needing a handbook on how to compile an inventory of historic resources or how to restore a house. Whether adding to a public, academic or organizational library, or developing a private collection, it is important to be knowledgeable about the organizations active in the field of historic preservation and to be on the mailing lists for their periodicals and other information. In addition to learning about the most recent publications from national and local organizations, it is often possible to receive advice and information in answer to specific questions. The National Trust for Historic Preservation, for example, functions as a clearinghouse of information on preservation.

One should be familiar with the locale and clientele to be served by the collection before selecting information resources. Activities and aims of preservationists vary according to regional differences in such matters as the structure of local government, local and state legislation, types of historic and cultural resources, various building materials, and the degree of community awareness of historic preservation. Information about the activities and publications of local private and governmental organizations is an important prerequisite for acquiring publications. For further advice on how to develop and organize collections of resources on historic preservation, write the Library of the National Trust for Historic Preservation, 1785 Massachusetts Avenue, N.W., Washington, D.C. 20036.

A select list of publications for initiating preservation collections follows.
Because of the above considerations the list is extremely limited. Only the
most generally useful books are included. Periodicals from several national
preservation-related organizations that include articles on current events as
well as information on recent publications have also been listed. Those interested in building more complete collections will want to supplement this list
according to their need for information. After assessing information requirements, use the previous chapter headings and the annotations to select relevant
publications. In order to augment an extensive collection, select freely
among the handbooks, "classics," bibliographies, and examples of local publications.

Brigid Rapp
Library Services Coordinator
National Trust for Historic Preservation

SELECT LIST

The items in the following select list for the basic historic preservation library are followed by entry numbers for referral to fuller description in the body of the text. The titles of the select list publications are preceded by an asterisk in the title index.

BOOKS

American Association for State and Local History. DIRECTORY OF HISTORICAL SOCIETIES AND AGENCIES IN THE UNITED STATES AND CANADA. 11th ed. Compiled and edited by Donna McDonald. Nashville: 1978. (1)

Bullock, Orin M., Jr. THE RESTORATION MANUAL: AN ILLUSTRATED GUIDE TO THE PRESERVATION AND RESTORATION OF OLD BUILDINGS. Norwalk, Conn.: Silvermine Publishers, 1966. (409)

Chambers, J. Henry. CYCLICAL MAINTENANCE FOR HISTORIC BUILDINGS. Washington, D.C.: Government Printing Office, 1976. (410)

Fitch, James Marston. AMERICAN BUILDING 1: THE HISTORICAL FORCES THAT SHAPED IT. Boston: Houghton Mifflin Co., 1966. (465)

Greiff, Constance M., ed. LOST AMERICA: FROM THE ATLANTIC TO THE MISSISSIPPI. Princeton, N.J.: Pyne Press, 1971. (629)

_____. LOST AMERICA: FROM THE MISSISSIPPI TO THE PACIFIC. Princeton, N.J.: Pyne Press, 1972. (630)

Hosmer, Charles Bridgham. PRESENCE OF THE PAST: A HISTORY OF THE PRESERVATION MOVEMENT IN THE UNITED STATES BEFORE WILLIAMSBURG. New York: G.P. Putnam's Sons, 1965. (82)

Lewis, Ralph H. MANUAL FOR MUSEUMS. Washington, D.C.: National Park Service, U.S. Department of the Interior, 1976. (552)

Lynch, Kevin. WHAT TIME IS THIS PLACE? Cambridge: M.I.T. Press, 1972. (540)

McNulty, Robert H., and Kliment, Stephen A., eds. NEIGHBORHOOD CONSERVATION: A HANDBOOK OF METHODS AND TECHNIQUES. New York: Whitney Library of Design, 1976. (370)

National Trust for Historic Preservation. AMERICA'S FORGOTTEN ARCHITECTURE. Edited by Tony P. Wrenn and Elizabeth D. Mulloy. New York: Pantheon Books, 1976. (90)

_____. ECONOMIC BENEFITS OF PRESERVING OLD BUILDINGS. Washington, D.C.: Preservation Press, 1976. (103)

_____. A GUIDE TO FEDERAL PROGRAMS: PROGRAMS AND ACTIVITIES RELATED TO HISTORIC PRESERVATION. Nancy D. Schultz, principal consultant. Washington, D.C.: 1974. (11)

_____. A GUIDE TO FEDERAL PROGRAMS FOR HISTORIC PRESERVATION: 1976 SUPPLEMENT. Compiled by Nancy D. Schultz. Washington, D.C.: Preservation Press, 1976. (12)

_____. A GUIDE TO STATE HISTORIC PRESERVATION PROGRAMS. Researched and compiled by Betts Abel. Edited by Jennie B. Bull. Washington, D.C.: Preservation Press, 1976. (104)

North American International Regional Conference, Williamsburg, Virginia, and Philadelphia, 1972. PRESERVATION AND CONSERVATION: PRINCIPLES AND PRACTICES. Edited by Sharon Timmins. Washington, D.C.: Preservation Press, 1976. (44)

Stephen, George. REMODELING OLD HOUSES: WITHOUT DESTROYING THEIR CHARACTER. New York: Knopf, 1973. (462)

ULI--The Urban Land Institute. ADAPTIVE USE: DEVELOPMENT ECONOMICS, PROCESS, AND PROFILES. By Melvin A. Gamzon, Nathaniel M. Griffin, Thomas J. Martin, W. Paul O'Mara, Frank H. Spink, Jr., Joseph D. Steller, Jr., and Margaret A. Thomas. Washington, D.C.: 1978. (448)

U.S. Department of the Interior. National Register of Historic Places. GUIDELINES FOR LOCAL SURVEYS: A BASIS FOR PRESERVATION PLANNING. By Anne Derry, H. Ward Jandl, Carol D. Shull, and Jan Thorman. Washington, D.C.: 1977. (187)

Warner, Raynor M.; Groff, Sibyl McCormac; and Warner, Ranne P.; with Weiss, Sandi. BUSINESS AND PRESERVATION: A SURVEY OF BUSINESS CONSERVATION OF BUILDINGS AND NEIGHBORHOODS. Edited by Frank Stella. New York: INFORM, 1978. (449)

Whiffen, Marcus. AMERICAN ARCHITECTURE SINCE 1780: A GUIDE TO THE STYLES. Cambridge: M.I.T. Press, 1969. (166)

PERIODICALS

AMERICAN PRESERVATION. (665)

APT COMMUNIQUE. (670)

CONSERVE NEIGHBORHOODS. (684)

HISTORIC PRESERVATION. (693)

LANDMARK AND HISTORIC DISTRICT COMMISSIONS NEWSLETTER. (701)

MUSEUM NEWS. (709)

PRESERVATION NEWS. (726)

SOCIETY FOR INDUSTRIAL ARCHEOLOGY NEWSLETTER. (730)

SOCIETY OF ARCHITECTURAL HISTORIANS NEWSLETTER. (731)

AUTHOR INDEX

In addition to authors, this index includes editors, illustrators, and translators, as well as contributors of forewords and introductions. Contributors to collected works are listed only if they have been mentioned in the entry. Corporate, or institutional, authors are listed in the Organization Index. References are to entry numbers.

Author Index

Author Index

Author Index

McKenna, H. Dickson 460
McMath, George A. 239
McNulty, Robert H. 370
Maddex, Diane 249, 821
Major, J. Kenneth 568
Malo, Paul 229
Manucy, Albert 203
Marcus, Grania Bolton 443
Marion, John Francis 307
Marsan, Jean-Claude 259
Martin, Graham 275
Martin, Thomas J. 448
Martin, Van Jones 206
Marusin, Sarah A. 190
Massari, Giovanni 431
Massey, James C. 181, 212, 819, 822
Matthew, Robert 334
Matuszeski, Bill 346
Mayo, Walter Longley Bourke, 8th Earl of 266
Melville, Ian A. 414
Melvin, Peter 33
Menges, Gary L. 10
Mercado, Osiris Delgado. See Delgado Mercado, Osiris
Mercer, Henry C. 394, 403
Michelsen, Peter 93
Mielke, Friedrich 58
Miller, Hugh C. 153
Miner, Ralph W. 88
Montague, Robert L. III 127
Moor, Jay Haden 99
Moore, Arthur Cotton 33, 249, 821
Moore, Charles 344
Moore, George 542
Morgan, William 240
Morison, Samuel Eliot 594
Morrison, Jacob H. 119
Morrison, Mary 206
Morton, Terry B. 525, 636
Moses, Robert 46
Motto, Sytha 515
Mulloy, Elizabeth D. 89, 90
Murfin, James V. 287
Murtagh, William J. 190
Myers, Denys Peter 493, 784
Myers, Phyllis 371, 372

N

Nannen, Howard 113
Nash, Roderick 612
Nash, Susan Higginson 531
Needham, Joseph 405
Neil, J. Meredith 163
Nelson, Lee H. 404, 811
Nicholas, Darrel D. 424
Nichols, Frederick D. 295
Niering, William A. 605
Noblecourt, André 656
Noël Hume, Audrey 623
Noël Hume, Ivor 494
Norman, Thomas 136
Norwak, Mary 506
Nutting, Wallace 201
Nylander, Jane C. 495

O

O'Connell, Merrilyn Rogers 14, 15. See also Rogers, Merrilyn
Olmsted, Roger R. 194
Olson, George T. 606
Olwell, Carol 195
O'Mara, W. Paul 448
O'Neal, William B. 295
Otto, John Solomon 563
Overby, Osmund 791

P

Pace, Valerie Sue Halverson 384
Page, Marian 511
Paher, Stanley W. 645
Pannell, J.P.M. 568
Papageorgiou, Alexander 345
Park, Helen 164
Parrondo Acero, Carlos de 269
Parry, Ellwood 647
Pepper, Adeline 296
Perrin, Richard W.E. 796
Perry, William Graves 531
Peterson, Charles E. 46, 397, 592
Peterson, Harold L. 497
Pevsner, Nikolaus 32, 157, 267, 615

Author Index

ORGANIZATION INDEX

Listed here are corporate authors of publications, as well as institutional sponsors of publications, conferences, programs, and studies. Included are firms
and organizations, government departments and agencies, and international
agencies. References are to entry numbers, except where the letter "p." indicates a page reference.

A

Advisory Council on Historic Preserva-
    tion 11; 12, 44, 79, 100,
    660–62
Alabama Historical Commission 738
Alaska Historical Society 739
American Association for State and
    Local History 1, 5, 15, 157,
    404, 428, 536, 551, 553,
    554, 618
American Association of Museums
    550, 709
American Association of University
    Women 299
American Canal and Transportation
    Center 586
American Canal Society 663
American Forestry Association 288
American Horticultural Society 623
American Institute for Conservation of
    Historic and Artistic Works 699
American Institute of Architects
  Chicago Chapter Foundation 139
  Committee on Historic Buildings
    409
  Institute Scholar Program 35
  New Orleans Chapter 300

  New York Chapter 313
  Pittsburg Chapter 241
  Portland, Oregon Chapter 310
  Washington Metropolitan Chapter
    301
American Institute of Planners 306
American Museum of Natural History
    557
American Philosophical Society 614
American Society of Architectural
    Historians. See Society of
    Architectural Historians
American Society of Civil Engineers
    571
American Society of Planning Officials
    88, 127, 306, 351, 437
Ancient Monuments Society 392,
    667, 668
Anderson Notter Associates 354
Architectural Heritage–Baltimore 432
Arizona, University of. College of
    Architecture 123
Arizona State Historic Preservation
    Office 740
Asociacion Española de Amigos de los
    Castillos 677
Association for Industrial Archaeology
    672. See also Society for
    Industrial Archeology

Organization Index

Association for Living Historical Farms
and Agricultural Museums 6,
532, 704
Association for Preservation Technology
669, 670
Association of American Geographers
607
Association Reconnue d'Utilité
Publique 735
Atlantic Conservation Center 388
Aurora Historical Society 219
Australia. National Estate Committee
of Inquiry 53
Australian Council of National Trusts
253
Austria. Bundesdenkmalamt 54, 718

B

Back to the City, Inc. 673
Bath Marine Museum 579
Belgium. Commission Royale des
Monuments et des Sites 675
Belgium. Ministère de la Culture
Française 256
Berkeley-Charleston-Dorchester
Regional Planning Council 145
Bicentennial Committee of Westchester
237
Boston Landmarks Commission 348
Boston Redevelopment Authority 348
British Tourist Authority 627
Brownstone Revival Committee 451,
674
Bucks County Historical Society 240,
403
Building Research Institute 47
Bureau of Governmental Research 349

C

California Historical Society 590
Californians for Preservation Action
741
Cambridgeshire and Isle of Ely County
Council 101
Canada. Department of Indian
Affairs and Northern Develop-
ment 186
Canada. Ministry of State for Urban
Affairs 126

Canadian Conservation Institute 678
Cape Provincial Institute of Architects
76
Caribbean Conservation Association 56
Carpenters' Company of London, The
397
Carpenters' Company of the City and
County of Philadelphia, The 397
Central New York Community Arts
Council 226
Centre de Recherches et d'Etudes
Océanographiques 426
Centro di Studi per la Storia dell'
Architettura 318
Citizens for Historic Preservation 751
Citizens Union Research Foundation
106
Civic Trust 60, 334, 680, 683
Clarke and Rapuano 604
Classical America 499, 681
Clinton County Historical Association
222
Colonial Dames of America 510,
512, 517, 518, 543
Colonial Williamsburg 91, 93, 502,
533, 534
Columbia Historical Society 781
Columbia University. Center for
Advanced Research in Urban and
Environmental Affairs 331, 435
Columbia University. Graduate
School of Architecture and
Planning 236, 402, 724
Committee for the Preservation of
Architectural Records 4, 682
Confederation of South Carolina Local
Historical Societies 767
Connecticut Trust for Historic Preserva-
tion 742
Conservation Foundation 371, 372
Conservation Trust of Puerto Rico 138
Cornell University. Office of Regional
Resources and Development 238
Corning Museum of Glass 429
Council for the Protection of Rural
England (formerly: Council for
the Preservation of Rural Eng-
land) 266, 598-600, 686-87
Council of Coventry Cathedral 652
Council of Europe 23, 28-31, 319-
24

Council of Planning Librarians 3, 10, 22

D

Daughters of the American Revolution 278
Delaware. Public Archives Commission 514
Delaware Valley Regional Planning Commission 124
Denver Landmark Preservation Commission 146
Denver Planning Office 146
Documentation Center for Education in Europe 30
Don't Tear It Down 743
Duluth, Minnesota. Department of Research and Planning 311
Dumbarton Oaks 615, 623
Dutchess County Planning Board 221

E

Early American Industries Association 679
Early American Society 191, 689
Edinburgh Architectural Association 334
Educational Facilities Laboratories 440
Eidgenössische Technische Hochschule, Zurich 77
European Conference of Local Authorities 23

F

Federal Writers' Project p. 79
Florida. Department of State 141
Fort Greene Landmarks Preservation Committee 225
France. Caisse Nationale des Monuments Historiques 706
France. Direction de l'Architecture 261
French and Pickering Creeks Conservation Trust 602
Friends of Iolani Palace 542
Friends of the Cabildo 208

G

Garden Club of Virginia 624
Georgia. Department of Natural Resources 173
Georgian Group 690
Georgia Trust for Historic Preservation 744
German Democratic Republic. Institut für Denkmalpflege 59
Gesellschaft für Schweizerische Kunstgeschichte 77
Great Britain. Department of the Environment 391, 439
Great Britain. Minister of Housing and Local Government 66, 336
Great Britain. Ministry of Technology 421
Great Britain. Preservation Policy Group 66
Greater London Council 102, 268
Greater Portland Landmarks 456

H

HABS. See Historic American Buildings Survey
HAER. See Historic American Engineering Record
Haines Lundberg and Waehler 604
Hardy Holzman Pfeiffer Associates 440
Hartford Architecture Conservancy 113
Henry Ford Museum 530
Henry Francis du Pont Winterthur Museum 501, 736
Heritage Canada 685, 692
Heritage Council of Texas Historical Foundation 771
Heritage Trust of Nova Scotia 257
Historical Commission of Metropolitan Nashville-Davidson County 244
Historic Alexandria Foundation 246
Historical Society of Michigan 787
Historical Society of Western Pennsylvania 545, 574
Historic American Buildings Survey (HABS) 169, 174-76, 180, 188, 249, 778-827

TITLE INDEX

Titles have been shortened wherever possible and subtitles have been included only if needed to give clarification. Titles of contributions to multiauthored works and titles of individual volumes of multivolume works have been listed only if they are mentioned in the entry.

References are to entry numbers, except where the letter "p." indicates a page reference. Where there are references to both citation and secondary mention of a title, the primary reference is underlined.

Titles of series are underlined; titles of contributions to multiauthored works appear within quotation marks; and titles which are included in the "Select List," which concludes the appendix, "Developing the Historic Preservation Library," are preceded by an asterisk.

In instances where the name of a conference differs from the title of its resulting publication, both are given.

Title Index

H

N

Title Index

SUBJECT INDEX

This index is alphabetized letter by letter and numbers refer to entry numbers.
Underscoring refers to main subject areas of interest.

A

Abandonment of property 377
   countering urban 382
Abbeys, guide to Scottish 271, 273
Action Housing, Inc. 115
Adaptive use 33, 45, 149, 432-49,
   450, 452-53, 459
Advertisements, Connecticut broad-
   side 543
Aeronautics, British museums serving
   568
Aesthetics
   bibliography on environmental 10
   in environmental policy 94
   in preservation aspects of town
      planning 76
Africa, historic preservation of urban
   centers in 333
Aged. See Elderly
Agriculture
   archaeology of American 570
   British museums serving 568
   See also Animal husbandry; Barns;
      Farms; Gardening
Alabama
   guide to historic houses in 514
   nineteenth-century architecture
      in 192

   periodicals published by 738
   See also Mobile
Alaska, periodicals published by 739
Alexandria, Va.
   guide to the Old Town of 306
   survey of early buildings of 246
Allegheny County, Pa.
   historic preservation in 364
   register of areas and buildings
      of 242
Allegheny Self-Study Program 368
Allentown, Pa. 346
Aluminumware 505
American Indians
   ancient sites of in New Mexico
      218
     in New York 238
   legislation and activities related
      to antiquities of 85
American Institute of Planners,
   statement on conservation/
   historic preservation 105
American Samoa. See Samoa,
   American
Anglo-Italianate architecture. See
      Architecture, Anglo-Italianate
Animal husbandry 472
Annapolis, Md.

Subject Index

guide to 306
historic preservation in 372
  case studies 115
  planning of 129
Anthropology 555
Antiques, dictionaries and encyclo-
     pedias of 474-75, 477, 481
  American 482-84
Antiquities, conservation and preserva-
     tion of
  in Germany, East 59
  in Hungary 70
  laws applicable to 561
  in Puerto Rico 252
  in the U.S. 416
  See also Archaeology, historical
Antiquities Act (1906) 85
Archaeology, historical 556-64
  bibliography on 560
  in garden restoration 623
  guide to information sources on 9
  investigation of in East Germany
    59
  in New York 238
  organizations and museums serving
    561
  in reconstruction of Fort Stanwix
    172
  survey of in Nebraska 216
  use and preservation of remains
    from 184
  See also Antiquities; Industrial
    archaeology
Archaeology, salvage 572
Arches, tendency of toward collapse
  411
Architects
  biography of Victorian 467
  directory of London 626
  guide to information sources on
    168
  of New Haven, Conn. 302
  of Philadelphia 312
  training of 397
  of Washington, D.C. 301
Architectural drawings
  of colonial St. Augustine archi-
    tecture 204
  HABS catalogs of 778-79, 812-14
  in industrial archaeology 568

of log cabins 593
of Washington, D.C. 251
Architectural surveys. See Surveys
    and inventories
Architecture
  bibliographies on 161, 163, 165
  of California 298
  of Cleveland 810
  of Connecticut inns and taverns
    543
  conservation and restoration of
    23, 342, 352, 396
    in the Americas 51
    bibliographies on 10, 19,
      21-22, 165
    in Chicago 153
    in Europe 24, 57, 83-84
    in the U.S. 83-84, 88,
      90
  controls in 117
  dictionaries on 159-60, 162
  of Fort McHenry 811
  of Georgia 173
  history of 187
    Canadian 470
  illustrations and descriptions of
    styles of 157, 166, 191
  influence of Britain on S. African
    76
  of Mississippi 292
  of Nantucket Island 826
  of New Bedford, Mass. 352
  of Newcastle-upon-Tyne 122
  of New Haven, Conn. 807
  of Newport, R.I. 156, 308
  of New Orleans 300
  of New York City 314, 805
    guide to research resources 4
  of New York State 309
  periodicals on 671, 700, 731
    record preservation in 682
  of Portland 310
  as socio-cultural expression 470-
    72
  of Tennessee 815
  of Tucson 123
  of the United States 500
    evolution of 385
  of Virginia 295, 534
  of the Virgin Islands 799

Subject Index

C

Cabinetmakers, English 476
Cabinet work 399
  Eighteenth-century tools for 403
California
  architecture of 193-95, 298
  guide to historic houses in 519
  historic preservation in 196-98
    laws of 115
  influence on domestic architecture
    167
  periodicals published by 741
  See also Monterey, Calif.; Sacra-
    mento; San Francisco; Santa
    Barbara, Calif.
California. Department of Parks and
  Recreation 196
California Historic Landmarks League
  196
Calligraphy, preservation of Japanese
  74
Canada
  architectural history of 470
  architecture of hotels in 258
  extant log cabins of 588
  farms and museums of 532
  historic preservation in 79, 397
    adaptive reuse projects 459
    planning of 126
  inventory of the sites of the
    American Revolution in 279
  periodicals about 692
    historic sites of 676
Canadian Inventory of Historic Building, manual for 186
Canadian National Railway, hotels
  of 258
Canadian Pacific Railway, hotels of
  258
Canals 585
  of Lowell, Mass. 151
  of New England 637
  of New York 238
  periodicals of 663
  See also Chesapeake and Ohio
    Canal National Historic Park
Candle making, programs for teaching
  of today 541
Cape May, N.J., history and architecture of 217

Capitol Building (Washington, D.C.)
  397
Capitols (cities), guide to United
  States 284
Carding, programs for teaching of
  today 541
Caribbean Islands, historic preserva-
  tion in 55-56
Carnegie International Center,
  seminar at (1975) 57
Carpentry 398-99, 592
  development of in England (1200-
    1700) 400
  early American 500
  eighteenth-century tools of 403
  See also types of carpentry work
    (e.g., Cabinet work)
Carriage and wagon making 399
Cartwrights 399
Carvings, early American 500
Casa Amesti (California) 814
Cast-iron fronts (architecture), of
  New York 224, 233
Castles
  conservation and restoration of in
    Hungary 70
  guidebooks to British 276
    to Scottish 271, 273
  lost and endangered French 633
  periodicals on 697
  Spanish 677
  See also Palaces
Cathedrals
  conservation and restoration of
    British 397
  guide to Scottish 273
    to U.S. 280
  See also Abbeys; Chapels;
    Churches
Ceilings, conservation and restora-
  tion of 420
Cement, composition of British 427
Cemeteries 548
  guide to European Jewish 270
    to New York State 309
  landscape design for 618
  of New Orleans 208
  photographs of New York City
    650
  surveys of Puerto Rican 252
  See also Tombs

Central America. See Latin America
Ceramics
   of the antebellum South 563
   conservation and restoration of
      551
   encyclopedias and dictionaries of
      antique 477, 484
   relating to ornamentation 485
Channel Islands, bibliography on the
      architecture of 158
Chapels
   adaptive reuse of 434
   British National Trust 272
Charleston
   architectural inventory of 46
   case studies on historic preservation
      in 115
   historic district legislation in 351
   historic houses of 524
"Charter of Venice" 51, 73
Cherry Hill (historic house) 523
Chesapeake and Ohio Canal National
      Historic Park 586
Chester, England, historic preservation
      in 66
Chestertown, Md., historic preserva-
      tion in 355
Chicago
   development rights transfer in 137,
      139
   HABS catalog for 782
   historic preservation planning in
      153
   lost and endangered landmarks in
      635
Chicago School of Architecture 153
Chichester, England, historic preserva-
      tion in 66
Chimneys 469
   drawings and photographs of
      English 486
   maintenance and repair of 454
   See also Fireplaces
Christmas, celebration of in colonial
      Virginia 502
Church architecture
   bibliography on 163
   of Scotland 271
   See also Towers

Churches
   conservation and restoration of
      24, 36
   adaptive reuse 434
   in Germany, East 59
   in Great Britain 101
   of England 275
   lost and endangered French 633
   of New England 637
   of Scotland 273
   of the U.S. 280
   See also Abbeys; Cathedrals;
      Chapels; Meetinghouses;
      Missions; Synagogues
Churchyards, preservation of
      European 36
Cincinnati, historic preservation in
      372
Cities and towns
   architectural survey of British
      266
   conservation and preservation of
      106, 327
   in Australia 254
   bibliography on 10
   in Europe 24
   in Great Britain 67, 134
   open spaces 604, 609
   guides to Scottish 273
   periodicals on 703
   photographs of American 649
   planned 46
   ruined, extinct, etc. 645
   See also Historic districts; His-
      toric urban centers; Land
      use, urban; Neighborhoods;
      Small towns; Villages
City and town life 469, 471-72,
      538, 548-49
   in the colonial period 537
   in early Virginia 468
   in New York City 580
   in the Victorian period 546
   See also Rural conditions
City halls, adaptive reuse of 432
City planning 153, 345
   bibliography of sources for 9
   historic preservation and 88,
      325, 341
   bibliography on 15
   in S. Africa 76

Subject Index

London legislation for 626
relation of history of to architectural surveying 181
in Washington, D.C. 306
See also Land use, urban; Regional planning
City traffic 333, 342
in Cuzco, Peru 329
in London 332
in St. Paul, Minn. 376
See also Pedestrian zones
Civic Amenities Act (Gt. Brit., 1967) 66, 134, 625
Civil engineering 180-81
Clay products, weathering of 418
Cleveland, architecture of 810
Clinton County, N.Y., architecture of 222
Clivedon (Pennsylvania house) 814
Cloth. See Textile fabrics
Clothing. See Costume
Coach-houses, conservation and restoration of Canadian 459
Coal industry, archaeology of British 566
Coastal zone management 605
in Europe 24
in Great Britain 272
in Japan 74
in the U.S. 94
College Art Association 48
Colonial architecture. See Architecture, colonial; Architecture, colonial revival
Colonial Williamsburg. See Williamsburg, Va.
Columbia University. Graduate School of Architecture 638
Program in Historic Preservation 45, 236
Columbus, Ga., adaptive reuse projects in 445
Comings, Marian 48
Commercial buildings. See Mercantile buildings
Commission des Monuments Historiques (France) 41
Commons areas 309
Communications, archaeology of British 566

Concrete, weathering of 418
Conference on Historic Site Archaeology 560
Connecticut
guides to historic houses of 517-18, 520
historic preservation planning in 130
inns and taverns of 543
open space preservation in 605
periodicals published by 742
survey of the natural and built heritage of 201
See also Bridgeport, Conn.; Hartford, Conn.; New Britain, Conn.; New Haven, Conn.; Norwich, Conn.; Waterbury, Conn.
Conservation. See Historic preservation
Conservation of natural resources, guide to information sources on 9. See also Landscape; Natural reserves; Open spaces
Convents, lost and endangered French 633
Cookbooks 502. See also Food
Cooking utensils. See Kitchen utensils
Coopers and cooperage 399
Cornell University, library resources of 10
Corning Museum of Glass 429
Cornwallis, Charles (Lord), description of Yorktown by 646
Cortes, Hernando, description of Mexico by 646
Costume
in American genre painting 549
preservation of Japanese traditional 74
as socio-cultural expression 472
Cottages, conservation and restoration of 459
Council of Europe 73
See also European Architectural Heritage Year (1975)

Country homes, English
decoration of 488
lost and endangered 627, 639
as sociocultural expressions 466–67
Country homes, Hungarian 70
Courthouses
handbook on conservation and restoration of 183
of Pennsylvania 242
Coventry Cathedral 652, 657
Covered bridges 595
of West Virginia 583
Craftsmen
biographical data on 478
of Williamsburg, Va. 533
See also Arts and crafts
Cultural history, buildings, objects, and sites in interpretation of 465–72
Cultural property, protection of 50
in the Americas 52
in Europe 28, 30, 57, 340
in Italy 340
in Japan 74
in times of war 656, 658–59
in the U.S. 87, 135, 419
in Yugoslavia 99
See also types of cultural property (e.g., Art)
Custom House Institute (N.Y. City) 128
Cuzco, Peru, historic preservation in 329
Czechoslovakia, historic preservation in 57

D

Dampness in buildings 414, 429–31
Dams, guide to U.S. 285
Danube, N.Y., historic preservation in 185
Death Valley. See Cities and towns, ruined, extinct, etc.
Decatur House (Washington, D.C.) 522, 525, 814
Decoration and ornament
conservation and restoration of European 36

dictionaries and encyclopedias of 474–75, 477–78, 480, 485
English eighteenth-century 488
evolution of American 285
as representations of social attitudes 488
Decoration and ornament, architectural 195
dictionary of 485
Deerfield, Mass. See Old Deerfield, Mass.
Delaware Valley
guide to historic houses of 518
historic preservation in 124
See also Wilmington, Del.
Denmark, historic preservation in 67
Denver
historic preservation planning in 146
nineteenth-century architecture of 199
Designers, biographies and lists of 476, 478
Detroit, history of the building of 214
Development rights transfer 114, 136–40, 153
District of Columbia. See Washington, D.C.
Docents 298
Domestic architecture. See Architecture, domestic
Doors, maintenance and repair of 362, 454
Doorways, drawings and photographs of English 486
Dovecotes, of the British National Trust 272
Downtown-Lower Manhattan Association 128
Drainage 414
Drama. See Theatre
Drayton Hall (Charleston), bibliography on 524
Drink, as socio-cultural expression 469, 472, 537–38
Duluth, Minn., guide to the architecture of 311
Dutchess County, N.Y., architecture of 221

Subject Index

E

Easements 88, 602

Eaves, maintenance and repair of 361, 454

Ecclesiastical buildings
adaptive reuse of 434
architecture of British 267
of Peruvian 329
conservation and restoration of
Hungarian 50
guide to New York State 309
See also Abbeys; Cathedrals;
Chapels; Church architecture;
Churches; Convents; Meetinghouses; Missions; Synagogues

Edinburgh, Scotland
the building of 273
historic preservation of the urban
center of 334

Education
historic preservation as a means of
60, 81
for historic preservation careers
24, 35, 44-45, 53, 58,
86, 104, 358, 388, 396
of the public toward historic
preservation 207
See also Architects, training of

Egypt, historic preservation in 326,
338

Elderly, displacement effect of historic districting on 371

Electrical systems 432

Electric power, archaeology of
British 566

Elevators 432

Eminent domain 121

Engineering
bibliography on historic 7
British museums serving 568
See also Civil engineering

England. See Bath, England; Chester,
England; Chichester, England;
Essex County, England;
Great Britain; Kent County,
England; London; Newcastle-
upon-Tyne, England; North-
umberland, England; United
Kingdom; York, England

Environment
concern for in pedestrians zones
331
condition of Australian 53
improvement of courthouse
interior 183
influence on American building
465

Environmental law 117

Environmental policy and planning
94
bibliography on aesthetics in 10
in highway construction 135
in the United States 135

Environmental protection, use of
development rights transfer
in 138

Epoxy compounds, use of for wood
repairs 425

Essex County, England, development
of wood construction in
400

Essex County, N.Y., architecture of
223

Ethnic groups
consideration of in historic planning 105
of Southbridge, Mass.
644
See also names of ethnic groups
(e.g., Finnish Americans)

Europe
guidebooks to Jewish landmarks
in 270
historic preservation in 23-24,
28-31, 36, 46, 57, 60-69,
93, 95, 325, 342
architectural 83-84
law of 327
planning of 125
urban centers 333, 340, 343
pedestrian zones in 331

European Architectural Heritage
Year (1975) 23-24, 58,
125, 434, 639
educational activities relating to
60
Spanish contributions to 269

Extended use. See Adaptive use

F

Fabrics. See Textile fabrics
Factories, surveys of 575. See also
    Industrial buildings
Fall River, Mass., adaptive reuse
    projects in 442
Farmhouses, conservation and restora-
    tion of Canadian 459
Farm land, tax incentives for preserva-
    tion of 114
Farms 649
    bibliography on 6
    of New England 637
    periodicals on 704
    photographic essay on 590
    of Scotland 271
    See also Agriculture; Animal
        husbandry; Barns; Outbuildings
Federal government
    environmental policy and 94
    in historic preservation 11-13,
        21-22, 41, 88, 95, 124,
        133, 155, 173, 221
        adaptive reuse projects 438,
            440
        in Canada 126
        laws of 116-17
Federal Land Use Policy and Planning
    Assistance Act (1972) 611
Fences 458, 588
    details of 204
    maintenance and repair of 362
    See also Gates
Festivals, preservation of Japanese
    traditional 74
Finance. See Historic preservation,
    economic and financial
    aspects of
Fine arts, evolution of American
    285
Finnish-Americans, examination of
    the cultural landscape of
    132
Fireplaces 469, 506
    maintenance and repair of 454
    See also Chimneys
Fire prevention 551, 553
Firewood, selection of 454
Flooding. See Dampness in buildings

Floor plans. See Architectural
    drawings
Floors and flooring 204
    English eighteenth-century 488
    treatment of 456
Florence, monument preservation in
    50
Florence, University of. Faculty
    of Architecture 417
Florida
    historic preservation planning in
        141
    influence on domestic architecture
        167
    See also Key West; Palm Beach;
        St. Augustine, Fla.
Florida, University of, preservation
    education at 45
Folk art, early American 500
Food
    convenience 506
    preservation of Japanese traditional
        74
    as socio-cultural expression 469,
        472, 537-38
Footpaths, survey of British 266
Ford (Henry) Museum (Dearborn,
    Mich.) 530
Fort Greene (Brooklyn, N.Y.) 225,
    230
Fortifications, adaptive reuse of
    434
Fort McHenry, architecture of 811
Fort Pitt Museum (Pittsburgh) 545
Fort Stanwix (Rome, N.Y.)
    archaeological investigations at
        559
    report on reconstruction of 172
Foundations, conservation and
    restoration of 408, 414
Framing (building), conservation and
    restoration of 408
France
    formal gardens of 615
    historic preservation in 41-42,
        67, 261, 326
        architectural 83-84
        of monuments 27, 46
        19th-century development of
            198

organizations 95
  theory and history of 25
influence on American architecture
  167, 208, 349
lost and endangered landmarks of
  633
periodicals on the houses of 735
  on the monuments of 706
preservation work by in Venice
  328
surveys and inventories of 261-62
See also Il-de-France; Paris
Friends of Cast-Iron Architecture
  (N.Y. City) 128
Furnishings 519, 521
  of Connecticut inns and taverns
    543
  encyclopedias and dictionaries of
    478, 483
  English eighteenth-century 488
  photographic sourcebook of 498
  technology in the development of
    501
Furniture
  conservation and restoration of
    European 36
  early American 500
  encyclopedias and dictionaries of
    473, 475, 477-79, 483
    English 476
  relating to ornamentation 485
  kitchen 506
  of Newport, R.I. 487
  as socio-cultural expression 471
Furniture making 399

G

Gables, maintenance and repair of
  454
Galleries. See Museums
Gamble House (Pasadena, Calif.) 298
Gardening 458
Gardens 456, 613-24
  conservation and restoration of
    616-18, 623
  in Japan 74
  in Virginia 624
  of Great Britain 272, 276
  inventory of Spanish 269

of the United States 285
  colonial 537, 616
  See also Landscape; Open spaces;
    Herbs
Gas lighting, American 493
Gates 434
Gateways, drawings and photographs
  of English 487
Gdánsk, Poland, historic preservation in 75
Georgetown (Washington, D.C.),
  architecture of 797, 800-
  804, 808
George Washington University, preservation education at 45
Georgia
  historic preservation in 173
  periodicals published by 744
  See also Columbus, Ga.;
    Savannah
Georgia. Historical Commission,
  history of 205
German Americans, arts and architecture of in Missouri 215
German Democratic Republic, preservation of monuments in
  59
Germany, Federal Republic of
  preservation of monuments in 58
  preservation work by in Venice
    328
Germany, periodical on art and
  monument protection in 688
Ghost towns. See Cities and towns,
  ruined, extinct, etc.
Glass
  conservation and restoration of
    43, 49, 551
  early American 500
  encyclopedias of antique 477
Gold, encyclopedia of antique 477
Good, Albert H. 48
Gothic revival architecture. See
  Architecture, Gothic
  revival
Gould (Jay) Greenhouse (Tarrytown,
  N.Y.) 170
Granaries, adaptive reuse of 434
Grand Central Terminal (N.Y.
  City) 337

Historic buildings 548
  British National Trust 272
  conservation and restoration of 43,
    47, 391, 397, 423
    adaptive reuse 436-37, 439,
      443, 446-50, 453, 459
    in the Americas 51
    bibliographies on 7, 10, 389,
      391-93
    building codes and 111
    in Canada 459
    in Europe 28-29
    in Germany, East 59
    in Great Britain 42, 69,
      101, 415, 436, 443, 450,
      599, 626
    international cooperation and
      programs 43, 318-26
    in Japan 74
    laws of 101
    manuals for 410-13, 415,
      419, 428
    in Massachusetts 433
    in New York City 374
    in New York State 443
    in Scotland 68
    in South Africa 76
    in Switzerland 77
    in the U.S. 46, 95
    urban renewal and 385
  of Delaware 514
  fire protection for 553
  lost and endangered London 626
  of Massachusetts 818
  of Mississippi 292
  of Newcastle-upon-Tyne 122
  of New Haven, Conn. 302
  of New Jersey 297
  of Newport, R.I. 308
  of New York City 313-14
  of Ohio 819
  of Philadelphia 307, 312
  surveys and inventories of 169,
    174, 181, 187, 820
    guidelines for 180
    in St. Paul, Minn. 376
    specifications for 176
  of the U.S. 285
    concerned with the Revolutionary
      War 290

  of Washington, D.C. 821
  See also Architecture; Dampness
    in buildings; Ecclesiastical
    buildings; Industrial build-
    ings; Log buildings; Mercan-
    tile buildings; Outbuildings;
    Public buildings; Rural
    buildings
Historic districts 180, 348-63
  conservation and restoration of
    adaptive reuse 445
    in Annapolis, Md. 129
    in Boston 348, 351
    in Indianapolis, Ind. 149
    laws of 351, 356-58
    in Lowell, Mass. 151, 354
    in Maryland 355
    in Massachusetts 356
    in New Bedford, Mass. 352
    in New Britain, Conn. 200
    in New Orleans 349
    in Newport, R.I. 156
    in New York City 230-33,
      236
    in Tombstone, Ariz. 148
    in Tucson 350
    zoning in 88, 350, 353
  establishment of 381
  evolution of designations for 132
  guides to New York City 305,
    314
  surveys of 187
    Spanish 269
  See also Development rights
    transfer; Historic urban
    centers; Neighborhoods
Historic Districts Act (Mass.) 356
Historic District Zoning Ordinance
    (Tucson) 350
Historic preservation
  administration and planning in
    15, 66, 83, 86, 102,
    104-9, 122-35
    bibliography on 105
  cartoons on 636
  description and documentation in
    157-269
  economic and financial aspects
    of 42, 67, 75, 103-4,
    106-7, 113, 115, 124,

132, 140, 146, 148, 183, 221, 325, 357-58, 369-70, 377, 381, 383, 386, 432, 435, 441-43, 445, 448, 456, 601, 603, 609
failures and losses associated with 625-59
general works on 1-22
historical and current overviews of 23-50
national and regional 51-99
history interpreted through 465-554
international cooperation and programs in 43, 49, 55, 73, 75, 95, 178, 318-29, 658
organizations and agencies for 1, 11, 13, 14, 16, 21, 35, 44, 54, 58, 94, 97, 126, 173, 244, 359, 388, 393, 412, 443, 561, 567, 625, 633
periodicals on 660-777
related disciplines 555-96
war and 651-59
See also subheading "conservation and restoration of" under types of structures (e.g., Industrial buildings, conservation and restoration of); "historic preservation in" under names of countries and states (e.g., Italy, historic preservation in); "maintenance and repair of" under architectural detail (e.g., Gables, maintenance and repair of)

Historic sites
application of photogrammetry to 179
British National Trust 272
conservation and restoration 50
adaptive reuse in 445
in the Americas 51-52
bibliographies on 7, 10
in the Caribbean 55
economics in 132
in Europe 29-30
in France 261
in Great Britain 69, 101

in Japan 74
laws 101
surveys 144, 187
in Switzerland 77
tax incentives for 114
in the U.S. 46, 95, 104
urban renewal and 385
interpretation of 298, 536-49
of Jefferson County, La. 209
lost and endangered French 633
of Minnesota 294
need for an international documentation center on 178
of New Jersey 297
of New York City 314
periodicals on 675
Canadian 676
of Philadelphia 307, 312
registers of 22
of the U.S. 282, 285-86
concerned with the Revolutionary War 287, 290
Historic structure reports 170, 172, 182, 185
Historic trees, American 288
Historic urban centers, conservation and restoration of 318, 330-47
in Edinburgh 334
in Egypt 338
in Great Britain 330
in Italy 73
in London 332
in New York City 337
in York, England 336, 341
See also Historic districts; Urban renewal
History, guide to information sources on 9. See also Cultural history; Oral history; Social history
Hitchcock, Henry-Russell 48
Hoboken, N.J. 346
guide to row houses in 451, 463
Holland, Leceister B. 48
Hotels
architecture of Canadian railroad 258
in Spain 321
See also Inns and taverns

Subject Index

House construction 195, 399
  history of English 401
House moving. See Moving of buildings, bridges, etc.
Houses. See Architecture, domestic
Housing, rural
  guide to Scottish 271
  of Switzerland 529
Housing Act (Gt. Brit., 1969) 66
Housing and Community Development Act (1974) 364
Hovey, Walter Read 48
Hudson Valley area, architectural inventory of 234
Humidity. See Dampness in buildings
Hungary, historic preservation in 57, 70
Huth, Hans A. 48
Huxtable, Ada Louise 168

I

Il-de-France, endangered architecture of 634
Illinois
  HABS catalog for 782
  measured drawings of the architecture of northern 812
  periodicals published by 746
  See also Chicago
Implements, utensils, etc.
  guide to American 494
  preservation of Japanese traditional 74
  See also Furniture; Kitchen utensils; Tools
Independence Hall (Philadelphia) 397
Indiana
  HABS catalog for 783
  periodicals published by 747
Indianapolis, development planning in 149
Indians. See American Indians
Industrial archaeology 180-81, 565-71
  periodicals on 672, 679, 730
Industrial architecture. See Architecture, industrial
Industrial buildings 573-76
  adaptive reuse of 434, 441-42, 445

archaeology of British 566
conservation and restoration of
  Hungarian 70
  of Newcastle-upon-Tyne 122
  of New York State 309
  See also Architecture, industrial; Mercantile buildings; types of industrial buildings (e.g. Factories; Mills)
Inland waterways, archaeology of British 566. See also Canals
Inns and taverns
  of Connecticut 543
  early American 537-38
Insurance, for "brownstones" 455
Interior decoration
  American nineteenth-century 499
  catalogs of products and suppliers for 490-91
  environmental aspects of courthouse interiors 183
International Centre for Conservation (Rome), preservation education at 45
International Congress of Historic Monument Architects and Technicians, Second, resolution of 51
International Council on Monuments and Sites 73
International law. See Law
International Monuments Year, report of 92
Interpretation 298, 536-49
Inventories. See Surveys and inventories
Iolani Palace (Hawaii), restoration of 542
Iowa, periodicals published by 748. See also Marshalltown, Iowa
Ipswich, Mass., historic preservation in 112
Iran, historic preservation in 326
Ireland, bibliography on the architecture of 158
Iron and steel industry, archaeology of British 566
Ironwork, drawings and photographs

of English 486. See also
Cast-iron fronts (architecture)
Irving, Washington, description of the
Bermudas by 646
Istituto Centrale del Restauro 653
Italy
gardens of 615
historic preservation in 42, <u>71-73</u>
following war 653
laws of 71, 321
of monuments 72-73
theory and history of 25
of urban centers 340
See also Florence; Pompeii, Italy;
Veneto, Italy; Venice

J

Jackson, Henry M. 79
Jails, in Pennsylvania 242
Japan, historical preservation in <u>74</u>,
79, 325
laws of 95
See also Tokyo
Jefferson, Thomas, Garden Book of
614
Jefferson Parish, La., historical
survey of 209
Jerusalem, preservation of the urban
center 343
Jewelry, encyclopedia of 483
Jews, European landmarks concerning
270. See also Synagogues
Johnson Hall (Johnstown, N.Y.) 185
Joinery 400
eighteenth-century tools of 403

K

Kent County, England, history of
265
Kentucky
periodicals published by 749
Shaker architecture in 188
Key West, historic preservation in
362
Kingston, N.Y., historic preservation
in 185
Kingston, Ontario, architecture of
260

Kitchens 502-6
as depicted in genre painting
497
Kitchen utensils 503, 505-6
as socio-cultural expressions 469
Kline, Donald C. 48
Knox, John, description of The
Plains of Abraham by 646
Krautheimer, Richard 48

L

Lancaster, Pa. 346
Landmarks
conference on 357-58
conservation and preservation of
106, 343
transfer of development rights
in 137, 139
directory of commissions for 359
European Jewish 270
lost and endangered 625-40
of Monroe County, N.Y. 229
of New Haven, Conn. 302
of New Jersey 296-97
of New York City 128, 221,
305, 313-14
periodicals on 701-2
plaques and markers noting
316-17
in Georgia 205
of the Revolutionary War 279,
297
of the San Francisco area 194
of Washington, D.C. 97, 249
See also Literary landmarks
Landscape 612
guide to New York State highway
309
survey of the British 266
See also Open spaces
Landscape architecture 180-81
history of 615
Landscape protection, in Great
Britain 69
Land use
guide to information sources on
9
laws of 611
in neighborhood conservation 375

London
  architectural survey of 268
  lost and endangered landmarks in 626, 631
  nineteenth-century photographs of 642
  preservation of historic centers in 332, 335
  war damage to 654
London. Historic Buildings Board 102
Long Island, architectural landmarks in 235
Long Island Historical Society 650
Longwood Villa (Natchez, Miss.) 526
Louisiana
  influence on domestic architecture 167
  periodicals published by 750
  See also Jefferson Parish, La.; New Orleans
Louisiana. State Museum 447
Louisville, historic preservation in 33
Lowell, Mass., historic preservation in 33
  adaptive reuse projects 442
  guide to 354
  planning of 151-52
Lublin, Poland, historic preservation in 75
Lumbering industry 592
Lynchburg, Va., adaptive reuse projects in 445
Lyndhurst (New York house) 814

M

McAndrew, John 48
Machinery
  in industrial archaeology 568
  museum displays of 530
  See also Tools
Maine
  HABS catalog for 784
  periodicals published by 751
Malls, compendium of American 331
Manchester, N.H., adaptive reuse projects in 442
Manhattan. See Greenwich Village; New York City; So-Ho-Cast Iron District (N.Y. City)

Manners and customs, preservation of Japanese traditional 74
Manor houses, Hungarian 70
Manuscripts 548
  conservation and restoration of 551
  in Japan 74
  as sources in industrial archaeology 568
Maps, as sources in industrial archeology 568
Marble, maintenance and repair of in Venice 328
Marshalltown, Iowa, case study of the courthouse in 183
Maryland
  domestic architecture of 210
  HABS catalog for 785
  historic preservation in 355
    planning of 142
  periodicals published by 752
  See also Annapolis, Md.; Baltimore; Chestertown, Md.
Masonry and brickwork
  composition of British 427
  conservation and restoration of 36, 49, 361, 408, 428
  early American construction with 402
  in early New Jersey 407
  See also Brick walls
Massachusetts
  domestic architecture of 191
  HABS catalog for 786
  historic buildings of 818
  historic preservation in 356
    adaptive reuse projects 433
  periodicals published by 753
  Shaker architecture in 188
  See also Boston; Fall River, Mass.; Ipswich, Mass.; Lawrence, Mass.; Lowell, Mass.; Nantucket, Mass.; New Bedford, Mass.; Southbridge, Mass.
Mechanical arts, evolution of American 285
Mechanical systems 432
Medals, early American 500
Meeks, C.L.V. 48

Subject Index

Meetinghouses, guide to U.S. 285
Memorials
  American presidential 289
  European Jewish 270
  of Schenectady, N.Y. 182
Memphis, historic preservation in
    364
Mercantile buildings 285
  adaptive reuse of 446, 449
  guide to New York State 309
  of New York City's seaport area
    582
Metal-work
  British museums displaying 568
  conservation and restoration of
    551
  dictionary of ornamentation of
    485
  early American 500
  weathering of 418
Mexican-Americans, of Tucson 123
Mexico
  description of by Cortes 646
  preservation law of 51
Michigan, HABS catalog for 787.
    See also Detroit
Middeldorf, Ulrich 48
Middle Atlantic states
  domestic architecture of 191
  photographs of the colonial heri-
    tage of 647
Mills
  adaptive reuse of 434
  conservation and restoration of
    Canadian 459
  lost and endangered French 633
  of Lowell, Mass. 151
  of New England 576, 637
  of New York 576
  periodicals on 720
  of the U.S. 285
Mines and mining
  archaeology of American 570
  British museums serving 568
  of New England 637
Minnesota
  guide to the historic sites of
    294
  periodicals published by 754
Missions, conservation and restora-
    tion of California 196-98

Mississippi
  guide to the architecture of 292
  periodicals published by 755
  See also Natchez, Miss.
Missouri
  arts and architecture of Germans
    in 215
  periodicals published by 756
Mobile, Ala., urban renewal in
    385
Mohawk-Hudson (N.Y.) Area
    Survey 571
Moisture. See Dampness in
    buildings
Monroe County, N.Y., landmarks
    of 229
Monterey, Calif., urban renewal
    in 385
Montreal
  architectural and environmental
    development of 258
  19th-century photographs of
    643
Monuments
  application of photogrammetry to
    177-79
  conservation and restoration of
    667-68, 675, 707, 737
    in the Americas 52
    in Austria 54
    bibliography on 395
    in Europe 28, 30
    in France 46, 261
    in Great Britain 61, 65,
      101
    international cooperation and
      programs for 43, 318,
      321, 323
    in Japan 74
    laws of 54, 61, 101
    opposition to 65
    in Poland 75
    in Russia 78
    in the U.S. 86
  dampness problems of 431
  European Jewish 270
  of France 262
  of Great Britain 272, 276
  inventory of Spanish 269
  of Jefferson Parish, La. 209

Pittsburgh; Reading, Pa.;
Sewickley, Pa.; York, Pa.
Pennsylvania. Historical and Museum
Commission. Register of
Historic Sites and Landmarks
124
Pennsylvania Station (N.Y. City)
335
Pewter, American 500, 505
Philadelphia
guide to 307
the architecture of 312
historic preservation in 117
urban renewal and 384
urban homesteading in 382
Philipse Manor (N.Y. State) 420
Photogrammetry 177, 179
in garden restoration 623
Photographs 548, 641-50
HABS catalogs of 778-79
in industrial archaeology 567
Pictures and picture hanging, English
eighteenth-century 488
Pittsburgh
adaptive reuse programs in 33
historic preservation case studies
of 115
history of 545
Pittsburgh History and Landmarks
Museum 33
Place names, guide to European
Jewish 270
Plains of Abrahahm, description of
J. Knox 646
Planned communities. See Cities
and towns, planned
Plants. See Gardens; Herbs
Plaster
conservation and restoration of
420
early American construction with
402
Plastics, weathering of 418
Point State Park (Pittsburgh) 545
Poland, historic preservation in 57,
75
Polish Americans, examination of the
cultural landscape of 132
Politics
the log cabin in American 569

of neighborhood conservation
369, 373
Pompeii, Italy, gardens of 623
Pope-Leighey House (Virginia) 814
Population, consideration of in
neighborhood conservation
375
Porches, maintenance and repair of
362
Porter, Charles W. 48
Portland
architecture of 239
guides to 310, 456
historic preservation in 364
Portsmouth, N.H., urban renewal
in 385
Post offices, adaptive reuse of 33
Potter, Edward T. 182
Pottery, early American 500
Power resources, archaeology of
566, 570
Poznań, Poland, historic preservation
in 75
Presidents (U.S.), guide to historic
places commemorating 289
Prison Ship Martyrs' Monument
(Brooklyn, N.Y.) 230
Property. See Abandonment of
property; Real property
Providence, R.I., historic preserva-
tion in
planning of 154
urban renewal and 385
Public buildings
adaptive reuse of 437, 446
architecture of British 267
conservation and restoration of
Hungarian 70
gardens for 618
See also Capitol building;
Capitols (cities); City halls;
Courthouses; Post offices;
Schools; Washington, D.C.
Puerto Rico
application of development rights
transfer in 138
historic preservation in 22, 104
inventory of monuments in 252
See also San Juan, Puerto Rico
Pumping stations, adaptive reuse of
434

Subject Index

Q

Queen Anne architecture. See Architecture, Queen Anne
"Quito Standards, The" 52

R

Railroads
archaeology of British 566
British museums serving 568
Canadian hotels 258
of New England 637
of New York 238
recreation potential of restored 544
survey of British 266
Railroad stations and depots
adaptive reuse of 440
of New York City 335, 337
portfolio of paintings of 584
Ramée, Joseph Jacques 182
Reading, Pa. 346
Real property 115, guide to information sources on 9
Recreation. See Outdoor recreation
Recycling. See Adaptive use
Regional planning, conservation and restoration in 105, 130. See also City planning; Land use; Open spaces
Religion
destruction in the name of 61
preservation of Japanese traditional 74
Religious buildings. See Abbeys; Cathedrals; Chapels; Church architecture; Churches; Ecclesiastical buildings; Meetinghouses; Missions; Synagogues
Remodeling for other uses. See Adaptive use
Renaissance architecture. See Architecture, Renaissance
Rensselaer County, N.Y., architecture of 223
Reservoirs, preservation of open space around 606
Resorts, of New England 637

Revolutionary War
guides to sites of 279, 287, 290
in New Jersey 297
monuments of 230
Rhode Island
domestic architecture of 191
HABS catalog for 791
periodicals published by 766
See also Newport, R.I.; Providence, R.I.
Richardson, H.H. 242
Richmond, survey and inventory of the buildings in 247
Road construction, environmental and historic impacts of 135
Roads
in early America 538
guide to New York State landscaped 309
historic markers along West Virginia 317
of New England 637
survey of British 266
See also Streets
Robie House 813
Rochester, N.Y., landmarks of 229
Rockefeller Center (N.Y. City) 337
Romanesque architecture. See Architecture, Romanesque; Architecture, Romanesque revival
Romania, historic preservation in 57
Roofs and roofing 204
early American 397
maintenance and repair of 36, 361-62, 408, 414
Roosevelt, Theodore, house of 527
Ropewalks, of New England 637
Row houses
of Boston 211
conservation and restoration of 460
adaptive reuse in 434
in Canada 459
in Germany, East 59
of London 335
of New Jersey 451, 463

of New York 227, 236, 335
buyers' guides to 451, 455, 463
periodicals on 674
Rubble walls. See Stone walls
Ruins. See Antiquities; Archaeology
Rumania. See Romania
Rural areas
bibliography on 6
land use aspects of historic preservation in 132
Rural buildings, conservation and restoration of Hungarian 70. See also Barns; Outbuildings
Rural conditions 549, 587-88, 590, 596
of the English upper-classes 466-67
Rural housing. See Housing, rural
Ruskin, John 25, 67, 73
Russia, historic preservation in 57, 78, 79

S

Sacramento, guide to the Victorian houses of 299
Sagamore Hill (historic house) 527
Sag Harbor, N.Y., historic preservation planning in 155
St. Augustine, Fla., domestic architecture of 203
St. Paul, Minn., historic preservation in 376
St. Paul's Cathedral 397, 411
Salem, Ore., historic preservation in 364
Salt Lake City, historic preservation in 103
Salvage archaeology. See Archaeology, salvage
Samoa, American, historic preservation in 104
San Francisco
architecture of 194-95
historic preservation in 197
urban renewal and 385
San Juan, Puerto Rico, historic preservation planning in 147
Santa Barbara, Calif., architecture of 193

Savannah, historic preservation in 103, 206
case studies of 115
planning of 150
Scandinavian countries, development of historic preservation in 198. See also Denmark; Sweden
Schools
adaptive reuse of 434, 437
of New England 637
Science, British museums of 567
Scotland
architectural guides to 271, 273
bibliography on vernacular architecture of 158
historic preservation in 68
See also Edinburgh, Scotland
Sculpture
American 500
conservation and restoration of Japanese 74
See also Statues
Sculpture, architectural, conservation and restoration of 43
Seals, early American 500
Seashores. See Coastal zone management
Seattle, historic preservation in 33, 103, 372
Seaver, Esther Isabel 48
Second Empire architecture. See Architecture, Second Empire style
Senate House (Kingston, N.Y.) 185
Sewickley, Pa. 242
Shadows-on-the-Teche (Louisiana house) 814
Shakers. See Architecture, Shaker
Shawnee County, Kans., architecture of 207
Sheboygan, Wis., survey of the architecture of 248
Shell-work, of Newport, R.I. 487
Ship-building and shipping 399, 568, 577-82, 637
Shoring and underpinning 408, 414
Shrines, conservation and preservation of British 69

Scientific, and Cultural
Organization (UNESCO) 27,
29
United States
architectural histories, inventories,
and surveys of 188–91
guides to historic houses of 507–
27
to historic sites of 278–317
historic preservation in 32, 41,
46, 48, 51, 79–98, 342
adaptive use 444
laws of 32, 100, 117, 119,
327
nineteenth-century development
of 198
of open spaces 601–3, 605,
610–12
planning of 104–9, 124–25,
127, 132–33, 135
of ruins 416
history of building in 465
preservation work by in Venice
328
See also subheading "in the U.S."
under subjects
U.S. Bureau of Ethnology 85
U.S. Corps of Engineers 152
U.S. Department of the Army, building maintenance manual for
419
U.S. Historic Preservation Act (1966)
96
U.S. Historic Sites Act (1935) 95
U.S. Library of Congress, role of in
the Historic American Buildings Survey 169
U.S. National Park Service 46,
189, 547
bibliography of 2
establishment of urban parks by
153
in the Fort Stanwix restoration
172
investment program of 152
report sponsorship by 56
Revolutionary War sites administered by 287, 290
role in the Historic American
Buildings Survey 169

U.S. National Park Service. His-
toric American Engineering
Record. Mohawk–Hudson
Area Survey 571
U.S. National Park Service.
National Parks Centennial
Commission 610
U.S. National Park Service.
Office of Archeology and
Historic Preservation
bibliography of projects of 7
historic place list of 189
U.S. National Park Service.
Office of Archeology and
Historic Preservation. Inter-
agency Historic Architec-
tural Services 410
Universities and colleges, role of
in urban renewal 386
Upholstering, English 18th-century
488
Urban areas. See Cities and towns;
City planning; Historic
districts; Historic urban
centers; Land use, urban
Urban design
historic preservation in 45, 137
183
in Savannah 150
of Nantucket, Mass. 826
Urban homesteading 382–83
Urban National Cultural Park Program 152
Urban renewal 88, 327
historic preservation and 108,
344, 384–86
in Philadelphia 384
in Providence, R.I. 154
in Savannah 150
of Washington, D.C. 97
See also City planning; Historic
districts; Historic urban
centers; Land use, urban
Utah
HABS catalog for 794
periodicals published by 772
See also Salt Lake City

V

Vanderbilt, Cornelius 291

Subject Index

Van Rensselaer family, house of 523

Veneto, Italy, conservation and restoration of the villas of 321

Venice
international cooperation for restoration activities in 328
lost and endangered landmarks in 628, 640
monument preservation in 50

Vermont
land use legislation in 611
periodicals published by 773

Vermont, University of, preservation education at 45

Vernacular architecture. See Architecture, vernacular

Victoria and Albert Museum (London) 639

Village greens. See Commons areas

Villages
architectural survey of British 266
British National Trust 272
conservation and restoration of European 24
of British 67
list of preserved and museum 528–35
lost and endangered French 633
of New Jersey 293
of Scotland 271, 273
of the U.S. 283, 291
See also Small towns

Villas and chateaux, conservation and restoration of 321

Vint, Thomas C. 48

Viollet-lec-Duc, Eugène Emmanuel 73

Virginia
architecture of 295
as socio-cultural expression 468
garden restorations in 623
HABS catalog for 795
periodicals published by 774
See also Alexandria, Va.; Lynchburg, Va.; Richmond, Williamsburg, Va.; Yorktown, Va.

Virginia, University of, preservation projects at 397

Virgin Islands
architecture of 799
historic preservation in 22, 104

Volunteer workers and organizations 173
in Australia 53

W

Wales, bibliography on the architecture of 158

Wall decorations, early American 500

Wallpaper 456, 489

Walnut Hill Historic District. See New Britain, Conn.

War, destruction resulting from 651–59

Warehouses, adaptive reuse of 434–35

Warsaw, Poland, historic preservation in 75

Washington (state), periodicals published by 775. See also Seattle

Washington, D.C.
bibliography on 171
guidebook to 315
the architecture of 301, 306, 806
HABS catalog for 781
historic buildings of 522
historic houses of 821
historic preservation in 97, 249
urban renewal and 385
periodicals published by 743
surveys and catalogs of the buildings in 249–51
See also Capitol Building; Georgetown (Washington, D.C.)

Washington, George. See Hasbrouck House (N.Y. City); Mount Vernon (Virginia)

Washington (George) University. See George Washington University

Waterbury, Conn. 346

JOURNEYS
IN DARKNESS AND LIGHT

Third printing December 2004

Earlier printings in a different format, by another publisher,
appeared in December 2003 and
February 2004

ISBN 1-4196-0002-8

Printed in the United States of America

Cover image: *Stranger*, appliqué by Rebecca Weiss

www.weiss-gallery.com
www.helgahenschen.com

Cover design and photo layout by Steven and Monica Ferry

To order additional copies, please contact us.
BookSurge, LLC
www.booksurge.com
1-866-308-6235
orders@booksurge.com